PLANNING MATTERS

PLANNING MATTERS

*The impact of development planning
in primary schools*

BARBARA MacGILCHRIST
PETER MORTIMORE
JANE SAVAGE
CHARLES BERESFORD

P·C·P
Paul Chapman
Publishing Ltd

Copyright © 1995, Barbara MacGilchrist, Peter Mortimore,
Jane Savage and Charles Beresford.

Paul Chapman Publishing Ltd
144 Liverpool Road
London
N1 1LA

British Library Cataloguing in Publication Data
MacGilchrist, Barbara
Planning Matters: The Impact of Development
Planning in Primary Schools
I. Title
372.1207

ISBN 1-85396-267-8

Typeset by Dorwyn Ltd, Rowlands Castle, Hants
Printed and bound by
Athenaeum Press Ltd, Gateshead, Tyne & Wear

A B C D E F G H 9 8 7 6 5

CONTENTS

Preface   vii
Acknowledgements   viii
Introduction   ix

1. The growth of school development planning   1
2. The development planning process   9
3. The complexity of development planning   22
4. Development planning and school improvement   34
5. The research design and our methodology   43
6. The national survey of LEAs   58
7. The headteachers' story   72
8. The classteachers' story   94
9. The emergence of different types of plans   118
10. The written plans   150
11. The classroom story   159
12. The governors' story   176
13. The LEAs' story   183
14. The theoretical implications of the research findings   192
15. The practical implications of the study   210

References   223
Subject Index   231

PREFACE

Improving schools is a goal which unites practitioners, academics and policy-makers alike. Seeking to achieve that goal, however, can sometimes unintentionally create the opposite effect. Whilst there is common agreement about some of the key characteristics which distinguish a successful school from a failing one, such as the quality of leadership and the staff's will to improve, there is often disagreement about the most effective means of becoming successful. The purpose of this book is to contribute to the school improvement debate: its focus is on *planning* as a strategy for school improvement. It seeks to explore and to answer the question – *does it make a difference*? Is it a process which enables schools to improve or is it an idea that in theory has an appeal but which in practice is a different matter? Like the best laid plans this book does not provide complete answers, rather it clarifies the debate and also opens up further questions which, in turn, will need to be explored by others.

ACKNOWLEDGEMENTS

Teamwork has underpinned our approach to this study. As a research team based at the Institute of Education, University of London, we met on 91 occasions to debate and come to agreement about the many facets of the project. We are convinced that working in this way has enhanced our individual and collective understanding about the relevant literature and research techniques and about the day-to-day work of schools. Naturally we are indebted to the headteachers, classteachers, governors and, not least, the pupils in the nine primary schools which participated so willingly in the research. The richness of the data is a reflection of the openness and generosity of all those concerned. Grateful thanks are also due to the officers and inspectors in the three local education authorities (LEAs) from which we drew the schools and also to those in the other 132 LEAs who found time to complete and return our questionnaire. An unexpected bonus was the willingness of academics within the Institute and those involved in related research in Denmark and Australia, particularly Lloyd Logan from Griffith University and Neil Dempster and Judyth Sachs from the University of Queensland, to engage in our debates, share findings and scrutinise our data. Finally, for providing the funding for the research we extend our gratitude to the Economic and Social Research Council, and for so patiently processing the manuscript we thank Kate Myronidis.

Dr Barbara MacGilchrist and *Professor Peter Mortimore*,
Co-directors of the Research,
Jane Savage, The Research Officer and
Dr Charles Beresford, The Research Associate

INTRODUCTION

WHY STUDY SCHOOL DEVELOPMENT PLANNING?

At the Institute of Education we are interested in many aspects of school effectiveness and school improvement. We have scrutinised numerous examples of studies of both effectiveness and improvement. We are constantly seeking to draw on their lessons and to translate these into concrete ways of helping headteachers, teachers and governing bodies improve the opportunities for learning within their schools.

We are aware of the investment of large amounts of time in school development plans (SDPs) and are conscious of the claims that are being made on their behalf. School development planning has been described as a 'bottom-up' approach to change which enables schools to accommodate and respond to 'top-down' reform in a coherent way (Maden and Tomlinson, 1991). It has been defined as 'a strategy for managing development and change to make the school more effective' (DES, 1989a, p. 4). It is also claimed that it provides an opportunity for forward planning at the level of the whole school which combines development needs arising from a school's own aims and values, with local and national imperatives (Davies and Ellison, 1992). Finally, it is also seen as a means to an end: a process for enabling a school to improve 'the quality of teaching and standards of learning' (DES, 1991a, p. 2).

These are just a few of the claims made about school development planning. It is a process which, in less than a decade, has been widely adopted by schools, local education authorities (LEAs) and central government and, as is obvious from these quotations, which is expected to serve multiple purposes – some of which are potentially in conflict with one another. Given the limited research evidence available on which to test the profitability of this investment, we felt it was important to carry out an empirical investigation into the efficacy of such plans and their impact on the learning opportunities of pupils. Many headteachers and teachers are endeavouring to use planning as a means of making sense of the school reforms, emanating from the 1988 and subsequent Acts of

Parliament, and of the many other changes which are taking place around them. In these circumstances, we felt it all the more important that their efforts should be guided by systematic research and sensitive evaluation. We have chosen to focus on primary rather than secondary schools because there is less research on this phase of schooling and we wished to use the opportunity to increase the research base evidence available about the work of primary schools. It is clear, however, that many of the lessons from the study of development planning are likely to apply to secondary schools and, indeed, to other kinds of educational institution.

AN OUTLINE OF THE RESEARCH

Our 32-month project began in September 1991. It had three main aims:

1. To carry out an empirical investigation of the implementation and impact of SDPs in primary schools in order to provide a contribution to knowledge in the form of a clear and detailed description of an innovative development.
2. To examine how the findings of this study can contribute to the theories of how change takes place in schools; in particular, to strengthen the link between school effectiveness and school improvement theory and practice.
3. To identify good practice and, if appropriate, to disseminate to policy-makers and practitioners.

We sought to answer the following questions:

- What impact do SDPs have on

  - the management of the school as a whole;
  - classroom management;
  - the professional development of teachers; and
  - the learning opportunities for pupils?

- Are some plans more effective than others?
- What are the key elements of successful practice and the implications of these for LEAs and schools?

We began the project with a set of general expectations drawn from previous research and from our own experience about the kinds of conditions necessary to enable schools to improve. They were that:

1. most staff and the headteacher can agree on a clear mission for the institution;
2. a systematic audit of current strategies and weaknesses is carried out;
3. a change plan is thoroughly thought through;
4. an outside agent is involved;
5. the implementation of the change plan is supported by all appropriate external authorities; and
6. an evaluation of progress is used formatively to support the implementation.

We wanted to find out the extent to which these expectations would be supported by our findings.

During our study, three specific hypotheses emerged – two from our detailed review of the literature and one from the data derived from our fieldwork – and formed an important focus for our investigations in the field.

The basis of our investigations was the plans and the planning processes of our sample schools. We collected plans for the school years 1992/3 and 1993/4. Where there was relevant supporting documentation, this was also collected. We wanted to find out who had actually written them, for which audiences they were intended, what formats had been adopted and how many components had been included in the plans.

The formal plans are one thing; the process of planning is quite another. We were interested in the length and pattern of the planning cycle and the nature of any review arrangements. We wished to examine the roles of many individuals – headteachers, their senior and more junior colleagues, governors and local authority representatives. Without infringing on the privacy of individuals we needed to get below the surface and to delve into the reality of what was happening in the schools and LEAs rather than simply deal with what 'was supposed to happen'. Our findings from this investigation, therefore, touch on the classroom experience of the pupils and their teachers, the organisation and management of schools, the views of governors and of responsible LEA officers.

In addition to the focus on the schools, and the LEAs in which they were situated, we also wished to explore the ways in which LEAs, across the UK as a whole, were promoting and using development planning as a strategy for school improvement. We decided, therefore, to collect information from all 135 LEAs in the UK in the anticipation that such a survey would provide a national context for the specific investigation into the relatively small number of schools and LEAs actually involved in the research project. Finally, drawing on the work of our fellow researchers – and particularly on our collaborators in Queensland, Australia – we wanted to identify an international picture of the use of development planning in schools.

As with all investigations into real situations we, as social scientists, faced role conflicts and had to find ways to reassure our respondents of their rights to anonymity (at the individual, school and local education levels) and of the need to respond as honestly as possible to enquiries. We are happy to report that the vast majority of those whom we interviewed during the study appeared to accept our reassurances and presented accounts which proved to be both frank and accurate. Inevitably, some discrepancies were recorded. These can occur because people genuinely have quite different perceptions of the same situation. They can also occur because people are sometimes unwilling to reveal themselves, their colleagues or their schools in a poor light. We attempted to deal with such instances by seeking views from a wide spectrum of respondents and by collecting observational as well as statistical evidence.

THE SHAPE OF THE BOOK

In the first four chapters of this book we trace, albeit briefly, the history of SDPs and indicate the nature of the progress of research on school development planning. We aim to provide a full account of British studies, carried out on this topic, and supplement this account with studies from abroad where these seem particularly relevant and where we are aware of them. We provide a description of the development planning process and make an analysis of key factors which need to be taken into consideration. We seek to describe the relationship between development planning and school improvement by drawing on a wide range of research literature. We then, in Chapter 5, describe our own research strategy. We reveal how we chose the schools; the range of evidence that we needed to collect; and the way we did collect, process and analyse it. In Chapters 6–13 we describe our main findings. In particular, we focus on the way we tried to make sense of the different views of respondents and to identify the overall pattern of what was happening in schools. We describe how, as a result of this analysis, four different types of SDPs, each with their own set of characteristics, emerged. We show how these characteristics determined the nature and the extent of the impact the plan had on the school as a whole, on teachers' own development and, most importantly, on the learning opportunities for pupils. We endeavour to demonstrate the ways in which we sought to check out the validity of this key finding.

In Chapter 14 we compare our findings with those of other research studies. We examine the level of agreement between both sets of findings and, even more interestingly, those areas where our findings do not fit the general picture. In this analytic section we focus down on three basic issues:

1. The scope and purpose of planning.
2. The methods of planning.
3. The value of planning.

Our final chapter addresses the implications of the study for both policy and practice. It is always tempting for researchers to claim a 'special' significance for their findings and we will endeavour to avoid this trap. More modestly, perhaps, we believe that some of our findings do challenge some of the received wisdom in the area of school management and we offer a series of potential implications for:

• working classrooms;
• schools;
• LEAs;
• the national scene; and
• the international scene.

We trust our study will prove to be timely. At its best, we believe time spent on development planning to be an excellent investment; but, at its worst, we are concerned that such activities distract heads and teachers from other tasks and, if there is no *pay off* in terms of increased learning opportunities, it dissipates their time and energy. It is hoped our findings will stimulate all those involved with the management of schools to learn from the evidence and, thereby, maximise the benefits from their labours.

1

THE GROWTH OF SCHOOL DEVELOPMENT PLANNING

This chapter provides a brief history of the introduction and expansion of school development planning in the English education system. It draws particular attention to the impact of the 1988 legislation on this innovation. In the final section it identifies a set of issues which any research study into the efficacy of development planning will need to address.

There is no government legislation which *requires* schools to have a development plan. In recent years, however, advice has been issued centrally (DES, 1989a; 1991a) which has clearly been based on the premise that all schools have, or should have, such a plan. In addition, at least three books have been published which offer a guide to schools on how to establish and implement a development plan (Hargreaves and Hopkins, 1991; Skelton *et al.*, 1991; Davies and Ellison, 1992).

Furthermore, there is no government legislation which requires LEAs to insist that their schools have a development plan. Yet from a national survey of primary and secondary headteachers in 1991 (Arnott *et al.*, 1992), it emerged that 98 per cent had an SDP. The concept of development planning appears, therefore, to have become embedded in the education system despite the lack of a statutory requirement.

The history of school development planning is short but complex. It concerns a series of strategies to influence, support, monitor and control the work of schools. The genesis of school development planning can be traced to national and local events in the 1970s and early 1980s. From being mainly a professional initiative stemming from development work within schools and between schools and local inspectors and advisers, SDPs became integrated into LEA policy and then into a government strategy to make schools more responsible and accountable for their own self-management. Prior to the 1970s, there is very little evidence of policy and practice concerned with SDPs, although the 'notion' of development planning at LEA level was encapsulated in the Education Act 1944 in respect of the need for a building programme to meet future demographic needs.

It is possible in the 1970s, however, to identify local and national initiatives that represent the early origins of SDPs. At a local level one of the largest local education authorities in the UK began to encourage schools to become more responsible for their own self-management. The Inner London Education Authority (ILEA) published in 1977 *Keeping the School Under Review* (ILEA, 1977). The purpose of this somewhat innovatory guidance for schools on the process of self-appraisal was 'to assist in the clarification of objectives and priorities, to identify weaknesses and strengths and ensure that due attention is given in turn to all aspects of school life' (*ibid.*, p. 1). It offered a framework for school self-review and provided a focus for a dialogue between schools and inspectors. It is significant that Eric Briault was the Chief Education Officer at the time when this initiative was first introduced. In an earlier publication for the Council for Educational Technology (Briault, 1974), he had already pointed to the need for schools to become much more proactive and innovative in relation to resource management. At that time he urged schools to establish arrangements for shared decision-making about the choice and use of the growing range of learning resources coming on to the market. It is also significant that the ILEA document emerged a year after the publication of the Auld Report on William Tyndale Junior School (Auld, 1976). Given the nature of the problems at William Tyndale, *Keeping the School Under Review* was a title with dual meaning. Whilst proposing self-review by schools, it was also an early move by an LEA to make schools more accountable for their actions and it raised the profile of the inspectorate in school development.

At a national level, education was also receiving a high profile at this time. A report on the DES (OECD, 1976) was critical of a lack of forward planning. So, too, was a report by a House of Commons Expenditure Committee (1976). Political concern about the education system was also growing. This concern was encapsulated in Callaghan's speech at Ruskin College in 1976. It is during this period that the seeds for school development planning were sown and were encouraged to germinate by other related activities. One concerned inservice education; the other, the curriculum. In the early 1970s the importance of inservice education and training (INSET) as a means of improving the quality of teaching had been emphasised in the James Report (DES, 1972). The report focused on the offsite training needs of individual teachers and recommended an expansion of INSET opportunities. However, by 1976 views about inservice education were changing. Doubts about the relationship between attendance at offsite courses and school improvement were being raised. Recommendations about the need to make INSET more school focused and for staff development policies linked to the identified needs of the school emerged (ACSTT/INIST, 1976). A further publication from the same source (1978) provided advice about how to establish a staff development programme and raised questions about the kinds of arrangements needed within a school to plan and review priorities. Thus, a link between staff development and school development had been created.

Two events in the late 1970s were related to the curriculum and encouraged the seeds of SDPs to establish firm roots, particularly in primary schools. In 1977 the Secretary of State commissioned a survey of LEA curriculum policies. In the report which followed, a wide variation in curriculum policy and practice across LEAs was revealed (DES, 1979). This raised questions about the need for more central control over the curriculum on offer in schools. The primary survey by Her Majesty's Inspectorate (HMI) published in 1978 contributed to this debate (DES, 1978). It revealed inconsistencies between schools in relation to the breadth and balance of the curriculum on offer and pointed to the need for improvements in curriculum development and management, not only in the classroom but also at the level of the whole school. The notion of school-wide policies on the curriculum had been initiated. By 1980 the Secretary of State had instituted a consultation exercise about the curriculum (DES, 1980).

This 1980 consultation resulted in the publication of *The School Curriculum* (DES, 1981). This contained explicit reference to the need for schools to have a more systematic approach to planning. It stated that 'Every school should analyse its aims, set these out in writing, and regularly assess how far the curriculum within the school as a whole, and for individual pupils, measures up to these aims' (*ibid.*, para. 18). Arising out of this was a requirement for all local authorities to produce a curriculum statement. This, in turn, led to LEAs either requiring or encouraging schools to develop their own whole-school policies on the curriculum. This move towards seeking ways of improving the quality of whole-school development was given added momentum by the DES publication entitled *Better Schools* (DES, 1985), in which the importance of whole-school policies, regular review and assessment was emphasised. It was this report which laid the foundation for a significant change in government funding arrangements for inservice education.

The LEA Training Grants Scheme was introduced in 1989 along with a new form of Education Support Grants. Both were aimed at improving the quality of inservice provision locally and required LEAs to address national priorities as well as locally identified needs. Consultation with, and the involvement of, schools in this process was encouraged and LEAs were held accountable for the appropriate use of the grants provided. The aim was to establish a framework for more effective planning and management of training. The scheme led to a much more co-ordinated approach to INSET in LEAs and increasingly schools were required by LEAs to establish INSET plans as a precondition for receiving a grant. A subsequent HMI report (DES, 1991b) confirmed that the scheme was encouraging a planned approach to staff development linked with identified priorities for improvement.

Another national initiative undertaken at this time provided support for schools in the process of identifying priorities for development. In 1984 the outcome of a Schools Council project was presented (McMahon *et al.*, 1984) in the form of 'Guidelines for Review and Internal Development in Schools' (GRIDS). The materials, which had been developed for the project through widespread trialling in primary and secondary schools, were designed to support a school's own self-review and were used widely on the growing number of management courses emerging at that time.

In parallel with these national changes, the first half of the decade saw the identification of some significant local initiatives that contributed to the national debate. It was through one of these that school development planning finally came to fruition. It was the work of one local authority in particular that resulted in SDPs receiving national attention. In a drive to raise levels of achievement, ILEA commissioned two reports, one on secondary education, the other on primary education. The findings of the secondary review, chaired by David Hargreaves, were published in 1984 (ILEA, 1984) entitled *Improving Secondary Schools*. The report recommended a planned approach to school development in which individual schools be required to establish priorities for improvement. In 1985 the findings of the primary review, chaired by Norman Thomas, were also published (ILEA, 1985). It was in this report, *Improving Primary Schools*, that a formal recommendation was made about SDPs as a result of committee members observing their successful use by individual schools:

> We recommend that every school should have a plan for development, taking account of the policies of the Authority, the needs of the children, the capabilities of the staff, and the known views of the parents. The plan should have an action sheet attached to it, showing what the responsibilities of members of staff will be and setting target dates. The plan should also show what, if any, outside assistance or special resources will be needed and indicate time scales; it should also show by what means the effects of the plan are to be assessed. The central purpose should be expressed in terms of the improvements sought in the children's learning.
>
> (*Ibid.*, para. 3.94)

This local initiative was to become a national recommendation a year later. In 1986 a report from the House of Commons Education, Science and Arts Committee (para. 14.167) included:

> We recommend that every primary school . . . should be required to operate according to a development plan agreed between it and the governing body and/or LEA, subject to the school's county or voluntary status. The plan should take account of the policies of the government, LEA, governing body, the capacities of the staff and the known views of the parents. The plan should have an action sheet attached to it showing what the responsibilities of members of staff will be and setting target dates. A plan might well take more than a year, and would be one of a continuing series. Such a plan should show what, if any, outside assistance or special resources would be needed. It should show by what means the effects of the plan are to be assessed. The central purpose should be expressed in terms of the improvements sought in children's learning. Agreement by the LEA and governing body would include agreement to the resources, including INSET, necessary to the plan's success.

Given that Thomas was an adviser to this committee, the source of this recommendation is self-evident. It is also worth noting that in a memorandum to this committee, the DES stressed the relationship between INSET and school-based developments. The changes in the wording from the original ILEA recommendations, however, were significant, and included the need for schools to take account of government policies and those of the governing body. It was at this stage that the impetus for SDPs changed from a local to a national one.

THE IMPACT OF THE 1988 AND SUBSEQUENT LEGISLATION ON SCHOOL DEVELOPMENT PLANNING

The Education Reform Act 1988 (DES, 1988a) had significant implications for school development planning. It resulted in the broadening of the purpose of SDPs to enable this innovation to provide the means whereby the requirements emanating from the 1988 and subsequent legislation could be accommodated by schools. It led to the government exerting pressure on schools to engage in development planning. Apart from the National Curriculum and the new assessment arrangements, the self-management of schools became a central plank of government policy. The requirement for LEAs to devolve funding to schools as part of the local management of schools (LMS) legislation (DES, 1988b) meant that schools would become increasingly responsible for resource management including premises, staffing, INSET and curriculum development. Evidence is now available that schools perceived SDPs as a solution to coping with the demands of the new legislation. As one headteacher (Glover, 1990) put it: 'There was a desperate need for a planned approach to 1988' (p. 23) and the school development plan provided a means of dealing with 'initiative overload' (p. 22).

In 1989 the DES commissioned Hargreaves and Hopkins to undertake a research project to provide guidance for schools and LEAs on school development planning. As a result of this initiative two publications emerged which were sent to every school in the country (DES, 1989a; 1991a). Both publications provided advice on ways of formulating, implementing and evaluating SDPs. In the same year, the National Curriculum Council (NCC, 1989) advised schools to establish a National Curriculum development plan. It was unclear what the difference was between this and an SDP, although in an HMI report on the early stages of the implementation of the National Curriculum in primary schools (DES, 1989b, para. 26) it was reported that

> The progress of drawing up, and the quality of, school development plans and curriculum development plans varied markedly. As might be expected, in authorities where development plans had been requested for some time the schools had less difficulty adjusting to the additional planning requirements than those with no such experience. Most of the schools needed to relate their school development plans more closely to the requirements of the whole curriculum, including the National Curriculum, and to identify the curricular demands upon individual teachers.

Additional guidance emanating from the Hargreaves and Hopkins project was made available by the DES to LEAs in the form of a paper (Hargreaves *et al.*, 1990). It indicated the kind of support and advice that LEAs needed to provide, particularly for schools experiencing difficulty with school development planning. Our survey of 135 LEAs (Beresford, 1994), which achieved 100 per cent response, revealed that the number of LEAs that had a policy on development planning by the academic year 1990/1 had increased significantly from 5 per cent pre-1988 to 83 per cent. There was every indication, therefore, that the 1988 legislation was a watershed in respect of the expansion of SDPs.

Three other government initiatives had a strong link with SDPs. The first concerned performance indicators. In 1989 the government commissioned a working party to identify a core set of performance indicators for judging the work of schools. The task proved to be more complex than anticipated and the findings were made available in the form of an *aide-mémoire* (DES, 1989c). Management was one of the six main sections identified. Under this heading seven out of ten indicators referred directly or indirectly to SDPs. By implication, the quality of school development planning was seen as a measure of school effectiveness.

In 1990, as part of the government's policy on local management, a School Management Task Force (SMTF) was established. Later that year the SMTF produced a report (DES, 1990) in which SDPs that incorporated a management and staff development policy were seen as a characteristic of successful schools.

The third initiative concerned significant changes in school inspection. In 1989 a report by the Audit Commission (1989a) on school inspection was published. The government had commissioned the report because it was concerned to highlight the need for LEA inspectors to be more rigorous about monitoring and reporting on the quality of work in schools. The report was critical of the number of LEAs in which inspection was not a high priority. It was said that inspectors or advisers were spending a disproportionate amount of time on development and advisory work. This subsequently led to a change in LEAs in the balance between inspection and development work with inspection receiving a much higher profile. Three years later, following the Education (Schools) Act 1992, SDPs were included in the national programme of inspections. In the draft *Framework for the Inspection of Schools* (Ofsted, 1992, para. 6.4), there was a section on management and planning in which inspectors were required to make 'a judgement on the quality of the school development plan, its usefulness as an instrument of change and development, its realism and the achievement of any priorities set'. Similarly, the subsequent Office for Standards in Education (Ofsted) inspection handbook (1993) provided criteria for the assessment of the effectiveness of a school's development plan. The focus of this document, however, was on the management of the process, not necessarily its impact.

A year later, in the evidence provided by the Department for Education (DFE) report to the School Teachers' Review Body (Gardiner, 1994), the promotion of SDPs as one of the steps taken to encourage improvements in school management was listed. For the same review body, however, Ofsted reported that recent inspections had revealed that whilst in primary schools the quality of SDPs had improved, monitoring and evaluating the standards achieved and the quality of work in classrooms was the most frequently neglected management task. The need for a stronger evaluative dimension was stressed if schools were to assess whether or not goals set had been achieved. It was reported that in half the secondary schools inspected in past years there had been significant weaknesses in the SDP. Again, the inadequacy of monitoring, evaluation and review was emphasised. Given the significant changes in the role of LEAs since 1988, not least the steady reduction and, in some cases, the total removal of a local infrastructure of advice and support, it is not clear to whom schools will turn for help in addressing and overcoming the kinds of weaknesses identified by Ofsted.

OVERVIEW

From this brief historical review of the introduction and expansion of school development planning, it can be seen that SDPs have been used in an attempt to meet the needs of different interest groups and to serve a growing range of purposes. Initially, individual schools, and then LEAs, used them for curriculum and professional development purposes. They were seen as a means of developing whole-school policies through the process of self-review, supported by the LEA. In turn, SDPs provided a vehicle for LEAs to encourage schools to be more accountable for the curriculum on offer and for the organisation of INSET related to school-wide priorities for improvement. The introduction of the National Curriculum and its assessment and changes in INSET funding both provided added impetus for a planned approach to change.

The introduction of LMS and of a national programme of inspection noticeably broadened the purposes of development planning. Its use as a management tool, rather than a developmental process, began to be emphasised in official documents. There appeared to be an expectation by central government that SDPs would enable schools to fulfil the additional planning requirements of the 1988 legislation, not least financial delegation. Skelton *et al.* (1991) offer this as the main rationale for school development planning. The pressure on schools from central government to have a development plan noticeably increased after 1988. By implication, SDPs were now being used as part of a means of controlling schools and making them more accountable. The focus on school development planning as a vehicle for meeting a school's own self-review, evaluation and development purposes was realigned as it became perceived as an external measure of a school's effectiveness.

The juxtaposition of these multiple purposes appears to be generally unquestioned, as does the perceived cause and effect relationship between school development planning and school improvement. The state of readiness of

individual schools to use development planning to meet these different requirements also appears to be taken for granted, despite the findings of Hargreaves
et al. (1990) about the necessity for LEA support and the subsequent criticism
from Ofsted (Gardiner, 1994). Although a coherent approach to support and
advice of a developmental nature, as opposed to inspection, is rapidly diminishing at LEA level, there appears to be an expectation that schools will be
able, at the appropriate time, to purchase support to meet their own identified
needs.

Underlying the multipurpose nature of school development planning is a
set of issues that research needs either to address directly or to take into
account. There is a potential conflict, or at least a tension, between development and accountability. Likewise, the balance between the use of development planning to control the work of schools and the extent to which it can
empower a school's own development will be a consideration not least because, increasingly, SDPs have become an innovation imposed from outside.
The relationship between a process – used as a management strategy to cope
with multiple change – and the notion of development planning as being a
school improvement strategy will also need to be examined. So, too, will be
the question of whether or not schools have been diverted too far from the
original central purpose of development planning, namely, to improve the
quality of pupil learning.

2

THE DEVELOPMENT PLANNING PROCESS

HMI and subsequent Ofsted criticism of SDPs has concentrated on different aspects of the planning process. Initially, concern was focused on the content of plans and on roles and on responsibilities (DES, 1989b). Five years later criticism was directed at monitoring and evaluation procedures (Ofsted, 1994). There is an apparent assumption that if schools concentrate on particular aspects of development planning, the quality of the overall process will automatically improve; the planning cycle, as a whole, appears to have been taken for granted. This chapter examines all aspects of the process in detail through a close scrutiny of the guidance which was available nationally in the early stages of our project. It reveals that development planning is much more complex than often portrayed in the literature.

> In its simplest form a SDP brings together in an overall plan, national and LEA policies and initiatives, the school's aims and values, its existing achievements and needs for development, and enables it to organise what it is already doing and what it needs to do in a more purposeful and coherent way.
>
> (Hopkins, 1991, p. 61)

The unifying nature of the development planning process is a common theme. Development planning is seen as a means whereby the planning for different aspects of the life and work of a school can be brought together in an integrated way. The process is said to enable priorities for development which incorporate local and national requirements as well as school-generated concerns to be established. The development planning process, itself, is portrayed as a rational approach to the management of change; a sequential process, the different stages of which form a planning cycle, as illustrated in Figure 2.1.

The problems associated with such an approach to school management are discussed in detail in Chapter 4. Basically, the process involves formulating, implementing and evaluating a plan for development in which short, medium and long-term targets for improvement are identified. This process enables those involved in a school to decide in advance what is to be done, how it is to be done and whether or not the desired outcomes have been achieved.

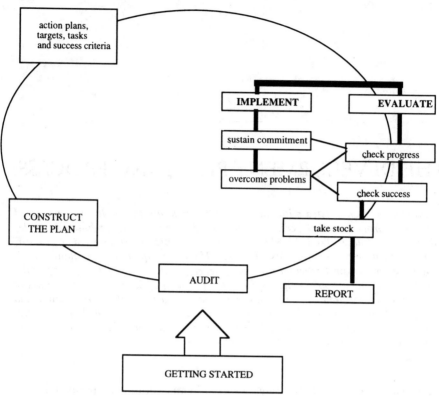

Figure 2.1   The planning process
Source: DES (1989a, p. 14)

The most substantial guidance available on development planning has been produced as a result of the School Development Plans Project referred to in Chapter 1. This DES-sponsored study was codirected by Hargreaves and Hopkins. The project involved field visits to 40 schools in 14 LEAs, discussions with governors, LEA officers and inspectors and an examination of a range of LEA documentary advice to schools on SDPs. As noted in Chapter 1, the project resulted in the publication of two DES practical guides on development planning for governors, headteachers and teachers (DES, 1989a; 1991a). An additional paper, written for LEAs, was entitled *The Management of Development Planning* (Hargreaves *et al.*, 1990). The purpose of this document, which was sent to all chief education officers by the DES, was to assist LEAs in establishing their policies and strategies for development planning in partnership with schools. It paid particular attention to diagnosing the difficulties some schools experience with development planning and the kinds of support needed in these circumstances. Hargreaves and Hopkins (1991) then published their own book on development planning. This was a compilation of the findings of their study and included an attempt to use some of the key principles of the school effectiveness, improvement and educational change literature to provide a rationale for development planning. In the same year, Skelton *et al.* (1991) published a practical guide to development planning for primary schools. The guide drew on the DES research project, some of the relevant literature (most noticeably in the field of management) and on the authors' own experiences of working in and with primary schools engaged in development planning. They drew, in particular, on the work of schools in one LEA where development planning appears to have been introduced successfully over a period of four years. Another guide to development planning was published a year later (Davies and Ellison, 1992). This book took the form of a management guide for senior staff in primary and secondary schools with a focus on the importance of development planning for effective and efficient self-management. It offered a step-by-step approach to designing and completing an SDP and used examples of actual plans written by a few schools and a reporting format developed by one LEA. The handbook did not draw on the findings of the DES project, and the use of the literature available was very selective and limited. Also in 1992, a further guide with a focus on business planning was published (Puffitt *et al.*, 1992).

What follows is a description of the development planning process drawing on the advice offered in the literature we have cited. Our description is interwoven with a commentary on the similarities and differences in the guidance provided by the various authors.

FORMULATING THE PLAN

The audit

There is agreement in the school development literature that in order to formulate a plan, schools need to begin by carrying out an audit. This is an information-gathering exercise: a means whereby current strengths and weaknesses are identified to enable a school to make informed decisions about future planning priorities. The audit 'serves to provide a description of the school as it is now' (Skelton *et al.*, 1991, p. 32). The importance of the context of the audit is emphasised in the advice offered. The DES guidance (1989a; 1991a) stresses that when conducting an audit, schools should take account of their own aims and values, LEA and national policies and initiatives, outcomes of appraisal interviews, recent reviews and inspections and the views of those working in the school or connected with it in the community. Davies and Ellison (1992) argue that defining or redefining the aims of the school is a necessary prerequisite for establishing an SDP, because the plan can then be used as a vehicle for realising aims in practice.

There are conflicting views about the length of the audit and the content of the exercise. There is a consensus that development planning must be an ongoing process in which outline plans for two to three years are mapped out and are supported by detailed action plans for any one year. The DES guidelines (1991a) discourage lengthy, comprehensive audits. Instead, a rolling programme of specific audits in key areas is advocated to enable schools to accommodate to the rapid pace of change. A menu of 12 options is identified from which schools can make a selection for an intensive audit in any one year (*ibid.*, p. 33):

- pupils' diversity and achievements
- curriculum provision and access
- assessment and recording
- pupil attendance, punctuality and behaviour
- teaching styles and methods
- responsibilities of the teaching staff
- school management and organisation
- relationships with parents
- partnership with the local community
- links with other schools and colleges
- school, LEA and national documents
- resources.

The DES advice is that two of these options, namely curriculum provision and resources, be audited each year. The reasons given concern the demands of the National Curriculum legislation and the need for financial and resource planning to support the construction and implementation of the plan.

Skelton *et al.* (1991, pp. 19–21) suggest a different approach. They identify six key areas for development:

- the developing curriculum
- the staff
- the school constituency
- buildings and sites
- organisational systems
- the climate.

The authors argue that these represent the important dimensions of a school and that every two to three years the six should be audited to provide a comprehensive picture of the school. They acknowledge that, having done this, all six aspects may not appear in the final plan.

Davies and Ellison (1992, p. 9) offer yet another strategy. They describe an SDP as a summary; a means of integrating separate plans covering 'core' and 'support' elements in the school. These are defined as:

Core elements	*Support elements*
• curriculum and curriculum development	• physical resources
	• pupil roll and marketing
• human resources	• management structures and approaches
• pupil welfare and pastoral care	• monitoring and evaluation mechanisms
	• financial resources

The authors argue the need for SDPs to cover all eight elements in any one year as part of a three-year, long-term plan. To avoid overload they acknowledge that it may be necessary to prioritise the elements to be considered in detail each year. Like Hargreaves and Hopkins (1991) they suggest that certain elements, for example the curriculum, be examined in detail annually. It is understandable, given the requirements of the National Curriculum, that all the guidance advises that the curriculum should be audited annually. However, beyond that, the difference between the approaches is significant. Interestingly, it is only the DES guidance that focuses attention on teaching and learning and, in particular, on pupil achievement.

Two further issues to be considered at the auditing stage are identified in the literature. These concern decisions about *who* is to be involved and *how* the audit is to be conducted. In many respects the content of the audit will determine who needs to be involved. The DES guidelines (1991a) suggest that governors select the content of the audit on the advice of the headteacher, following consultation with the staff. The more comprehensive audit suggested by the other writers points to the need for a wider constituency of involvement which includes parents, pupils and others concerned with the work of the school. The practicalities of achieving this, however, are not addressed. Skelton *et al.* (1991, p. 34) identify issues to be considered when deciding who is to be involved in planning and argue for the need for an external view to avoid the risk of 'the staff becoming victims of their own institutional culture'. All the sources of advice agree that regardless of who is involved, there is a need to clarify roles and responsibilities in the process.

It is likely that the content of the audit will also determine, in part, the strategy chosen for carrying out the review. The DES guidance (1991a, p. 5) identifies three kinds of strategies from which schools can choose:

- getting an external perspective
- using a published scheme
- designing their own approach.

It lists the strengths and weaknesses of each and suggests that schools have found in practice that a combination of strategies best serves their needs. Such a combination enables evidence to be gathered about different aspects of the life and work of the school upon which to establish priorities for future action. The increasing difficulty of schools having access to an LEA perspective, other than in the context of an inspection, is an issue raised in Chapter 1.

The construction of the plan

On completion of an audit, a school is now deemed ready to construct a plan for development. A consistent message in the literature is the need for the plan to be realistic and achievable. Hargreaves and Hopkins (1991, p. 40) identify four processes in constructing a plan:

- taking account of the context
- consulting about possible priorities
- making a decision on the priorities
- writing up and publicising the plan.

The same contextual issues as for the audit are also seen to apply at this stage. In addition, schools are advised to use the findings of the audit along with information about available financial resources. Davies and Ellison (1992) stress the importance of setting educational priorities into a financial context and offer advice on how this can be achieved.

Common to all the advice is the need to obtain agreement about which priorities will be included in both the long-term two- to three-year plans and the detailed one-year plan. The necessity of effective consultation and decision-making procedures in order to turn a long list of priorities into a shortlist of manageable, coherent priorities is emphasised. Davies and Ellison (1992) suggest that separate plans for each of the eight elements be drawn up through a process of decision-making about short and long-term priorities and that the governors and the senior management team make the final decision about the overall SDP. The eight elements concern school-wide management issues. This fact, coupled with the approach to decision-making advocated, does raise questions about the degree of ownership the teaching staff as a whole is likely to have of the priorities for development chosen.

Hargreaves and Hopkins (1991, pp. 42–3) take a different approach. They recommend the identification of three or four major priorities and that, in order to achieve this, the governors, headteacher and staff review the findings of the audit and:

- consider urgency, need and desirability
- estimate size and scope
- distinguish between root and branch innovations
- forge links between priorities.

The first strategy speaks for itself not least because some priorities will be unavoidable because they are linked with legislation. The second has particular relevance for manageability. It concerns the need for schools to consider the scope and complexity of priorities and warns against schools taking on too many major priorities of considerable size and scope in any one year. Closely related to this is the third strategy. Hargreaves and Hopkins draw on the metaphor of growth in relation to bringing about change. They point to the fact that 'a school may lack roots of sufficient strength and depth to support the branches of innovation which represent its growth from existing practice. Development planning involves two kinds of change: root innovations that generate the base on which other, or branch innovations, can be sustained' (*ibid.*, p. 43).

Hargreaves and Hopkins advise schools to assess whether or not sufficient roots, or foundations, exist for the implementation of an identified priority. They put forward the view that such a distinction can assist headteachers in deciding upon the sequencing of priorities. The fourth strategy concerns the extent to which links between priorities can be established so as to achieve coherence where possible. It is argued that this can strengthen the plan itself and encourage collaboration. Whilst this advice has a ring of 'common sense' about it, it is likely to require skilled leadership and a degree of confidence to adhere to, particularly if the school has recently been inspected and the head-teacher is under pressure to produce results quickly.

The need for a systematic approach to obtaining agreement about the content of the plan is a consistent recommendation in the guidance available. What is less clear is where responsibility lies for actually approving the final plan. Skelton *et al.* (1991) make no mention of this specific part of the process. By implication, they see achieving consensus within the school as the key factor. Davies and Ellison (1992) link approval of the plan with budgetary decisions that involve joint decision-making between the senior management team and the governors. In contrast, Hargreaves and Hopkins (1991) state explicitly that governors should approve the plan before it is published. Very little reference is made in the advice of the need for, or the possibility of, external approval of the plan, for example, by the LEA. This is an interesting departure from the original House of Commons Select Committee recommendation described in Chapter 1.

In general, the exact involvement of the LEA at the formulation stage is unclear in the national guidance available. Whilst some reference is made to LEA proformas for SDPs in the DES documents, it is only in the Hargreaves *et al.* (1990) guidance for LEAs on the management of development planning (which is amplified in the subsequent book by Hargreaves and Hopkins, 1991) that the important role of the LEA in supporting schools in the development planning process is emphasised.

The publication of the plan

All the guidance offers advice about the format for the publication of the development plan. The general consensus is that the published plan should, in the words of Davies and Ellison (1992, p. 75), be 'concise, understandable, relevant, usable, and clear'. The DES guidance (1989a, p. 10) suggests that the length should be no more than four to five pages and should include:

- the aims of the school
- the proposed priorities and their timescale
- the justification of the priorities in the context of the school
- how the plan draws together different aspects of planning
- the methods of reporting outcomes
- the broad financial implications of the plan.

The uniqueness of each school's plan is often emphasised and it is stated that it will be for schools to decide the final format. Skelton *et al.* (1991, pp. 166–7), for example, emphasise the importance of an agreed format within the school. They argue that it:

- demonstrates involvement
- provides a focus for action
- provides a means of presenting the plan
- provides a means of assessing progress.

Skelton *et al.* also suggest that a summary plan of the key targets and time-scales might be the most appropriate format for wider circulation, perhaps for pupils and parents for example. This could then be supplemented by more detailed plans indicating how the plan is to be put into action. They then go on to identify criteria which need to be taken into consideration when deciding the format. It should (*ibid.*, p. 108):

- contain realistic targets
- include a timescale
- define responsibilities
- outline resource and financial needs
- be presented as simply as possible.

Davies and Ellison (1992) disagree. They recommend that detailed action plans for the coming year, including objectives, targets and success criteria, be published in the overall plan. There appears to be a mismatch between this recommendation and the criteria for the published plan. What is at issue here is the audience for the plan. It is only Skelton *et al.* (1991) who describe two types of published plan. These authors make a distinction between a general plan for wide circulation and a detailed, practical document for those directly responsible for implementing the plan. The need to ensure that the plan is a working document likely to lead to action seems to us to be an important issue: the transition between formulating and implementing a plan for development receives much attention in the literature.

IMPLEMENTING THE PLAN

> The hardest part of development planning is making things happen: turn-ing good intentions into something that makes a difference to the quality of pupils' learning.
>
> (DES, 1991a, p. 8)

Establishing an action plan

All the guides focus on the importance of translating priorities into an action plan; a working document which details specific targets, tasks, timescales, responsibilities, resource implications and review procedures. Skelton *et al.*

(1991) emphasise the need to set realistic, achievable targets that are clearly expressed and understood by those responsible for implementing them. They argue (p. 66) that, wherever possible, targets 'should be stated in such a way as to identify the level of success on completion'.

The DES guidance (1989a) takes up a similar point and stresses the importance of identifying success criteria related to each target at this stage in the planning process. Success criteria are seen (p. 11) as 'a form of school-generated performance indicator . . . the means for evaluating the plan . . . the evidence needed to judge successful implementation'. Davies and Ellison (1992) emphasise the value of school-generated success criteria and suggest that the level of achievement acceptable in relation to each success criterion be built in at the planning stage. Hargreaves and Hopkins (1991) provide a much more detailed description of success criteria. Unlike the DES guidance, which only equates success criteria with quantitative measures, they argue that they can also be qualitative in nature. Their use in development planning is seen (*ibid.*, p. 140) as distinctive in that success criteria:

- refer to future rather than past performance
- relate to a planned target designed to improve performance
- are chosen by the persons who set the target
- influence the way the target is designed
- emphasise success rather than failure
- are a key component at each stage of development planning.

Hargreaves and Hopkins (*ibid.*, p. 141) argue that such criteria can exert a positive influence on ways of thinking and ways of working in that they can:

- promote desirable goals for schools
- suggest standards appropriate to such goals
- guide the action needed to achieve agreed standards
- distinguish between process and outcome
- indicate the evidence needed to judge success
- help in reporting success
- shape further action if the degree of success falls short of expectation.

In relation to success criteria, Skelton *et al.* (1991, p. 68) warn against the danger 'of attempting to measure the immeasurable'. They refer to Eisner's (1979; 1985) distinction between 'instructional' objectives (targets) and 'expressive' objectives (targets), the former being much more conducive to measuring outcomes than the latter. They argue (1991, p. 67) that there are some profound differences between these two kinds of objectives or targets which have 'implications for the way in which targets are evaluated, for the way job descriptions are defined and for the way success is measured'. Skelton *et al.* also offer advice as to how targets can be set in relation to these differences.

Whilst the aims of success criteria and the recognition of the need to identify both qualitative and quantitative 'measures' are laudable, it is only Skelton *et al.* who begin to unpack some of the underlying difficulties of this aspect of the planning process. The complex issues concerned with assessing the general effectiveness of a school and the value it adds to pupil progress and achievement are ignored in the guidance despite a growing literature in this area (Nuttall *et al.*, 1989; Smith and Tomlinson, 1989; Gray and Jesson, 1990; Cuttance, 1992; Gray, 1993; Sammons *et al.*, 1993; Mortimore *et al.*, 1994). There also appears to be an assumption that schools already have the knowledge and skills necessary to create their own success criteria. This is a questionable assumption, not least in the light of Ofsted's (1994) criticism of this aspect of development planning.

The need to build evaluation into the action plan is clear. A strong message from the Hargreaves and Hopkins study, which is endorsed by Skelton *et al.* (1991), is that implementation and evaluation must be linked to ensure that evaluation helps to 'shape and guide the action plan rather than being a post-mortem upon it' (DES, 1989a, p. 14). It is probably for this reason that there is a recommendation in the DES guidance that regular progress checks be built into the action plan before it is implemented.

Once targets and success criteria have been agreed, the DES guidance (1989a) focuses on the need to identify specific tasks in relation to each target and who will be responsible for achieving these tasks within a given timescale. Skelton *et al.* (1991) concur with this advice and emphasise that, if necessary, job descriptions may have to be refined or renegotiated to ensure that targets can be met. Both sets of guidance refer to the need to resource the action plan adequately in terms of finance, materials and INSET. 'Action plans cannot be implemented properly unless they are carefully coordinated with the INSET planning' (DES, 1989a, p. 12). Both identify the need to create links between appraisal concerned with the professional development of individuals, and staff development concerned with the development of the school as a whole. This detailed advice on the establishment of an action plan is in contrast to the limited advice from Ofsted about action planning (1993) and a lack of clarity about the relationship between a post-Ofsted action plan and action planning as part of the development planning process.

Implementing the action plan

Davies and Ellison (1992) pay little attention to the implementation process. By implication, they appear to assume that there will be no gap between the rhetoric of the written plan and the reality of practice. Hargreaves and Hopkins (1991, p. 67), however, warn of the dangers of assuming that an action plan will automatically be acted upon: 'Experience suggests that implementation does not proceed on automatic pilot.' They identify (*ibid.*, p. 65) the activities required to make the plan work:

- sustaining commitment during implementation
- checking the progress of implementation

- overcoming any problems encountered
- checking the success of implementation
- taking stock
- reporting progress
- constructing the next development plan.

They also provide detailed advice on each of the activities listed. Likewise, Skelton *et al.* (1991) emphasise the importance of people management and identify a range of strategies for supporting and motivating staff. The possible involvement of others in the implementation of the plan, such as pupils, governors and LEA personnel, is seldom referred to by any of those commenting on school development planning.

EVALUATING THE PLAN

Procedures for monitoring the plan

It is in their description of the evaluation process that Davies and Ellison (1992) confirm their mechanistic and, what appears to us to be, a somewhat simplistic view of development planning. They argue for a value-added approach which enables a school to examine the links among inputs, processes and outputs. In itself, this is a reasonable suggestion, but no mention is made of the potential difficulties underlying such an approach; rather, schools are simply advised to be clear about which form of evaluation is being used.

Hargreaves and Hopkins (1991) take a different approach. They argue that monitoring must serve two functions. It must enable an ongoing evaluation of the implementation process itself and its management, as well as providing the means whereby the extent to which targets have been achieved can be assessed. Skelton *et al.* (1991) develop this theme even further. They stress the need to monitor action throughout the planning process and draw attention to the kinds of evidence to look for beginning with the audit stage.

Reviewing and evaluating outcomes

Taking stock and reviewing outcomes is described in the guidance available as the final stage in the planning cycle. The first DES guidelines (1989a, p. 17) state that the purpose of taking stock is to:

- examine the success of the implementation of the plan
- assess the extent to which the school's aims have been furthered
- assess the impact of the plan on pupils' learning and achievement
- decide how to disseminate successful new practices throughout the school
- make the process of reporting easier.

This process is a means of fulfilling a 'mini audit'; a necessary preparation for reporting progress and constructing the next plan.

Procedures for carrying out success checks, based on the success criteria for the targets established during the construction of the action plan, are described in the DES guidance (1989a). Skelton *et al.* (1991) draw attention to the complex nature of the task of evaluating the extent to which targets have been achieved. They warn (*ibid.*, p. 125) against simplistic checks that simply focus on whether or not an activity has taken place: 'Even when something has been done, there is no guarantee that it has achieved what has been intended.' They advise schools to use a wide range of evaluation strategies and suggest a systematic process to conduct the review. Hargreaves and Hopkins (1991) stress the role that development planning can play, particularly during the evaluation phase, in enhancing the professional judgement of teachers. They suggest that teachers' judgements can be refined through discussion, seeking agreement on standards, observing one another and reading relevant literature. They argue the need for professional judgement to be complemented by a combination of qualitative and quantitative evidence. There is no mention of the possible role of others in evaluating outcomes, such as governors and outside agencies.

Reporting progress

The result of the review provides the information needed for reporting progress. There is agreement in the guidance that the outcomes of the planning cycle should be reported upon but, with the exception of Skelton *et al.* (1991), scant attention is paid to this aspect of the process. There is a consensus of opinion that the governors should be kept informed and the DES guides suggest that they receive an annual progress report. In respect of parents, the DES guides suggest ways in which they may be informed, although the right of parents to have access to SDP reports is unclear. The DES guides are alone in making reference to the possibility of reporting to pupils. Despite the fact that Davies and Ellison (1992) see an SDP as a basis for an external audit and evaluation of the school by the LEA or other external agency, they do no more than raise the question as to whether or not it is appropriate to provide a report for the LEA. Whilst the DES guides make no mention of LEAs, Skelton *et al.* (1991) maintain that they need to receive reports to assist with meeting statutory obligations. The authors go on to argue that the content and format of SDP reports should vary depending on the audience and purpose which, in turn, will determine the frequency of reports.

Recommencing the planning process

The reporting process signals the 'end' of the planning cycle. It is at this point that schools are advised to start again and construct the next plan. However, all the sources of guidance agree that plans do not have a discrete beginning and end. They are said (Hargreaves and Hopkins, 1991, p. 72) to represent a continuous cycle of development in which priorities and specific targets may be achieved, refined or perhaps changed because of factors such as:

- any lessons learnt from taking stock of the implementation of the original plan
- the outcomes of the school's annual audit of curriculum and resources
- the outcomes of any specific audit undertaken as part of the school's rolling programme of audits
- changes in national and local policies and initiatives
- the changing needs and circumstances of the school
- any slow-down or acceleration in progress.

The message in the guidance offered is that the process of development planning provides a flexible framework which enables schools to plan ahead but, at the same time, be able to respond to changing circumstances. Skelton *et al.* (1991, p. 15) maintain that 'school development planning should be about maximising success and reducing failure'. They refer (p. 16) to the findings of Hargreaves and Hopkins (1991) which suggest that schools go through three stages in relation to SDPs:

- the need for and creation of a plan
- an understanding that the processes involved in creating and implementing the plan are important
- an understanding that the effective management of those processes is the real key to success.

Hargreaves and Hopkins (1991, p. 4) argue that

> The production of a good plan and its successful implementation depend upon a sound grasp of the processes involved. A wise choice of content for the plan as well as the means of implementing the plan successfully will be made only when the process of development planning is thoroughly understood.

3

THE COMPLEXITY OF DEVELOPMENT PLANNING

This chapter focuses on some of the complex issues which underlie development planning. As well as commenting on aspects of the process itself, it provides an analysis of key factors concerned with the purpose of development planning; the context within which planning takes place; and the content of plans and their outcomes. It draws attention to the potential gap which can occur between the rhetoric of plans and the reality of their impact in practice.

What is clear from the quotation that ended the last chapter is that the success of development planning is seen as conditional; it depends on the knowledge and actions of those using the process. Hargreaves and Hopkins (1991, p. 83) claim that their book

> like most guidelines on school development plans, consists of a recipe of advice which, if followed sensibly and creatively, should help a school to achieve its aims and manage change successfully . . . The school's response to development planning is a reflection of its culture. Some schools respond to the advice as intended and find the advice helpful and relatively easy to put into effect. Other schools cannot or do not respond as expected; and yet it is often precisely these schools which are in greatest need of this advice. The consequence is that the gap between the most and the least effective schools tends to widen.

They conclude that the solution to this problem is the establishment of a particular kind of strategic partnership between schools and LEA officers. The process itself goes unquestioned.

On the one hand, Hargreaves and Hopkins (*ibid.*, p. 86) argue that there is a relationship between successful development planning and school effectiveness yet, at the same time, they argue that a school's ability to use development planning successfully is 'not intended as a measure of school effectiveness'. This apparent contradiction is compounded in the description provided of the characteristics of schools that have difficulties with development planning. The diagnosis of difficulty invites the reader to place schools along a continuum of strengths and weaknesses. The characteristics illustrated reflect the findings of some of the research literature on school effectiveness (Rutter *et al.*, 1979; Purkey and Smith, 1983; Mortimore *et al.*, 1988). They go on to argue that there are conditions that schools need to take account of and tensions they need to resolve to maximise the development planning process. The conditions and tensions identified draw on the findings of the school effectiveness and school improvement literature, although the authors acknowledge that their review of the literature is limited and for this they have been criticised (Hutchinson, 1993). Despite this, they claim (Hargreaves and Hopkins, 1991, p. 110) that there is 'a great deal of similarity between the characteristics of the "effective school" and our description of the management arrangements appropriate for sustaining school development planning'. 'We are pleased to report that other school improvement research is consistent with our general advice' (*ibid.*, p. 117). This begs the question as to whether a school has to be effective before it can be successful at development planning or whether development planning can, in itself, help to make a school more effective.

Hargreaves and Hopkins claim that development planning can respond to the subtle nature of change in school because it concerns the school as a whole, its culture and its management. However, the recipe nature of the process model they describe could well encourage schools to ignore the subtleties of change and take a rather mechanistic approach to school development. A restructuring process that does not touch the underlying culture of the school (Fullan and Hargreaves, 1992) could be the result. This would defeat the central argument of the authors. There appears to be a tension between the acknowledgement in the book that schools have been described as non-rational organisations (Patterson *et al.*, 1986) and that change is a complex rather than a smooth process, and the scientific approach to development that is portrayed. There are those who have warned of the dangers of mechanistic management models (Taylor, 1976; Bottery, 1988) and those who have argued that goal-orientated models of management can result in a narrowing rather than a broadening out of educational outcomes (Bush, 1986). Hargreaves and Hopkins accept that development planning is in its infancy, yet they appear to have no hesitation in expressing a strong conviction about the key role of development planning as a means of improving schools.

Skelton *et al.* (1991, p. 189) also recognise that development planning is in its infancy. They point out the dangers of perceiving it as a more rational process than it really is and state that 'development planning cannot, by itself, create an effective school'. They argue (*ibid.*) that 'There is a necessary and strong element of rationality and careful, analytical thought is vital if effective development plans are to be produced'. They attempt to strike a balance between warning the reader about the inherent difficulties of systematic planning, and promoting development planning (*ibid.*, p. 6) as 'the most important tool we can use to create a clear direction from the many demands being placed upon us'.

There are very few conditions and tensions identified by Davies and Ellison (1992). They choose to ignore totally the research literature about the complexity of change in schools and offer advice within a narrow management paradigm. Whilst they acknowledge that there can be difficulties with a rational approach to planning, they claim that proactive management is the answer. They provide advice on the characteristics of effective planning and argue (*ibid.*, p. 11) that development plans should be 'the central feature of the school's management activity'. They present development planning as a systematic approach to management driven by financial considerations.

A similar, unquestioning approach to development planning is taken in the DES guidance. It ignores the difficulties identified in the study by Hargreaves and Hopkins and is prescriptive in style. Although the guidance acknowledges that it is easier to construct a plan than to implement one, a mechanistic approach to the management of people is taken. The assumption is that all schools will, in the words of Hargreaves and Hopkins, follow the advice 'sensibly and creatively'.

SPECIFIC ISSUES

A number of specific issues related to the development planning process that need to be clarified to provide a clearer framework for this study have been identified by this preliminary analysis. These concern the nature of the process itself and the conditions needed for it to be used successfully in schools. Five key aspects of development planning that require further analysis concern the

- purpose,
- context,
- process,
- content and
- outcomes

of development planning. All five are closely inter-related but need to be discussed in detail.

The purpose of development planning

What is clear from our brief examination of the literature is that development planning is seen to fulfil a wide range of purposes. There is general agreement that the ultimate aim of development planning is to improve the quality of pupils' learning, although little or no evidence is provided to substantiate this claim. The few case studies there are in the available guidance tend to focus on the plan and the planning process. Those writing about their experiences of development planning tend to do likewise and, where outcomes are mentioned, these are related to teachers, not pupils (Jordan, 1989; Glover, 1990; Biott *et al.*, 1994; Newman and Pollard, 1994).

Beyond this generalised rationale for development planning, a range of other purposes has been identified. These all concern the use of development planning as a means of exercising control over the work of schools. There are those who argue that the purpose of development planning is to bring about externally imposed change (Wallace, 1991a; Hutchinson, 1993). There are also those who argue that SDPs empower schools to take control over their own development (Hargreaves and Hopkins, 1991). There is a tension between these two different but related perspectives which is likely to have implications for schools. Externally imposed SDPs may well place schools in a reactive, defensive mode and may result in a lack of ownership. Internally produced and controlled SDPs could well have the opposite effect. There is research evidence emerging, for example, to show that imposing SDPs on schools does not necessarily achieve the desired outcomes (Wallace, 1991b; Cuttance, 1992; Hutchinson, 1993).

In the Australian context, SDPs have been introduced to facilitate the restructuring of the educational system (Cuttance, 1994). They have been described as 'a useful management process essential in the trend towards the decentralisation of educational authority' (Dempster and Drew, 1992, p. 1). In Scotland, SDPs are seen as a means of fulfilling the requirements of the Parents' Charter (SOED, 1993). In the context of England and Wales, it appears that they enable schools to meet the new requirements of self-management linked with recent legislation. The introduction to the first DES guidance (1989a) refers to the 1988 Act and states that SDPs are the means whereby schools can realise the goals of government legislation. Skelton *et al.* (1991) argue that one of the main purposes of SDPs is to enable schools to be more publicly accountable. Our LEA survey of development planning revealed that SDPs were increasingly being used by LEAs for monitoring and inspection purposes rather than as a means of identifying ways in which support for schools could be coordinated. In addition, SDPs are also seen as one of the performance indicators of a school's effectiveness (DES, 1989c).

Some of those who advocate the external purposes of development planning claim that it can also fulfil the internal purposes of schools, not just as a coping strategy but as a means of establishing a long-term, systematic approach to development (Skelton *et al.*, 1991; Davies and Ellison, 1992). As described at the beginning of this chapter, one purpose of SDPs is to enable schools to have an integrated approach to planning. It is claimed that they provide a means whereby planning for different aspects of the school's work can be brought together. All the guidance points to the extent to which SDPs can support whole-school planning and encourage shared decision-making. It has been found that SDPs can provide an agreed structure and enable a school to set goals for managing change (Bolam *et al.*, 1993). Even though West and Ainscow (1991) argue that a feature of the increased autonomy of schools is a corresponding loss of autonomy at teacher level, they claim that, whilst SDPs are a vehicle of control at the level of the whole school, this is not necessarily in conflict with the notion of teachers exercising their own professional judgement in the context of whole-school priorities. Hargreaves and Hopkins (1991) also take up this theme and argue that the central purpose of SDPs is to empower schools: to enable teachers to manage change and new innovations more successfully. They claim that school development planning can change the culture of schools.

Underlying the multiple purposes attributed to development planning are two particular issues which need to be addressed. There is an assumption frequently made that development planning makes schools both more efficient and more effective. In the national guidance offered, these two words are frequently used synonymously. The planning process is thus seen as an efficient management tool. The assumption is that by using the process schools will automatically become more effective. West and Ainscow (1991) warn against accepting such an assumption. They make a sharp distinction between efficient and effective planning, arguing that efficient management practices, such as those incorporated within the development planning cycle, may not necessarily contribute to the effectiveness of the school. What is needed, they claim, is for each school to define what is meant by effectiveness in order to enable an agreed set of goals to be established. In this model the planning process becomes the means of achieving these goals and the outcomes of the process can then be assessed in the light of the success of the goals (*ibid.*, p. 9):

> Neither the understanding without the skills to operate the model, nor the operational skills without the understanding of the wider purposes of the school constitute a satisfactory basis for educational management. The aim must be to manage resources efficiently towards the achievement of objectives which constitute effective educational outcomes for pupils.

This warning by West and Ainscow is echoed by Constable *et al.* (1991), who caution that it cannot be assumed that SDPs will always lead to improvement.

These concerns raise the whole question of the focus of development planning, not least if its ultimate aim is to bring about tangible improvements in pupils' learning. The very term *development* implies growth and continuous improvement, yet SDPs are seen as all-embracing, 'a plan of plans' (Wallace, 1989) with, if Davies and Ellison's (1992) advice is followed, at least eight different elements. What is interesting in the guidance is that Hargreaves and Hopkins (1991) and Davies and Ellison (1992) recognise that even planning for maintenance – that is, stability and continuity – is important and necessary. Davies and Ellison slide over this issue by calling SDPs 'school management development plans'. Hargreaves and Hopkins take a different approach. They discuss the tension between development and maintenance and argue that the choices a school makes about the balance between maintenance and development in any one year are a reflection of the school's management arrangements which, in turn, are an outcome of the culture of the school. They argue (*ibid.*, p. 17) for the need for schools to 'maintain some continuity with their present and past practice, partly to provide the stability which is the foundation of new development and partly because the reforms do not by any means change everything that schools do now'. They conclude that 'Development planning is therefore about both ensuring maintenance and supporting development. An aim of the development plan is to move a new development into the school's maintenance activity' (p. 18). Clearly this argument has important implications for the content of a development plan and a school's ability to sustain developments and ensure that they become institutionalised.

The context of development planning

The current state of knowledge about the management of change and the problems associated with school improvement initiatives need to form a backcloth to development planning. Over and above such considerations, any study of development planning needs to take account of the national, local and individual context of schools (Dempster *et al.*, 1994). In relation to the national context in England and Wales, West and Ainscow (1991, p. 43) point to the apparent contradiction between schools being required to work with centrally prescribed policies whilst, on the other hand, having greater control over their own management: 'Though this can create tensions it also provides opportunities and challenges that may well facilitate improvements in schooling.'

The local context is frequently identified as an important sphere of influence in relation to development planning. Hargreaves *et al.* (1990, p. 7) argue that 'The approach taken by LEAs to development planning is likely to be a major factor affecting the success of schools in development planning and its own success in responding to ERA'. They draw attention to issues LEAs need to consider if they are to provide the kind of context in which development planning can succeed. The issues concern the LEA's attitude and policy towards development planning; the LEA's own development plan; the use the LEA makes of SDPs; the support system for development planning; and the relationship between inspection and development planning. The guidance stresses the need for a partnership between the LEA and schools to provide general and specific support for schools, and suggests a set of strategies for achieving this. Hargreaves *et al.* conclude their advice to LEAs by quoting from an Audit Commission Report (1989b):

> Schools and colleges will need support in the new environment. That support should not maintain the institutions in a 'client' or subservient role. Rather it should be designed to assist them to achieve autonomy (page 6). Development and planning at institutional level can be encouraged and facilitated by the central education department. That means helping schools establish systematic arrangements for taking decisions about priorities, for example by encouraging the preparation of school development plans (page 7).

As has already been established, the continued availability of support at LEA level for development planning is in doubt yet there is evidence that, without such support, there are schools which will continue to be unsuccessful at development planning (Constable, 1994). Hargreaves and Hopkins (1994, p. 21) argue that 'we are certain that with regard to school improvement it is very difficult for schools to go it alone . . . development planning is a means of combining accountability with help and intervention with collaboration. This is what 'pressure' and 'support' is about'.

What is clear from the literature is that the nature of the school's own context is a crucial factor in development planning. There are at least two key issues that need to be considered. The first concerns the school's understanding of and attitude towards development planning. Hargreaves and Hopkins (1991) draw attention to the relationship between a school's understanding of development planning and the effectiveness of the plan. As described earlier, they found that the initial reaction to development planning was to focus on the plan, the production of a document, often as a result of SDPs being imposed from outside. This kind of reaction tended to give way to a recognition that the planning process was more important than the publication of a written document. In turn, this led to an understanding that all important was the management of planning itself. Both the school's collective understanding and attitude towards development planning, coupled with those of the LEA, are likely to be some of the key factors affecting the impact of development planning at all levels within the school.

The second issue concerns the extent to which the culture of the school is likely to support or inhibit development planning. Hargreaves and Hopkins (1991, p. 123) claim that school development planning can have a significant impact on the culture of the school. They argue that development planning

> is not just about implementing innovation and change but about changing the culture of a school to improve its capacity to manage (other) changes. Where a school lacks the appropriate culture, development planning is a means to achieving it. The recognition by schools of this fact is the real and important condition of development planning. This is the key insight.

An issue emerging from the School Growth Planning Project in Canada (Stoll and Fink, 1992) concerns the importance of establishing trust and shared meanings. These are seen as preconditions for school development. Hargreaves and Hopkins argue that effective teamwork is central to development planning, but rather than waiting for this to be the norm, they suggest that simply engaging in the process itself can help to establish new roles and relationships and improve teamwork. Since their study, however, evidence has emerged that achieving teamwork (Newman and Pollard, 1994) and the involvement of teachers (Biott *et al.*, 1994) in development planning are complex issues which rely, in part, on the skilful leadership of the headteacher (Levine, 1994). Hargreaves and Hopkins (1991, p. 23) also argue that 'success in development planning depends on the quality of a school's management arrangements or on action that is taken to improve those arrangements'. Skelton *et al.* (1991) place much emphasis on practical strategies for team building, making meetings efficient, decision-making and developing job descriptions. They stress the relationship between the nature of leadership in the school and the extent to which delegation, combined with authority and accountability, is encouraged to enable plans to be put into action. As far as the literature is concerned, a common theme is that the type of leadership and management exercised in the school will determine not only the extent to which plans are implemented but also the relationship between plans and the overall aims of the school. Caldwell and Spinks (1988) describe the many failures of goal-setting and policy-making endeavours in the past and argue that school management needs to ensure that plans and budgets reflect goals and policies.

Shared aims which provide a clear focus for the school are also seen as a necessary context for development planning. Davies and Ellison (1992) argue that without a mission and a corporate set of aims, a development plan can have no substance. Hargreaves and Hopkins (1991) agree. They argue that the auditing process must be set within the context of the school's mission and declared aims and values. Development planning itself is seen by them as providing a context for a school to review and perhaps refine aims.

Beyond issues concerned with the school's general understanding of development planning and the prevailing culture, there are other contextual factors which have a bearing on development planning. In all the guidance given, reference is made to the need for schools to devise plans that reflect not just the aims of the school but also national and local priorities, any targets identified from appraisal interviews and any recommendations resulting from an inspection. Hargreaves and Hopkins (1994) have raised questions about the relationship between school development planning and the national programme of inspections in respect of the extent to which they can be complementary and mutually supportive.

In addition, the availability of resources will, of necessity, have a bearing on development planning. There are those who argue (Paisey, 1992) that it will be finance which will ultimately determine the school plan. There is an obvious tension here between resource-led decision-making and the view advocated in much of the guidance that development planning should shape the use of resources which, in turn, should support and serve the needs of the plan.

The process of development planning

A consistent theme in the guidance available is the dual importance of the need to manage all aspects of the development planning process and to keep these under regular review whilst, at the same time, managing the implementation of the development plan itself and evaluating the extent to which targets have been achieved. Attention is drawn to the setting of realistic targets and the allocation of adequate resources to achieve them. The need to avoid a gap between the rhetoric and the reality is also stressed. So too is the potential danger of so much time and energy being taken up with the planning process, that it becomes an activity in its own right, separate from the main purposes of the school (West and Ainscow, 1991). This is a useful warning of the need to avoid confusing 'means' with 'ends', an issue to which we will return in due course.

An aspect of managing the SDP process which receives much attention in the literature is how teachers can be drawn into the process in such a way as to feel a sense of 'ownership' in relation to the plan and so that they will become committed to implementing it (Newman and Pollard, 1994). West and Ainscow (1991) argue that there is likely to be a relationship between the extent to which teachers contribute to the plan and its outcome. They suggest that a balance needs to be struck between whole-school development planning priorities to which all teachers will subscribe and be expected to implement, and encouraging the personal, professional development and autonomy of the classteacher. It is likely that if teachers perceive management as a process that does not involve them, then their commitment to development planning will be questionable (Hargreaves and Hopkins, 1991). The study by Biott *et al.* (1994) has revealed that the participation of the whole staff in development planning, however, is uncommon, and Hargreaves and Hopkins (1994) suggest that participation needs to be selective to ensure that classteachers feel that it is worth while to be involved. There is agreement in all the guidance offered about the importance of establishing a programme of staff development that links with the priorities that have been agreed. Such a programme needs to provide the staff with the necessary knowledge and skills to implement the plan.

One other issue needs to be considered. It concerns the notion of development planning as a cyclical process, and the relationship between this and other planning cycles that schools have to take into account. In his study of development planning in a small number of schools, Wallace (1991a) found that the formal annual plans of the schools were supplemented by informal developments which arose in response to unforeseen circumstances emerging during the year. In support of his argument for more flexible planning, as opposed to the cyclical nature of development planning, he suggests (*ibid.*, p. 181) that 'While planning procedures based on an annual cycle may be effective for schools in a stable environment, they may work less well in one which is more turbulent and unpredictable'. In support of his argument he makes the point that schools have traditionally planned for the academic year which neither coincides with the financial year nor the government's planning cycle for inservice training grants. The validity of Wallace's hypothesis remains to be verified. Whilst he is obviously correct in stating that there is an inconsistency in the planning cycles which schools have to accommodate, his view of the development planning process as a rigid, annual cycle of activity does not match the version provided by, for example, Hargreaves and Hopkins (1991). They advocate a type of evolutionary approach to planning (Louis and Miles, 1992) as opposed to discrete annual plans. In the second DES guidance (1991a) the issue of conflicting planning cycles is also addressed and examples are provided of ways in which schools can resolve this problem. Nevertheless, the perception those in schools have of the planning process and the advice and support offered by the LEA in connection with different planning cycles are likely to have a powerful impact on the procedures adopted by the school.

The content of development planning

It has already been established that SDPs have to be multipurpose. Any discussion about the content of SDPs, therefore, needs to consider issues to do with the number of priorities identified in the plan and the nature of those priorities. Given that the content of the plan is expected to reflect national, local and individual school priorities, this places schools in the difficult position of having to decide what to put in the plan and what to leave out. There is general consensus in the literature that issues to do with the curriculum, resourcing and staff development should always be included in the plan. Beyond this, there is conflicting advice in the guidance available about which other aspects of the work of a school should be included. Schools are advised, on the one hand, to agree a set of priorities which are manageable and achievable whilst, at the same time, they are encouraged to include up to eight different dimensions of the work of the school in any one plan (Davies and Ellison, 1992).

It could be argued that SDPs have become more of an all-embracing management tool than a plan which has, as its focus, the recognition that the 'central purpose should be expressed in terms of the improvements sought in the children's learning' (ILEA, 1985, para. 3.94). The original intention of development planning as defined by the Thomas Report (see Chapter 1, p. 4) appears to have been redefined in the context of the 1988 legislation. The balance between SDPs working in the interests of efficiency as well as effectiveness in relation to pupil learning remains to be ascertained. Such a situation may well lead to schools incorporating into any one plan an unrealistic number of targets. Cuttance (1994) has also found that headteachers tend to overestimate the progress they have made in implementing developments. It could encourage headteachers to lose sight of the link between the content of the plan and the overall aims of the school. In other words, it could blur rather than sharpen the focus of the planning process.

Three main strategies for avoiding such a situation can be identified in the advice on offer. These concern achieving a balance among short, medium and long-term priorities; between maintenance and development priorities; and between root and branch developments. Development planning is seen as a continuous process in which schools can establish a rolling programme of priorities to be addressed. As such, schools are encouraged to identify short-term priorities which can be achieved in any one year and medium and longer-term priorities that are sketched out in more general terms and are refined and worked towards over several years. Given the amount of external demands placed on schools in recent years, the extent to which short-term priorities made in response to external demands end up replacing long-term priorities linked to the identified aims of the school remains to be seen.

Planning for development could well give the impression that schools should always be working on new priorities. Yet schools have been advised that the content of any plan should include maintenance as well as development priorities (Hargreaves and Hopkins, 1991; Davies and Ellison, 1992). This is an important consideration and could well be one of the key issues in evaluating the long-term effects of development planning. Schools which perceive the content of SDPs as always having to do with new developments are unlikely to include within the plan the need to maintain past practice or to sustain the implementation of recent priorities. Such an approach, as described by Hargreaves and Hopkins (1991, p. 88), could well lead to a situation in which the school is overwhelmed with new priorities and in the long term the 'school's rhetoric about innovation is far in advance of its practice'.

It is in this context that Hargreaves and Hopkins (1991) identify the difference between root and branch priorities as described on page 14. They argue that schools need to develop appropriate structures and policies that will support a range of other developments. By way of example, Hopkins (1991, p. 62) argues that

> Strong roots to support the curriculum and teaching aspects of the development plan are provided by a well-developed staff development policy, or a history of collaborative work among the staff and with the school's partners. When such roots are lacking, there is a danger that some of the planned branch innovations will wither and die.

Hopkins goes on to argue that schools need to recognise that their management arrangements underpin so many innovations and as such may well have to be a priority for development in their own right. A school's ability to be able to discriminate between root and branch developments and to use this conceptual framework at the audit stage of the development planning process to decide on the sequence of priorities could well be an important consideration in determining the impact of development planning in a school.

There is one further issue concerned with the content of development plans which needs to be considered. It involves the extent to which those in schools, having decided which priorities are to be included in the plan, go on to identify success criteria in relation to each of these. The guidance urges them to establish targets and to link these with specific outcomes through the identification of success criteria. However, as already noted, frequently insufficient attention is given to the potential difficulties of deciding the nature of the evidence to be gathered and on what counts as success in implementing targets for improvement. Whether or not many headteachers currently have the knowledge and skills to fulfil this key aspect of the development planning process is not clear.

The outcomes of development planning

It is significant that this is the aspect of development planning about which so little is said. Development planning is recognised to be in its infancy despite claims made about its likely outcomes. Evaluation is seen as a major part of the planning cycle and schools are encouraged to evaluate the outcomes of the management of the process itself as well as estimating how successful the school has been in achieving the targets set. The extent to which those in school monitor the process in action and the nature of the evidence gathered will determine their ability to assess its impact over time. It is at this stage that a school's initial focus for development, the link between the priorities chosen and the identified aims of the school, and the quality of the management arrangements put in place to ensure the plan is implemented, all have an important bearing. So, too, will the headteacher's understanding of the purpose, context and processes involved in this strategic approach.

The literature available on development planning concentrates on the impact of the process in relation to such issues as the potential or actual changes in approaches to management (Glover, 1990); difficulties in adhering to the plan (Wallace, 1994); and changes in professional relationships and teacher involvement (Biott *et al.*, 1994; Newman and Pollard, 1994). Little attention has been paid so far to the impact of development planning on teachers and pupils in the classroom. This is despite the fact that in much of the guidance development planning is seen as a means to an end. It is said to be a process which will lead not just to an 'empowered school' (Hargreaves and Hopkins, 1991) but also to improvements in the quality of pupil learning; a process which will enable a school to develop and improve over time. The extent to which this rhetoric of development planning in practice becomes a reality will be an important focus of our research.

4

DEVELOPMENT PLANNING AND SCHOOL IMPROVEMENT

Chapter 1 identified many of the reasons why the idea of school development planning was adopted very quickly by practitioners and policy-makers. Chapters 2 and 3 used the development planning literature to reveal the complexity of the process itself and the factors associated with it. This chapter draws on a much wider range of literature to examine the potential relationship between development planning and school improvement.

The difficulty of putting plans into practice is a common theme in the literature. Fullan (1991, p. 5) argues that there is a tendency to underestimate grossly the meaning of change and that 'the interface between individual and collective meaning and action in everyday situations is where change stands or falls'. Such a view is shared by those who, in common with Fullan, have studied the different dimensions of change and development in schools (Cuban, 1988; Joyce and Showers, 1988; Nias *et al.*, 1989; Rosenholtz, 1989). Sergiovanni (1992) has warned of the danger of the plan becoming the substitute for school improvement or its outcomes. The literature points out that schools differ in their capacity for change (Dalin, 1989), and that policy development is a very complex process in which schools need to be prepared for the realities of change. Efforts to change need to be flexible and planning needs to be sensitive to local circumstances (Lagerweij and Voogt, 1990).

Hopkins (1991) also argues that change must not be equated with improvement and claims that too often school improvement attempts ignore key contextual factors. A significant theme emerging from the school improvement and change literature is the importance of a school's culture in relation to its capacity for change and development (Lieberman, 1988; Hargreaves, 1989; Rosenholtz, 1989; Hopkins, 1991; Nias *et al.*, 1992). Internal factors which need to be taken into consideration include: the type of leadership (Rutter *et al.*, 1979; Mortimore *et al.*, 1988; Leithwood, 1992); school organisation (Miles and Ekholm, 1985; Louis and Miles, 1992); prevailing attitudes (Fullan, 1985; Fullan and Hargreaves, 1992); the need for a united effort to improve (Chrispeels, 1992; Louis and Miles, 1992); and the micropolitical constraints on action (Ball, 1987; Rossman *et al.*, 1988; Sarason, 1990). In this context, Fullan (1991) maintains there is a need to combine the findings of school effectiveness research with that of the change literature. Independently of Fullan, it has been argued that a synthesis of the school effectiveness and school improvement research is now needed (Reynolds *et al.*, 1993; Stoll and Reynolds, 1994) and it has been suggested that, not unlike the concept of school growth planning, school development planning is a means by which school effectiveness criteria can be integrated with school improvement strategies (Hopkins, 1991).

Hargreaves and Hopkins (1991, p. 109) claim that 'Our work fits into a current emphasis in educational research on the characteristics of effective schools and the strategies for school improvement'. They argue (*ibid.*, p. 16) that 'Successful schools realise that development planning is about creating a school culture which will support the planning and management of changes of many different kinds'. This raises a fundamental question about school development planning. If this systematic, but flexible, approach to planning is to achieve its aim of improving the quality of teaching and learning, how can a school best institutionalise the process? It would seem that the answer to this question is that, as well as acquiring the necessary skills for development planning, it is even more important for those in a school to understand the nature of its culture and the conditions most likely to lead to the successful use of development planning.

Patterson *et al.* (1986) identify five dimensions of schooling which, in their view, represent the reality for headteachers, teachers and those involved in the work of schools. For example, the diffuse nature of educational aims means that schools have to cope with multiple and sometimes conflicting goals, coupled with the unpredictable impact that external influences can have on the system. They also identify the uncertainties which can arise because of the ways in which power is distributed throughout the system. Within schools they argue that the very nature of the processes involved in decision-making will lead, inevitably, to solutions which represent some form of compromise. Lastly, they point to the fact that approaches to teaching will themselves be variable depending on a whole range of circumstances. They could well have added a sixth dimension, namely, the varied nature of learning itself, to strengthen even further their argument that schools are complex organisations which do not necessarily behave in a logical, predictable manner. Added to this, there is research evidence that there are complex differences between schools and that they differ from one another in multidimensional ways (Southworth, 1987; Mortimore *et al.*, 1988; Nuttall *et al.*, 1989; Sammons *et al.*, 1993).

The identification of the importance of the culture of an individual school in determining a school's ability to bring about improvement from within (Deal and Kennedy, 1983) is a recognition of the complexity of schools. The compatibility of an innovation with the school's culture is becoming increasingly recognised as of fundamental importance (Sackney, 1986; Fullan, 1991; Fink and Stoll, 1992; Fullan and Miles, 1992; Louis and Miles, 1992). Four key conditions for successful school growth planning were identified in the Halton Study (Stoll and Fink, 1992). These were a shared vision; climate setting; the development of collegiality; and a sense of mission. It is argued that these fundamental conditions appear to blend together to create a culture for change. Fullan (1988, p. 29) argues that 'Strategies are needed that more directly address the culture of the organization' if schools are to improve. Reid *et al.* (1987, p. 136) claim that 'effective school . . . improvement requires a change in the culture of the school'. Hargreaves and Hopkins (1991) take up this theme and claim that school development planning can transform the culture of a school. Deal (1990) argues that to transform an organisation is to alter its fundamental character or identity. The difficulties in achieving such second-order changes have been identified in the literature (Cuban, 1988; Rossman *et al.*, 1988). An important outcome of this research will be to judge if such a claim really does have substance.

A DEFINITION OF SCHOOL CULTURE

Given that a school's culture is so important in determining its ability to improve, it would seem appropriate to attempt to define what exactly is meant by the term *school culture*, as distinguished from a broader concept of culture, through an examination of views which have been emerging in recent years from within and outside education.

What is immediately obvious from the literature is that it is not easy to define school culture and that it is a complex concept (Hargreaves, 1993) and an often neglected topic (Reynolds and Packer, 1992). The definitions that are provided appear to be derived from views about the purpose of an organisation and the best means by which it can fulfil that purpose. Hargreaves and Hopkins (1991, p. 17) define school culture as 'the procedures, values and expectations that guide people's behaviour within an organisation'. Like Deal (1987), they describe it (p. 17) as 'the way we do things around here'. They go on to argue that management arrangements are the most vital expression of a school's culture. By management arrangements they mean the frameworks which guide school policies and communication and decision-making procedures; the clarity of roles and responsibilities; and the existence of teamwork. It would seem to be a definition that tries to combine an instrumental view of management with an interactionist one. It recognises that it is the process factors such as a guiding value system and collaborative planning (Fullan, 1985), as well as organisational factors, such as policies for monitoring performance and achievement (Purkey and Smith, 1983), which need to be combined to help form a school's culture. Hargreaves and Hopkins (1991, p. 23) claim that 'effective development planning depends on the quality of management arrangements in the school'. In support of their argument they put forward the view that 'Management is about people: management arrangements are what empower people. Empowerment in short is the purpose of management' (*ibid.*, p. 15). These authors are critical of definitions of management which focus on structures and procedures. They argue that this can lead to a false divide between teaching and management and can perpetuate the notion that 'managers manage and teachers teach' (*ibid.*). The extent to which the procedures inherent in development planning help break down this divide remains to be seen.

The definition of school culture given by Hargreaves and Hopkins illustrates some of the difficulties of attempts to define this concept. Whilst recognising that a school's culture is an expression of its values and expectations, they appear to equate, too readily, culture with management. They move very swiftly from a definition of school culture to a definition of management arrangements. Such a position risks ignoring the subtle nature of culture as expressed, for example, in Schein's (1985, p. 6) definition: 'the deeper level of basic assumptions and beliefs that are shared by members of an organization, that operate unconsciously, and that define in a basic "taken-for-granted" fashion an organization's view of itself and its environment'. Nias *et al.* (1989, p. 12) also argue that 'the beliefs and values of a group . . . lie at the heart of its culture'. Like Deal and Kennedy (1983), they identified the difficulties that can arise when subcultures within a school prevent the development of shared values across the school as a whole. Chrispeels (1992), like Hargreaves (1993), argues that concepts of school culture drawn from anthropology do not completely reflect the complexity and multidimensional nature of schools. She identifies a close relationship among a school's climate, curriculum and instructional practices and structures and procedures, and the culture of a school. In relation to this, she agrees with Hargreaves and Hopkins (1991) that a school's organisational structures both reflect the culture and help shape it in ways, she argues, which can inhibit rather than facilitate pupil achievement. Implicit within Chrispeels' dimensions are issues concerned with the relationship between the culture of a school and the way it is led and managed.

MANAGEMENT AND LEADERSHIP

There are those who argue that primary schools have a distinctive culture (Southworth, 1987), and that their complexity is not well represented in models of organisational management derived from industry and commerce. Southworth argues that to change views about management requires a rethink about leadership in schools. Schein (1985, p. 171) argues that 'Leadership in organizations consists of building and maintaining an organizational culture. Management is mainly concerned to build and maintain an organizational structure – both culture and structure, leadership and management are necessary if an organization is to become highly effective'. Louis and Miles (1992) also distinguish between the two whilst emphasising that both are essential. They define leadership as establishing a mission for the school; giving a sense of direction. Management involves designing and carrying out plans, getting things done, working effectively with people. In the literature on organisations outside education, new ideas have emerged about successful innovative organ-isations. Fullan (1992a) draws on this work to argue the need for a significant change in our understanding of school culture and, in particular, a change in views about the role and purpose of headship. To do this, he describes the work of Block (1987), which argues for the need for organisations to move away from bureaucratic, hierarchical procedures which engender dependency and can stifle personal initiative and responsibility. Instead, he urges a move towards organisations which are led and managed in such a way as to em-power those working in the organisation to shape and develop it through a process of perpetual learning. Bennis and Nanus (1985) in their study of ninety top leaders support this approach. They found that all the leaders in their study were perpetual learners who enabled and stimulated others to learn. They argue that the culture of a learning organisation is when all involved have a shared focus on the long-term vision. This is achieved because there is trust in the leadership, the vision of the organisation is well communicated and staff are empowered to become agents of change.

In part, it was this recognition of the notion of the learning organisation which led to the establishment of the School Management Task Force (SMTF). In the report entitled *Developing School Management: The Way Forward* (DES, 1990), a new approach to school management development was pro-posed. The SMTF recommended that at the practical level of the school, man-agement development must be integrated with the professional development of the whole staff in a collective effort to improve the quality of learning. The report equated schools with learning companies and urged that support and training for management development be directed at schools so that all who work in them could have a stake in management.

The themes in the SMTF report echo the approaches to educational leader-ship outlined by Patterson *et al.* (1986). They identify three core concepts: managing the culture of the organisation; strategic planning; and empower-ment. In describing how the culture of an organisation can be managed they stress, as Bennis and Nanus (1985) have done, the importance of identifying and articulating the guiding beliefs of the school and of keeping them con-stantly under review. The description of strategic planning has some similari-ties to development planning in that it encourages an audit of the external environment combined with an audit of internal organisational needs. They caution (*ibid.*, p. 61) against a fixed long-term plan seeing the goal of strategic planning being 'to produce a stream of wise decisions designed to achieve the mission of the organization in which there is a need to accept that the final product may not resemble what was initially intended'. This bears a close resemblance to Louis and Miles's (1992) recommendation about evolutionary planning. The concept of empowering others equates with the notion of man-agement already noted in relation to the work of Hargreaves and Hopkins.

Despite attempts to broaden out an understanding of what management in schools is about (Handy, 1984), and despite studies about ways in which teachers can best gain such an understanding (Ouston *et al.*, 1992), research has demonstrated that traditional views about management and leadership, many of which were derived originally from outside education, still prevail (Southworth, 1987). In the past, school management was seen as something which happened outside classrooms. It was to do with systems and procedures, the skills for which could be learnt offsite at inservice courses. Leadership was equated with the role of the headteacher who was deemed responsible for establishing the vision for the school and for managing the school with the assistance of senior colleagues. Handy's (1984) description of school cultures exemplifies this approach. From his perspective as an industrial management specialist he applied his model of management cultures to schools. In the early 1980s, through the use of a questionnaire, followed up by a subsequent period of observation, he identified four types of school cultures. There was the personal, informal *club* culture which revolves around a headteacher who has a network of power which is likened to a spider's web. There was the *role* culture which signifies a hierarchical role system which has formal procedures for managing the organisation. Such an organisation is managed rather than led by the headteacher and can be resistant to change. In contrast, he found the *task* culture which is responsive to change in a less individualistic way than a club culture. It is built around co-operative, not hierarchical, groups and is usually a warm, friendly and forward-looking culture. Finally, there was the *person* culture which is a very individualistic one. The latter organisation is used by each member as a resource for developing their talents rather like stars loosely grouped in a constellation. Handy found aspects of all four cultural types present in any one school and found from his study that no two schools were the same. He argues that it is the task of management to gather the different cultural forces together using the strengths of each in the right places, and that if schools are to improve headteachers and teachers need to rethink the way they are organised. At that time, he warned of the dangers of educationalists taking on theories of management from the world of industry and commerce which are, themselves, changing and evolving. He recommended that schools have an open, consultative policy structure for making decisions and deciding priorities which enables all staff to have an opportunity to contribute to school policy. He supported the traditional primary-school philosophy of an emphasis on teaching pupils rather than school subjects and suggested that classroom teachers be seen as managers of learning.

The arguments developed by Handy and others from outside education (Peters and Waterman, 1982; Peters, 1987) about the nature of developing organisations has both influenced and been supported by recent educational research. Fullan (1992a), for example, argues that current work on leadership needs to be grounded in an understanding of organisations. He also argues for the importance of the professional culture of schools. By this he means a culture in which there is an openness to new ideas, the giving and receiving of help and a sense of collegiality which has, as its focus, instructional improvement. He calls this 'interactive professionalism' and describes it as both a strategy and an outcome of leadership and management. Such a view is supported by many others in the field.

Bolam *et al.* (1993) argue that professional working relationships help to shape the culture of the school. Miles (1987) stresses the importance of power sharing in schools. Hall (1987) and Mortimore and Mortimore (1991) argue that teamwork in schools, not the single leadership of the headteacher, is all important in bringing about change. Bolam *et al.* (1993) found that the concept of a senior management team in primary schools had been established in the majority of primary schools in their study. Eraut (1988) stresses the importance of teachers' professional learning, and Cuttance (1992) argues for quality management that binds the process of accountability and professional development into one structure. Rosenholtz (1989) found that schools with shared meanings among teachers were the 'moving' schools, namely, those striving for continuous improvement. As indicated in the previous chapter, the characteristics of developing organisations are reflected in some of the underlying principles of development planning.

Southworth (1992), in an overview of the literature on leadership, cautions about creating new categories or descriptions for leadership, such as the move from transactional to the more favoured transformational leadership (Burns, 1978; Beare *et al.*, 1989; Leithwood and Jantzi, 1990) or the contrasting models of instrumental and expressive leadership (Etzioni, 1964; Foster, 1989). He argues that the complexity of schools requires a responsive style of leadership that, as Alexander (1992) has suggested, operates at any one time as best fits the purpose in hand.

Reynolds and Packer (1992) describe the changed nature of school leadership and the neglect of research in affiliated areas concerning school culture and school interpersonal and psychological processes. The recent research of Nias *et al.* (1989) has attempted to address this issue. These authors found, in their staff relationship project in primary schools, that all five schools they studied were at varying stages in developing a collaborative culture but that social cohesion did not necessarily lead to curriculum development. They considered that any connection between personal staff relationships and curriculum development appeared ambiguous. In the follow-up study (1992), they argue that systemic and cultural change in schools as workplaces and in teaching as a profession are intimately linked and that these links represent a powerful route to educational reform. Whether school development planning can offer such a routeway remains to be seen. It could be, for example, that development planning offers a means of contriving collegiality which Hargreaves (1991) argues could be an initial strategy for effecting cultural change.

A REDEFINITION OF SCHOOL CULTURE

From this review of the literature on school culture and the related concepts of management and leadership it would seem that no one definition can adequately represent the complexity of schools. Clearly, the culture of an organisation is expressed through the ways in which those who belong to the organisation feel, think and act. From the literature, there appear to be three inter-related generic dimensions through which the culture of the school is expressed. The ways in which they are demonstrated will determine the extent to which a school is able to work towards its own continuous improvement. The three dimensions reflect the complexity of schools and the different aspects of each concern some of the key issues identified in the literature review. The three dimensions are: *professional relationships; organisational arrangements;* and *opportunities for learning.*

Professional relationships

Professional relationships concern how the headteacher and staff relate to, and work with one another and, in turn, their relationship with, and attitude towards others, for example, pupils, support staff, governors, parents and external agencies. The quality of leadership, and the extent to which there is shared leadership, are essential aspects, as is the degree to which there is a shared sense of purpose in respect of the school's aims. The degree of collegiality is also a key factor. In particular, the extent to which there is openness, teamwork and professional support, as well as a respect for the professional judgement of individual teachers and, consequently, a balance between independence and interdependence amongst the staff, are crucial.

Organisational arrangements

These concern two key aspects: the management of the school's structures and systems; and the management of the school environment. The nature of the management structures and systems are an important indicator of a school's culture. Roles and responsibilities, decision-making procedures including staff meetings and communication systems, together with financial management, are all key factors. So, too, are policies in respect of such issues as pupil grouping and pastoral care, including attendance, discipline and the system for rewards. The arrangements for ensuring the quality of the school environment are also important considerations. These include, for example, the general appearance and condition of the school building and the playground, and the use made, in classrooms and public areas of the school, of the display of pupils' work.

Opportunities for learning

Opportunities for learning concern both pupils and adults. The extent to which there is a focus on both and the nature of that focus are key factors. For pupils, access to the curriculum and the type of curriculum on offer, coupled with approaches to teaching and learning, are important indicators of a school's culture. So, too, are the prevailing attitudes and expectations about what it is possible for pupils to achieve, including equal opportunities issues and the provision of special educational needs. For teachers, all important is their professional development and their attitude towards their own learning. The balance between opportunities provided for whole-staff development and individual development is an issue along with the type of inservice activities planned by the school. The extent to which the school is a learning community which is continuously working towards its own improvement is also a key indicator.

These three dimensions are a practical manifestation of the underlying beliefs and values of a school community. All three are amenable to change so that not only are they an expression of the present culture but they can also help shape and change the future culture of the school. Hargreaves and Hopkins (1991, p. 79) argue that:

Development planning transforms the culture of the school by:

- promoting a shared vision for the school
- creating management arrangements that empower
- providing for every teacher a role in the management of the school and opportunities for leadership
- encouraging everyone involved to have a stake in the school's continuing improvement
- generating the commitment and confidence which springs from success.

They conclude (*ibid.*) that 'Over time, the creation of such a culture is both an indicator and a test of the quality of development planning, the purpose of which is the well-managed school with confident teachers who know that their pupils attain the highest standards of achievement'. Whilst other writers on development planning have not made such a substantial claim they have, nevertheless – if only implicitly – supported the view that school development plans can bring about deep-rooted change in schools (Maden and Tomlinson, 1991; Skelton *et al.*, 1991). The research evidence for such a claim, however, is more questionable.

Arising from the analysis of the development planning process in Chapters 2 and 3 and from the examination of the relationship between SDPs and school improvement in this chapter, two specific hypotheses to be investigated in the field were identified:

1. The impact of development planning on the school as a whole will be determined by

   - the purpose for which development planning is used;
   - the internal and external context of the school;
   - the understanding and application of the process; and
   - the content of the plan.

2. The extent to which school development planning is a school improvement strategy will be manifested in changes in the culture of the school, in particular, changes in

   - professional relationships;
   - organisational arrangements; and
   - opportunities for learning.

5

THE RESEARCH DESIGN AND OUR METHODOLOGY

This chapter describes in detail the ways in which we designed and conducted the research. It describes how the sample was chosen, the kinds of evidence collected and the techniques used for gathering and analysing the data.

ETHICAL CONSIDERATIONS

A systematic approach to all aspects of the research was adopted, not least because of its substantial qualitative nature (Miles and Huberman, 1994). Working practices were agreed in order to provide a common framework within which we, as individual members of the team, could operate. A regular pattern of meetings, held weekly in term times, was established. The agenda for these meetings always included a period of discussion before team decisions were made about different facets of the research. The meetings were minuted to enable a step-by-step record to be kept of the research. Procedures for communicating with schools and others were agreed, including the production of regular information bulletins.

Ethical factors were an important part of our considerations. For example, we decided that our observations should be non-participatory so as to maintain an as objective as possible perspective. Issues of confidentiality were addressed in respect of information received from those participating in the research. We also agreed that at no stage would the identity of LEAs, schools and participants be revealed and assurance was given that when the research was published the findings would be reported in an anonymous form. Prior to publication the schools would be provided with a draft of the findings to obtain feedback on the emerging issues. We explained at the outset, however, that it was not our intention to provide individual feedback or to negotiate about the findings, as has occurred in some other studies (Nias *et al.*, 1989; 1992). Confidentiality was also assured within the schools with which we were working. This enabled our research team to gather information on the differing perspectives and roles of those working within and with schools.

43

Permission from parents of the pupils studied in the sample was not sought, although it was agreed that their rights, and those of any others, to refuse to participate would be respected. We also chose to restrict attention to the formal life of the school and not to seek to use other information acquired in casual conversation or observed in teachers' off-duty behaviour.

CRITERIA FOR THE SELECTION OF THE SAMPLE SCHOOLS

We decided at the outset of the ESRC project to work in nine primary schools across three LEAs. Whilst the criteria for the selection of the sample schools were determined by the research team, the size of the sample reflected the funding available. Our focus on primary schools was to provide much-needed additional research data on this phase of schooling. The criteria for the selection of the schools were that these should provide as wide and as varied a sample as possible. Variation in size, type and status of school, catchment area and organisation were all deemed important. So, too, was the need to include schools with a range of experience of development planning, and with head-teachers with different lengths of headship experience.

To meet the criteria about varied catchment area and also to enable approaches to SDPs by LEAs to be studied in more detail, we decided to select three schools from three LEAs that were representative of urban, suburban and semi-rural settings and had been involved in development planning for varying lengths of time. Three LEAs which met these criteria were approached to obtain their agreement to be involved in the research. Once this was achieved, local officers and inspectors were provided with the selection criteria for the schools. Between them the LEAs had over 700 primary schools from which to choose. They were asked to nominate for us six schools per LEA which were engaged in school development planning and might be interested in participating in the research.

Data from the headteacher of each of the 18 schools nominated were gathered through the use of a semi-structured telephone interview, designed by the research team. All the headteachers gave permission for these interviews to be tape recorded. Each interview began with an explanation of the project, the personnel involved, the research procedures to be used and the ethical parameters of the project, not least the issue of voluntary involvement and confidentiality. The following information was then gathered.

Information on the school

The information included the number of pupils, how they were organised into teaching groups and whether it was anticipated that these arrangements would continue in the following academic year. In addition, information was gathered on the numbers of full-time staff including the headteacher and the number of part-time staff and their total workload; the status of the school, for example, county or denominational; the type of school; and details of the catchment area.

Information on the headteacher

This included the length of time that the headteacher had been in post and whether this was the first or subsequent headship. We were interested to see if the previous responsibilities of the headteacher or the length of time in post were related to the plan which was in operation or being developed in the school.

Information on the SDP

Information was collected on how many development plans had been experienced, the number and type of cycles and the stage in the cycle that the headteacher and school were at now. The research team wanted to work with schools which were just starting to think about and use SDPs as well as schools which had been involved in school development planning for considerable periods of time.

Information on the components of the plan

Probes used to elicit information focused on whether there were components relating to curriculum, staffing and inservice training, premises, management and finance. The nature and number of the components included in the school's development plan were of interest to the team as it was thought they could be an indicator of the school's understanding of the nature of the plan, and the complexity of both the plan itself and the planning processes associated with it.

Information on the format of the plan and whether it was LEA led

We wanted to gather this information to be able to examine the influence of, support from and attitude towards SDPs and planning from LEA and national sources. We made a particular note of the degree of involvement the LEA was said to have and whether the school was expected to use a standard format for the SDP devised by the LEA.

The involvement of others

The involvement of teachers, support staff, governors, parents and other representatives from the school and the wider community was probed. The nature of their possible involvement in terms of consultation or other types of interaction was also examined. It was anticipated that information gathered from this set of questions would help us to build up the picture of the headteacher's understanding and the degree to which development planning was perceived to be a shared process.

The headteacher's attitude towards development planning

We were interested to know the headteacher's views about SDPs in general as well as, specifically, about their impact on the school. We probed the headteacher's perceptions about the benefits and disbenefits of development planning to help us select schools with different attitudes towards this innovation.

The willingness of the school to participate in the research

The discussion in the telephone interview reiterated the need for the research team to select a balanced sample of different kinds of schools. Arrangements for our next contact after the research team had selected the sample schools were also discussed. The majority of the headteachers initially interviewed expressed positive views about future involvement, with many also wishing to discuss the issue further with their staffs before making a definite commitment.

The choice of schools

Each school was discussed in detail by the full research team and its characteristics were plotted against the selection criteria. The final selection of the nine sample schools was made in March 1992, and Tables 5.1 and 5.2 give the details. The LEA personnel who had provided us with the initial lists of schools to contact knew in advance that they would not be informed of which schools

Table 5.1   The general characteristics of the nine schools in the sample

	Size									
	Large (>400)			Medium			Small (<200)			
Type	JMI	JM	I	JMI	JM	I	JMI	JM	I	Total
Working class	1				2					3
Middle class							1*			1
Mixed	1			1*			1		2	5
Total	2	0	0	1	2	0	2	0	2	

Note:
* = Church school.

Table 5.2 The range of headship experience and experience of development planning in the nine schools in the sample

| Experience of planning | Length of headship | | | | | | |
| | −1 year | | 1–3 years | | +3 years | | |
	Initial	Plan + process	Initial	Plan + process	Initial	Plan + process	Total
1-year planning cycle	1		2				3
1 × 3-year planning cycle		1	1*				2
Subsequent						4*	4
Total	1	1	3	0	0	4	

Note:
* = Church school.

would eventually participate in the project as part of the research team's efforts to protect confidentiality wherever possible.

Although the nine schools met the criteria as far as was possible and provided a sample not unrepresentative of the generality of primary schools, they were atypical in other respects. It was recognised that account would need to be taken of a number of potentially limiting factors. The schools had been identified by LEA personnel as interested in development planning. The LEAs themselves had been selected from 135 possible choices. All the headteachers presented a positive attitude towards SDPs and all were willing to work with the research team to help explore their impact. We recognised that our participants were strongly in favour of development planning and realised that this would bias them. Furthermore, the fact that the added stimulus of involvement in the project was likely to increase the schools' awareness of the use of SDPs and so cause a halo effect. We were well aware, therefore, that this was not a random sample and that as a result of this and other factors – not least the limited size of the sample – our ability to generalise from the findings would be limited.

SOURCES OF EVIDENCE

Our overall aim was to collect a wide variety of information from as appropriate a group of respondents as possible. It was anticipated that this would enable the team to triangulate the accounts of past and present development plans and to compare these with any available documentary evidence. We also decided to observe classroom practice and to audit pupils' work as a way of investigating the impact of the plan at the classroom and individual pupil levels and of comparing these with whole-school developments. No specific 'value-added' outcome data for individual pupils were collected. It was not possible to obtain this type of data for several reasons. The priorities chosen by individual schools would be likely to differ and would have necessitated a wide range of baseline material and outcome assessments to be collected. There was no systematic use of any internal tests used by all the sample schools in the research project, and external test results in the form of national Standard Attainment Tasks (SATs) were not available because of industrial action. Even if these data had been available they would have been of limited value as the SATs themselves had been changed from year to year.

One focus of our study was an examination of the processes and impact of development planning from the perspective of the headteachers and class-teachers in the sample schools. We decided, therefore, that the main source of evidence would be these two groups. Our aim was to obtain data from head-teachers and classteachers which would provide a detailed account – from their own perspectives – of the different facets of development planning and its impact. However, in recognition of the potential shortcomings in respect of the validity of such data (Ackroyd and Hughes, 1981; Stone, 1984; Cohen and Manion, 1985), we also decided to use other sources of evidence to enable cross-referencing and comparison with other forms of data (Cannell and Kahn, 1968). In addition to drawing on governors' responses, therefore, documen-tary evidence related to each school's development plan was also collected. Additionally, evidence from classroom observation and other school docu-ments was drawn on to verify the headteachers' and classteachers' accounts.

To obtain evidence from classrooms we decided to study two classes in each school and to track the pupils in each of the 18 classes in 1992/3 through into the 1993/4 academic year to provide information on the pupils' experiences over time. We also wanted to examine and compare structures that were in place in each classroom which related to the school's development plan such as the National Curriculum, LEA guidelines and initiatives, whole-school policies and individual classteacher initiatives. Agreement within and between schools was a major concern and interest for us.

Before selection was made of the two classteachers the research team would be working with in 1992/3, the research officer was able to attend staff meet-ings in five of the sample schools to share information about the project and the nature of the work to be undertaken in school. Following this, head-teachers suggested the names of classteachers who were interested in working with us. In the vast majority of cases these names were given to the research team after extensive discussion between headteachers and their teaching staffs. The research team was anxious to work with as wide an age range of pupils as possible. This was achieved as in several schools there were more than two classteachers who were interested in working with the research team. In the 1992/3 academic year, therefore, classroom observations were made across the full primary age range from nursery through to classes containing year-five and six pupils.

At the start of the academic year 1993/4 our strategy for the selection of classteachers was different. In this second full academic year of the research project, the classteachers were selected because they were now teaching the pupils who had been observed in 1992/3. Whilst this methodological structure had been made clear to the schools at the beginning of the research project and discussed with headteachers during 1992/3, this did not appear to have been an over-riding factor when headteachers and, in some cases, their staffs were making decisions about which staff would teach which particular classes. The 18 1993/4 classteachers did not, on the whole, appear to be as carefully hand picked by the headteacher as the first cohort had been.

Three of the 1993/4 classteachers were involved in both years; two, because they were the only full-time classteachers in their school and one because she was teaching the same class of pupils as she had done in the previous year. Subsequent chapters will examine the similarities and differences between the two cohorts of classteachers with which the research team worked.

Some of the classteachers, headteachers or other members of staff in the sample schools had worked with, or come in contact with, members of the research team in different contexts, for example, through their mutual involvement in initial teacher training, advisory and inspection work or through other previous work experiences. In these cases it was particularly important for us clearly to establish our different roles and responsibilities as researchers. These were carefully discussed at the start of the research project and the change in roles does not appear to have caused any lasting or significant problems.

External sources of evidence were also drawn on to cross-check the validity of the data obtained from the schools. We decided to seek the views of LEA personnel linked to the schools in our sample and, in an attempt to provide a wider context for understanding the data, we also decided to obtain information about school development planning at a national level from all the LEAs across the UK.

THE TECHNIQUES USED FOR DATA COLLECTION

A combination of qualitative and quantitative data-collection techniques was employed. Qualitative data-collection techniques were used because we considered that these best suited the main purposes of our study (Bryman, 1988). To obtain the data needed from the headteachers and classteachers it was decided to use semi-structured interviews with both groups. This was to enable the collection of data concerned with a range of behaviours, opinions, events and facts. It would allow our enquiry to be open and for underlying beliefs and attitudes to be probed. It was deemed necessary to use a standard semi-structured interview schedule to enable responses within and between groups to be compared. Each school's written development plan related to this time period was also collected. In the nine schools there were, therefore, three forms of data collection:

1. Semi-structured interviews with headteachers, two classteachers in each of the two academic years of the project (1992/3 and 1993/4), the chair of governors and a parent governor.

2. Classroom observation in two classes following the same pupils across two academic years in each sample school using an instrument designed by the team, and a modified observation schedule (System for the Classroom Observation of Teaching Strategies – SCOTS) used in the Junior School Project (Mortimore *et al.*, 1988).
3. Systematic collection of documents relating to SDPs and each school's priorities, such as the plan itself, policy statements and guidelines, minutes of meetings, information about inservice courses, staff development programmes and reports to governors. Other documents collected were those relating to teachers' work in the classroom, such as termly plans and records of work completed.

In the LEAs three forms of data collection were also used:

1. A questionnaire sent to the 135 LEAs in the UK (apart from the Channel Islands).
2. A sample of LEA SDP documents provided voluntarily by those LEAs which chose to submit such data to the project.
3. Semi-structured interviews with the inspector, adviser or officer most closely associated with each of the sample schools.

THE DEVELOPMENT OF THE RESEARCH INSTRUMENTS

Every instrument used in the project was discussed by the whole research team and many drafts were produced and piloted with individuals who were not in the sample school group. We are indebted to the schools and individuals who helped the development of the research in this way. Each instrument included information as to its purpose on the front page. It also included information on the top of each page relating to the instrument number, page number, school or teacher code number, date completed and the initials of the researcher involved. No instrument was labelled with individual staff or school names so as to ensure confidentiality within and outside the project. The content of each instrument was determined by its purpose. The instruments seeking information about past, present and future development plans and planning processes drew on the SDP literature and on the findings of the literature on school effectiveness, school improvement and educational change.

The interview schedules

In respect of the known advantages and disadvantages of interviewing techniques (Tuckman, 1972; Ackroyd and Hughes, 1981; Stone, 1984; Cohen and Manion, 1985; Powney and Watts, 1987), a number of factors were taken into account when we were constructing the schedules. Care was taken to create questions which could be triangulated across the semi-structured interview schedules to enable the different perspectives of those interviewed to be compared and contrasted at the analysis stage. To strengthen the reliability of the schedules (Cannell and Kahn, 1968), close attention was paid to the grouping and sequencing of questions, the wording of questions and the probes and prompts to be used by the interviewer (Bradburn and Sudman, 1979). The nature of the questions were varied to meet a range of purposes within the one instrument. Some were closed questions concerned with factual information. These were precoded. The majority of questions, however, were much more open ended and sought to collect explanations, descriptions and opinions about behaviour and events. For these kinds of questions it was decided to postcode the responses so as not to impose any limits and, in due course, to enable the data to drive the analysis. The instruments devised by the team have been made available to a concurrent Australian project concerned with SDPs (Dempster *et al.*, 1993).

The headteacher interview schedules

Three instruments were developed specifically for headteachers. The purpose of the first was to collect background information about the headteacher, in particular: work history, initial training and inservice courses; other significant influences; and general involvement in school development planning. The other two focused directly on school development planning. The purpose of one was to gather background information about the school's present development plan and planning processes. The other focused on the collection of information about the headteacher's estimation of the impact of previous development plans.

For the next instrument, we chose four main areas of investigation: the origins of the plan and the school's state of readiness for development planning; the formulation of the plan; its implementation; and the headteacher's understanding of educational change. For the instrument concerned with the perceived impact of previous development plans seven issues were explored: when the school first had a development plan and who was responsible for formulating and implementing it; any significant changes in the formulation of plans; any significant changes in the implementation of plans; previous major areas for development and the degree of satisfaction with the outcomes of these and whether they had been sustained; the extent to which these past developments had made a significant impact on the school as a whole, on classroom practice and on pupils' learning; main lessons learnt; and the impact on the headteacher's role and any changes in understanding about development planning.

The classteacher interview schedules

Three instruments were also developed for classteachers. The purpose of the first instrument was to provide general background information about each teacher. Questions concerned data about work history; initial teacher training;

inservice qualifications and courses; current practice; and other significant influences. The other two instruments focused specifically on school development planning and, in many respects, they mirrored the headteacher instruments already developed. Care was also taken to ensure that the sequencing and wording of the majority of questions were the same or similar to those used for headteachers for triangulation purposes.

The aim of our next instrument was to gather information from classteachers about the school's previous and present development plans and planning processes and their impact. Issues related to six key areas were investigated: benefits and drawbacks; the origins of the plan; the formulation of the plan; the implementation of the plan; understanding of educational change; and any significant changes arising from past experience of development planning. The purpose of our third instrument was to review the impact of the 1992/3 SDP from the classteachers' perspective. This instrument was devised towards the end of the academic year because the research team was of the view that, until then, we had not elicited sufficient information about the classteachers' perceptions of the impact of development planning in respect of benefits and drawbacks and lessons learnt. It was also realised we had not specifically asked headteachers whom the school communicated with about the outcomes of the plan at the end of the planning cycle. From a preliminary analysis of the headteachers' responses, this had emerged as a relevant issue. These three aspects of development planning were included, therefore, in this supplementary instrument.

The governor interview schedules

Two instruments were designed for the governors although the majority of the questions were the same for each and mirrored, as far as possible, those asked of the headteachers and classteachers. The only difference between the two instruments was the factual information section at the beginning of each which focused on the different responsibilities of the chair of governors and the parent governor and their personal histories.

The LEA inspector/officer interview schedule

This instrument was designed with two purposes in mind. We wanted to compare the approach taken to SDPs in the three LEAs in the sample with the responses received from the national survey. We also wanted to be able to make a comparison between the view LEA personnel had about each school's approach to development planning and the view held by those in the school.

The classroom observation schedules

The classroom observation schedule designed by the team was to facilitate the collection of *hard* evidence of activities in the classroom which were related to priorities in each school's development plan(s). A header of information included on the top of the first four pages of the schedule was designed to be completed in advance of the observation visit. It enabled the priorities identified in the school's plan or documentation associated with the plan, as well as those identified during the course of the semi-structured interviews, to be recorded.

The first page of the schedule was used to record priorities from previous SDPs. The second page was used for noting ongoing priorities, the third, for new priorities and the fourth, for future developments. This structure enabled information to be collected about the tensions and balances between the different phases of development planning and to link these with the teaching and learning context of the individual school, staff and pupils. The schedule enabled information about priorities to be revised and updated in the light of new information obtained from documentation and staff interviews at the beginning of the 1993/4 academic year. We therefore included space to record any responsibilities said to be linked with priorities, be they at an individual, group or whole-school level. There was also room to note if a priority had been initiated from outside the school.

Seven categories of evidence to be collected were recorded on the instrument. These were

1. display – general;
2. display – pupils' work;
3. pupils' work in books/folders;
4. ongoing interaction and behaviour;
5. resources;
6. teacher planning; and
7. teacher record-keeping and assessment.

The final page of the instrument had a different structure. It was designed to be completed at the start of each observation visit and served to focus attention on what was happening in each classroom. It included the production of a general sketch map of the whole classroom and provided prompts concerned with the furniture, seating arrangements and any priorities for which there appeared to be no evidence in the classroom. It proved to be a useful source of evidence relating to change over time. There was also space on the fifth page for any general comments and for the collection of basic statistical information on:

- the numbers of boys and girls who, as far as could be ascertained by observation alone, fell into the following ethnic groups: white, Asian and Afro-Caribbean;
- the total numbers of girls, boys and pupils in the classroom; and
- the total number of classteachers, other teachers and adults in the classroom and their sex.

Our second classroom observation instrument was the SCOTS schedule (System for the Classroom Observation of Teaching Strategies). SCOTS was devised by Powell and Scrimgeour (1977) and used as the basis for the research project directed by Powell to study teaching (1985). This SCOTS instrument was simplified, shortened and used as one of the classroom observation instruments on the Junior School Project (Mortimore *et al.*, 1988). It was this latter version, with very minor amendments, which was used by our research project. In its original version the SCOTS schedule was intended as a system to measure 'aspects of teacher behaviour and teacher-pupil interaction' (Powell, 1985, p. 8). Predetermined categories to measure a small number of simple behaviours were utilised. Powell (*ibid.*, p. 13) describes how 'the initial choice of variables was made on a judgmental basis, factors that had struck us during our initial observations as potentially important being selected'. These arguments also apply to the version used in this project. This instrument, therefore, provided a subjective view based on the personal perspective of the researcher and was therefore subject to some bias. It proved to be a useful additional source of information, however, which, though limited, helped to build up a clearer and wider-ranging picture of the 18 classrooms studied in the research project. Like all other instruments it was piloted in non-sample schools before being used by the research officer in the project schools. The use of the instrument was also discussed with the project co-ordinator of the Junior School Project.

Fifteen categories were used for the observations:

1. Control of pupil learning activities.
2. Pupil responsibility for managing own work.
3. Pupil choice of work activities.
4. Teaching situation.
5. Organisation of work.
6. Industry.
7. Interpupil co-operation.
8. Pupil talk.
9. Pupil movement.
10. Pupil motivation.
11. Reinforcement.
12. Teacher audibility.
13. Pupil self-discipline.
14. Pupil/teacher social relationship.
15. Apparent teacher attitude to class.

Each category was allocated a numeric value using a five-point, Likert-type scale. These numerics matched detailed statements which provided the 'best match' against the specific category being observed.

The LEA questionnaire

This instrument was designed to enable us to conduct a national LEA survey. We wanted to obtain as comprehensive a picture as possible about LEA policy and practice in relation to SDPs and, in particular, the degree of guidance and support being provided for schools. We took care to ensure that many of the questions mirrored those to be asked of our sample schools to enable comparisons to be made. Chapter 6 provides details about the specific questions included. The questionnaire was piloted in three contrasting LEAs not involved in the project and was then modified before being distributed.

FIELDWORK

The code of practice for interviewing

In recognition of the strengths and weaknesses of interviewing procedures (Brenner *et al.*, 1985; Cohen and Manion, 1985; Kerlinger, 1986), the research team agreed a code of practice for each interviewer to follow in the interests of seeking to minimise bias (Kitwood, 1977; Cohen and Manion, 1985). It included the preparation of respondents, adherence to the questions and their wording, the use of agreed probes and prompts and, where possible, the recording of responses verbatim. Other than for the telephone interviews, tape recorders were not used as we deemed them to be too intrusive.

The headteacher interviews

Between March and April 1992 the research officer interviewed all the headteachers in order to collect background information about them, the school, the staff and the pupils. Between May and June 1992 two members of the team administered the two other instruments. This provided an opportunity for two colleagues to work together in the field and to observe one another's practice and adherence to procedures. It was decided that one would ask the questions on each occasion and that both would, independently, scribe the responses of the headteachers. This would provide an opportunity to check the reliability of the recording of the data. To substantiate this further, a third member of the research team checked and compared the handwritten accounts for their accuracy. In addition, both members of the team were able to provide feedback to one another on the role each played in the conduct of the interview and the response and attitude of the headteacher. This provided a valuable research training opportunity. We were aware, however, that by visiting together to interview the headteachers, special care would be needed to prepare the headteachers for this. At the commencement of the interview we sought to allay any fears they might have had and to answer any questions about the way we intended to proceed. The response from all the headteachers was positive. The average length of each interview was two hours. In the second year the research officer conducted a short semi-structured interview with the headteacher to update information on the school's 1993/4 priorities and to obtain the headteacher's evaluation of progress made since the start of the research project. Data collection in the schools was completed by Easter 1994.

The classteacher interviews

These were all conducted by the research officer. The first two sets of inter-views were completed between June and November 1992. The average length of each interview was one and a half hours. In the case of the third instrument, the teachers were interviewed between June and November 1993. This inter-view took approximately twenty minutes.

The classroom observations

The first classroom observation visit took place in the second half of the autumn term 1992 and the second and third visits in the two spring term half-terms. The fourth and final observation visit of 1992/3 took place in the second half of the summer term 1993. This visit was an opportunity to update statistical and personnel information to ensure that we gathered, as far as possible, a full picture of the 1992/3 plan and planning processes. We also used this to collect advance information relating to the 1993/4 SDP. Two further observation visits were made to classrooms in 1993/4. One, in the second half of the autumn term, the other, in the first half of the Easter term. Chapter 11 provides additional details about the fieldwork in relation to these observations.

   Although many of the classteachers had initial concerns about their involve-ment in the project, particularly the classroom observation stages, we were given open and, in our considered view, honest access to schools, classrooms, planning and record-keeping. In addition we were made to feel welcome by all pupils, staff and members of the school community. Classteachers and head-teachers were generous with their time and provided open access to and addi-tional copies of relevant school records and documentation. Confidentiality at all levels was widely respected by participants in the project schools.

The governor interviews

All the governor interviews were conducted by an experienced researcher and were completed in the spring term of 1993.

The LEA interviews

The interviews with the primary inspector, adviser or officer who worked most closely with each of the nine sample schools took place in June and July of 1993. They were conducted by the research associate and provided a comple-mentary and, in some cases, contrasting perspective to the views expressed by the headteachers of the schools concerned.

The LEA survey

The LEA questionnaire was sent out to all 135 LEAs in England, Scotland, Wales and Northern Ireland. The form was addressed to the Chief Education Officer or Director of Education as appropriate. We obtained a 100 per cent response to the questionnaire and received documentation relating to SDPs from over forty LEAs. An evening presentation in one of the project LEAs reporting on SDP procedures to headteachers was also attended by two members of the research team. This helped to gain a clearer picture of the style and expectations of policy and practice relating to SDPs in this LEA though similar meetings were not held in the other two LEAs.

DATA ANALYSIS TECHNIQUES AND PROCEDURES

The chosen analysis techniques ranged from a detailed content analysis of the respondents' interview responses, to qualitative and quantitative analyses of the LEA data, documentary evidence, classroom observation and, where appropriate, pupils' work. Like the development of instruments and data collection in the field, as far as possible, a systematic approach to the analysis of the data was adopted. In recognition of the amount of data to be gathered we decided to use the Statistical Package for the Social Sciences (SPSS) to facilitate the analysis of coded data and to help with the exploration of the complex triangulation possibilities.

In an attempt to strengthen the validity of the data, a set of principles were established to guide our analysis:

1. Qualitative data were to be quantified where appropriate (Miles and Huberman, 1984; 1994).
2. Every effort would be made to establish coder reliability (Tuckman, 1972). For example, data coded by one member of the team would be cross-checked by another or, in some instances, by the team as a whole.
3. There would be triangulation within and between different forms of data (Cannell and Kahn, 1968; Cohen and Manion, 1985).
4. Early conclusions would be avoided. Instead, every effort would be made to re-examine the data from different perspectives using a variety of methods (Kitwood, 1977).
5. Other researchers would be invited, where possible, to check the validity of aspects of the data analysis.
6. As indicated in an earlier section, feedback from the schools on the emergent issues would be obtained.

The next eight chapters describe the outcomes of our analysis of the range of data gathered.

6

THE NATIONAL SURVEY OF LEAs

This chapter describes our national survey of LEAs which was carried out towards the beginning of the project. Following an outline of the approach taken in this survey, the responses from LEAs in England and Wales are summarised, together with comments on the context in Scotland and Northern Ireland. Four types of LEA involvement in school development planning are identified in the final part of the chapter.

THE AIM AND METHODOLOGY OF THE SURVEY

The aim of the survey was to find out the different ways in which LEAs in the UK viewed the process of primary-school development planning. The specific objective was to enquire about policy and practice in the translation of such views into support for schools in their planning. It was intended that the outcomes of this survey would contribute to the project by providing a national context for the research findings in the nine schools and the three LEAs in the sample.

Any survey of LEAs involves organisations which differ considerably in size, style and context. The comments in this chapter relate to LEAs in general and have not been weighted to recognise the various sizes of LEA, which, at the time of the survey ranged in 1992 from one to 1,065 primary schools. However, analysis of the responses indicated that the size of the LEA was a less significant variable in determining approaches to school development planning than its type under the categories as shown in Table 6.1.

In most LEAs the form was completed by the chief inspector or adviser or the senior primary inspector or adviser. Their positive attitude to the enquiry was evident, both in the quality of the comments and in the quantity of locally produced materials which were sent. We are of the view that the 100 per cent response rate from the 135 LEAs in England (110), Scotland (12), Wales (8) and Northern Ireland (5) was a remarkable measure of the recognition by senior officers of the importance of school development planning in primary schools.

The first three questions asked for basic data about the authority; the next three asked about policy and practice; two questions then asked about how the

Table 6.1 Categories of LEAs

		LEAs		Schools	
		n	%	*n*	%
England	Counties and islands	41	30	12,951	52.1
	Metropolitan districts*	36	27	4,407	17.7
	London boroughs	33	24	2,091	8.4
Wales	Counties	8	6	1,841	7.4
Scotland	Regions and islands	12	9	2,524	10.2
Northern Ireland	Education and library boards	5	4	1,042	4.2
UK total		135	100	24,856	100.0

Note:
* Belfast, a metropolitan district, is included under Northern Ireland rather than with the other metropolitan districts.

authority used the plans; a further question asked about locally produced material; and finally there was space for comments.

In the introduction to the enquiry form we emphasised that comments would be valued, whether the authority had a well-developed system of school development planning or no activity in the area at all. Authorities were also assured that their individual responses were confidential to the research team and would not be identifiable in published reports of the outcomes of the project. The responses to each of the main questions are summarised next.

PREVALENCE OF SCHOOL DEVELOPMENT PLANNING

Does your LEA have a policy that all primary schools should have SDPs?

The response to this initial question indicated that the norm in England and Wales was for LEAs to expect primary schools to have SDPs. Two LEAs indicated that this was not a policy as part of the formal culture of the LEA, and this issue is picked up in later responses.

The notes accompanying this question stated 'The use of the term "policy" here is intended to include written guidelines and strategies supported by Chief Officers, rather than relating only to policies that have been formally agreed by Elected Members of Authority Committees'. Several respondents commented that the LEA, particularly the inspectors and/or advisers, strongly encouraged such planning but that it was not mandatory.

If so (i.e. if your LEA does have such a policy), when was this policy first implemented?

There was a scattered distribution of the first LEAs to develop a policy before 1988. This could have been the result of a variety of factors:

- The significance of the early work in ILEA.
- The significant effect a few individuals had on their LEAs.
- Mobility among relevant inspectors, advisers and officers who were involved in early developments. Also some other LEAs may have been wrongly omitted from the early stage by respondents appointed more recently.

The counties in this first cohort tended to be larger, together with a few urban areas.

The impact of the 1988 Act on planning was noticeable, particularly the introduction of the National Curriculum in England and Wales. At this stage there was no correlation between the size of the LEA and the date of introducing SDPs. However, the impact of networking across LEAs on promoting initiatives and shifting attitudes had been recognised by the DES and funding for collaboration between LEAs was incorporated into the early stages of the GRIST/LEATGS/GEST funding. This may have influenced the spread of development planning. For example, the effect on the introduction of school development planning in the Greater Manchester area may well have been linked with such funding, as grant aid was used in that area to employ a regional co-ordinator to promote such collaboration.

It was noticeable that in the following two school years, 1989/90 and 1990/1, development planning was introduced in adjacent LEAs. In several cases, inspectors and advisers said they were accustomed to meeting together, for example on inservice issues. From the responses it seemed that individual inspectors, advisers and officers had a considerable influence over whether school development planning was encouraged in primary schools. This led to some welcoming and others resisting the change in LEA policy, and subsequently influencing neighbouring LEAs. A pattern emerged relating to adjacent counties regardless of their size. As well as a steady growth among London boroughs, the spread of SDPs in the metropolitan districts became more pronounced during 1989/90, with about half of the districts starting such planning. The result was that the majority of districts in all the conurbations except the West Midlands had introduced SDPs by the end of 1990. The following year the West Midland group then began to come together, except for Birmingham, which differed significantly in size from the other LEAs. Other groups of adjacent LEAs in London, the north east and in north Wales also began at this time. The number of LEAs which had a policy on development planning by the academic year 1990/1 had increased significantly from 5 per cent pre-1988 to 83 per cent.

Finally, in 1991/2, the year in which the survey took place, almost all the remaining authorities embarked on development planning. There were comments from some respondents to the effect that such policies were currently being considered, but that LMS had led LEAs to reduce the introduction of new policies in non-mandatory areas. Only two LEAs in England and Wales did not have a policy on SDPs, and one other was developing a policy at the time of the survey.

What proportion of schools had SDPs for 1991/2?

This question required a high level of knowledge from the LEA respondent. Where a system was well developed this would have posed little problem, but nevertheless the replies did indicate that SDPs were in place in the majority of the LEAs in England and Wales by 1991/2. Five LEAs reported in response to this question that they were still at an early stage. In the case of three of these LEAs, half of the schools were said to have an SDP; in one LEA it was claimed that a quarter of the schools had one, and in the fifth LEA none of the schools were said to have begun development planning.

CONTENT

Has your LEA provided guidance to primary schools about the content or process of school development planning in primary schools?

All respondents except three Inner London boroughs and two Scottish regions said they had provided guidance. As schools in these authorities would have received guidance from ILEA prior to 1990 or the Scottish Education Department (SOED/HMI, 1991), it seems likely that schools in every authority would have had access to some guidance.

Is there an expectation that any of the following should be included: curriculum; staff; finance; organisation; premises; context?

The form included some grouping of issues and definitions which were adopted for the purpose of the survey. These were intended to ensure that misunderstandings about management issues were reduced:

Curriculum	Teaching and learning styles; curriculum materials and resources; assessment, recording and reporting; special educational needs; policies, for example, equal opportunities; continuity between phases.
Staff	INSET; management development; governor development.
Finance	Budget; LMS; management of resources.
Organisation	Administration; system development.
Premises	School environment; sites and buildings.
Context	Internal – ethos and climate; external – links with parents, community and governors; local and national government; communications – involvement and participation.

The DES strongly advised the production of National Curriculum development plans at both school and LEA level in Circular 5/89, although this was not a requirement under the Education Reform Act 1988. All the LEAs in England and Wales indicated in their responses to this survey that they expected schools to include curriculum issues in their planning. Similarly, all LEAs in England and Wales reported the inclusion of staff development. It was clear from the replies that staff issues were considered to be as vital a part of planning as curriculum issues. Nine of the LEAs in England and Wales which encouraged curriculum and staffing did not expect organisational issues to be included. There was no particular correlation between this and the size of the LEA.

The phasing of the introduction of LMS in primary schools had been later than that relating to the introduction of the National Curriculum, so it was expected that financial issues would not yet be included in many areas. There were some LEAs which did expect financial but not property issues to be included. Some of these LEAs were well advanced in LMS, but had retained property services.

The response from LEAs in England and Wales to the question about context contrasted with that in Scotland, where 'ethos indicators' are now a dimension of the HMI materials on performance indicators and school development planning. Again, it was more common for adjacent LEAs to take a similar approach than it was for isolated ones. There was no close correlation with the year in which planning was introduced or with the size of the LEA.

INVOLVEMENT IN PLANNING

Is there an LEA policy that people in particular roles should be involved in the planning process with the headteacher?

The use of the term 'policy' led some LEAs to comment that 'expectation' would be a more appropriate term for their style. Three LEAs indicated that no others were expected to be involved in the planning process with the headteacher. In all other LEAs, some of the following were said to be involved: the teaching staff (90 per cent); deputy head (87 per cent); governors (84 per cent); inspector/adviser (72 per cent); support staff (46 per cent); LEA officer (30 per cent); parents (27 per cent); and pupils (10 per cent). Four per cent did not answer this question and 3 per cent identified other roles.

Views about the role of the deputy headteacher in development planning appeared to vary slightly. Three of the four smallest rural LEAs in England and Wales, one in Scotland and the largest metropolitan district indicated that teaching staff, but not the deputy head, were involved. Conversely, two expected the deputy head to be involved, but not necessarily the other teaching staff.

Less than half of the LEAs expected support staff to be involved in development planning. Although none of the LEAs in Northern Ireland claimed they were involved, the pattern of response to this among LEAs in England and Wales was random in relation to their size and location.

Parents were said to be involved in development planning in a quarter of the LEAs all of which were situated in a swathe of adjacent home counties from the south west to the East Midlands, and in the London boroughs. Three London boroughs expected parents but not inspectors or officers to be involved. The contrast between London (42 per cent) and the other metropolitan areas (19 per cent) was particularly noticeable. Two of the three LEAs in our sample said parents were involved but the evidence from the schools suggested that involvement was rare in practice. We surmised, therefore, that actual involvement other than the legally required representations on governing bodies was likely to be considerably lower than the responses from the LEAs suggested. One-third of the LEAs which cited parents said that pupils were also involved.

The UK figure relating to the involvement of governors was lower because in Scotland this function is carried out by the school board. The only English LEAs indicating at that stage that governors were not involved were one county, four London boroughs and three metropolitan districts.

The responses about the involvement of LEA personnel reflected the fact that at the time of the survey the relative functions of inspectors, advisers and officers differed across the UK and were indeed changing. In almost every LEA where officers were said to be involved, so too were the inspectors and advisers. In the majority of LEAs which involved officers, there was an expectation that the LEA would approve the plan.

Do the plans have to be approved by the LEA?

Several respondents were aware of the changing relationship between the LEA and schools. This was reflected in the fact that it was said that 'policies' in non-mandatory areas no longer needed to be 'approved' since the advent of LMS. A previous question had asked whether the LEA had a policy that all primary schools should have plans, whereas this question asked whether the plans have to be approved by the LEA. As all but two of the LEAs in England and Wales indicated that there was such a policy, but only 26 per cent indicated that the plans had to be approved, it would seem that, in England and Wales at least, the purpose of such policies where they existed may have been to promote good practice rather than to control the content of the plans.

ANALYSIS

Does the LEA collect the plans?

All but three of the 41 counties in England were said to collect the plans. Clearly, the majority of LEAs expected to be kept informed of the outcomes of the planning process. In England, a few LEAs (13 per cent) expected both the priorities and the whole plan, but more expected the full plan than simply a synopsis of the priorities (60 per cent: 42 per cent). All the Welsh LEAs expected the full plans. Twice as many metropolitan districts and London boroughs expected the full plans as compared with those expecting summaries.

Does the LEA analyse the plans?

Six LEAs said they did not collect or analyse the plans, including three metropolitan districts in the West Midlands conurbation. 'Partial analysis' was carried out by the majority of LEAs, but this could mean that LEAs did not analyse all the data that schools were expected to submit. For example, in some cases staff development data was said to be analysed but premises data was not. Alternatively, it could mean that LEAs sampled the data across all the categories rather than analysing responses from all schools.

'Extensive analysis' varied with the size of the LEA, and was most commonly reported among the counties in England (42 per cent) followed by London (39 per cent), metropolitan districts (25 per cent) and Wales (25 per cent). Handling such analysis may require either a very small LEA or a larger one which has sufficient human and technical resources and structures to carry out such analysis and then integrate the data into monitoring and support systems.

Are particular aspects analysed?

Eighty per cent of the LEAs in England and Wales reported that they analysed the extent to which schools were using the development plan to introduce the National Curriculum, and 56 per cent of them included other areas of the curriculum as well. Staff development followed closely behind, with almost three-quarters of the LEAs in England and Wales analysing SDPs in connection with GEST funding bids (72 per cent) and other staff development planning (70 per cent).

Financial planning featured in analysis by less than half of the LEAs (46 per cent) and other organisational issues in less than a third (31 per cent), which is lower than might be expected four years after section 33 of the 1988 Act required each LEA to prepare a financial scheme for LMS with provision for yearly updating. Only a quarter of the LEAs analysed premises (25 per cent) or contextual (24 per cent) aspects of the plans. In the case of premises, the LEAs which were most and least advanced with the introduction of LMS may well have ignored this aspect, either because they saw this as a school issue or because their property divisions already had separate and well-established ways of identifying maintenance and development priorities.

USE OF SCHOOL PLANS BY LEA STAFF

Do LEA staff refer to SDPs and/or planning processes

In inspections?

The responses illustrated the variation in the role of the LEA inspector just before the changes under the Education (Schools) Act 1992 which led to the establishment of Ofsted. The pioneering work in school development planning and inspection in the former ILEA was evident in the 97 per cent response to this question from the London boroughs, which included the former ILEA. The evidence that 86 per cent of the metropolitan districts and counties were also using school plans for inspection 'often' was significant. Only four LEAs – two in Wales and two English counties – indicated that plans were never used for inspections, and half of these used planning processes but not plans. Apart from those in Scotland and Northern Ireland where roles differ, this indicated that the subsequent formalisation of Ofsted inspections, requiring the school plan as part of the background paperwork, was less of a novelty in most LEAs in England and Wales than it would have been a few years earlier.

As part of their monitoring of schools?

'Monitoring' reflected the role that LEA advisers had had prior to the introduction of the harder-edged 'inspector' role. All LEAs in England and Wales claimed to use plans to a greater or lesser extent as part of the monitoring process.

As part of their support of schools?

Much less use appeared to be made of data from plans for supporting schools in areas where inspection and advice had already been separated, except in Northern Ireland. Support tended to require a range of various types of information. Given the extent of curriculum and staff development data which the plans contained, this finding may indicate that many LEAs waste the potential benefits of better targeted support which could result from developing appropriate systems and strategies.

COMMENT

Taken together, the responses to these three questions illustrated the different emphasis given by various types of LEA to the use of plans and planning processes. The London boroughs responded that plans were normally used as a dimension of inspection. All but one borough used plans often, and the exception used them occasionally. They were also normally used in the monitoring process, though four boroughs only used them occasionally for this purpose. Only 45 per cent of the boroughs used them often in determining their support for schools. The same proportion said they did so occasionally, but three (9 per cent) stated that they did not.

In the metropolitan districts it appeared that plans were used as much for monitoring as for inspecting, and the pattern of not using them nearly as much for advice mirrored that in London. In the counties they were used for monitoring more than for inspecting, and more emphasis was given to using them in determining support for schools. In Wales the emphasis in using plans was on monitoring, in Northern Ireland on support and in Scotland on monitoring and support.

There was a divergence between the views of the nine schools in the three LEAs which were involved in our project and the claims of the LEAs responding to the national survey. It was noticeable that most of the schools in our sample considered that the role of the LEA in development planning was not significant. This disparity is explored further in the chapters which describe the outcomes of the interviews with school and LEA personnel.

SUPPORT MATERIALS

The questionnaire invited LEAs to indicate whether any guidelines or inservice materials had been produced for primary schools, and requested copies where feasible. The quality and quantity received in response to this appeal was most encouraging. The advice was presented in a range of ways from skeletal suggestions to detailed guidelines. Most of these had been developed by working parties involving inspectors, advisers and headteachers, and in some areas teachers, governors and officers had also been thoroughly involved. Subsequent contact with some LEAs indicated that we had been sent only a modest selection – some LEAs had produced extensive materials that were available on sale or only within the authority; others were in the process of revising earlier guidance or producing new materials. Some of the materials reflected an awareness of the research literature and developments elsewhere, while others appeared to be pragmatic responses to the need to promote the planning process, develop managerial skills or obtain data in a more co-ordinated way.

Most LEAs appeared to have produced a considerable range of training materials and guidelines, many of which were relevant to school development planning. Some of these had been displayed at HMI curriculum materials conferences and elsewhere in recent years, but the indications from the responses were that many more had been produced for specific purposes. Most of this wealth of material had been produced by former teachers working as lecturers, advisory teachers, centre wardens, advisers, inspectors and officers in the LEAs.

Regional variations

Wales

Local government and education in Wales, except universities, comes under the Secretary of State for Wales. In 1972 the Local Government Act reduced the former 13 county councils to eight. The 1993 Act reversed the process, and it is anticipated that from 1995 the eight counties and 37 district councils will become 21 unitary authorities, using some of the former county names.

Apart from one LEA, which was starting school development planning during the survey period, adjacent LEAs in Wales began in the same year. There were similarities between the approaches of LEAs to development planning throughout Wales. All but one LEA involved inspectors, and none explicitly involved parents in planning, other than as governors. Most LEAs expected to approve plans, which was unusual in England. All said they collected the full plans, though only two claimed to analyse them extensively. All the LEAs said they used them for monitoring the introduction of the National Curriculum. The inclusion of Welsh in the National Curriculum for Wales, and the distinct approach to curriculum change taken by the Welsh Office, appeared to underpin a particular interest among LEAs in Wales to monitor the introduction of the National Curriculum.

In general, Welsh LEAs used SDPs proportionately less for inspection and monitoring purposes than English LEAs, but more than LEAs in Scotland or Northern Ireland. The same proportion were said to use the plans in supporting schools as in the English counties, though, in common with other parts of the UK, only half as many LEAs used planning processes as used written plans in supporting schools.

Scotland

The nine regional and three island authorities are responsible for strategic planning in education. The regions span some of the smallest and the largest in the UK, ranging from Orkney with 24 primary schools to Strathclyde with 1,065 (which represents 42 per cent of the primary schools in Scotland). The legal system and Scottish Office work alongside but separate from those of England and Wales. The National Curriculum, LMS and GEST funding do not apply in Scotland. The Audit Unit was set up by the Scottish Office as part of the school inspectorate. It expects headteachers to involve school boards increasingly in issues to do with standards and quality. These include school development planning, school self-evaluation, staff development, appraisal and devolved management. School boards were given specified functions under the Schools Boards (Scotland) Act 1988. They have fewer powers than governing bodies in England and Wales, and headteachers are merely required to consult them on the exercise of their responsibilities. The intention of the Act was to give parents more say in the running of schools, and to give schools a parental perspective on their work.

Scottish HMI have worked in three regions to develop and pilot guidance materials on SDPs, which have been published since our survey. The variation between the responses reflected the extent to which regions were aware of this work or had been actively developing their own approach. Three-quarters of the regions had provided some guidance to schools about planning. A higher proportion of the authorities in Scotland than in England and Wales expected schools to submit their plans for approval and analysis, particularly concerning staff development. Contextual and ethos issues were given more importance than in England and Wales, and this is reflected in the HMI materials available. The Scottish Office have been proactive in sponsoring research, ensuring that the findings are disseminated effectively to schools, and promoting the link between school development planning and school effectiveness.

At the time of the survey (spring 1992) the Scottish regions and islands were in three categories:

1. Three were at the stage of implementing policy and practice in school development planning.
2. Six were developing policy and had some practice.
3. Three were at an initial stage – one with policy but no practice; one where policy was being developed; and one where there was some practice but no policy yet.

Northern Ireland

County councils were dissolved as units of local government in Northern Ireland in the reorganisation of 1973, when they were replaced by 26 district councils and nine area boards. Some functions which were the responsibility of local authorities were transferred to government departments. The administration of primary schools in Northern Ireland is covered by five education and library boards. These boards have statutory powers to provide advisory and support services to schools under the Education Reform Order and all the boards recommended that primary schools should have development plans. However, they do not have the authority to determine what is in a development plan, or to insist that the schools submit their plans, or to inspect schools. It is for the individual school to decide whether it should have a development plan and what this should contain.

The Department of Education is responsible for central policy, coordination, legislation and financial control of the education and library services. It is concerned with the individual and the quality of life, including leisure, recreation, culture, relaxation and entertainment. The inspectorate advises on the educational, as distinct from the administrative aspects, and makes use of school plans as part of this process where they exist.

The Regional Training Unit has produced inservice training materials and organises residential management courses which are followed up and supplemented by the boards. For example, in the South East Board, schools inform the board of their priorities over one- and three-year periods. The board supports the schools by monitoring progress and evaluating the achievement of targets in their plans.

All the boards reported that they had introduced policies between 1990 and 1992 that primary schools should have SDPs. Two of the boards estimated that about three-quarters of their schools had introduced plans, and the other three boards estimated that about one-quarter of their schools had done so. At the time of the survey, three-quarters of the LEAs in the UK reported that almost all their schools had plans, so the introduction of plans in Northern Ireland was happening later than in most areas. All the boards reported that they had provided guidance to schools about development planning, in common with 96 per cent of the LEAs. They all expected the full range of issues to be included – curriculum, staff, organisation, finance, premises and context – and claimed to use the plans 'often' in their support of schools. The boards all expected the headteacher, deputy head, teaching staff and governors to be involved in the planning process.

Information from the Northern Ireland Office, however, had indicated that this similarity of approach across the province depended more on the schools' approach to planning than the boards', and indeed the subsequent questions to the boards revealed a range of practice. In common with other parts of the UK, the boards appeared to vary most when they were in their first cycle of school development planning. As the proportion of schools increased, the tendency was to encourage schools to focus on priorities and for the board to find such information more useful for selective analysis and application.

DISTINGUISHING BETWEEN THE LEAs

From the analysis of the responses about the different LEA approaches to the content and process of school development planning it was possible to identify differing profiles of LEAs along a continuum from low to high levels of involvement. The factors used to indicate the level of involvement were primarily taken from the LEAs' responses to the national survey, modified in the light of other evidence from LEA materials, our case-study data and the combined NAHT/Birmingham survey of headteachers (Arnott *et al.*, 1992; 1994).

A typology was generated based on the extent to which the LEA was involved in school development planning, from '*minimalist*' through to '*supportive*', '*proactive*' and '*systematic*'. LEAs were then allocated to these four types of involvement on the basis of their response to the areas of questioning described earlier in the chapter. Most weight was given to the questions concerning the extent of support and guidance for the planning process from the LEA and the extent and quality of use made of school plans by the LEA.

Owing to the commitment in our study to respect confidentiality, it is not appropriate to include a map which would effectively illustrate the incidence of each type of LEA. However, it is feasible to summarise the data in the form of positive descriptions of different types of involvement as follows.

Minimalist: up to 10 per cent of the LEAs were included in this category

The LEA considered that the encouragement of school development planning was increasing unnecessary bureaucracy. Schools were said to be responsible for their own management, and that the role of the LEA was to monitor the extent of the success or failure of the process. Paperwork between schools and the LEA was minimalised in order to focus staff time in schools and the LEA on teaching and management rather than on documentation related to accountability. The LEA recognised the necessity of complying with central government mandates to avoid criticism or loss of grant. It expected schools to submit plans relating to the introduction of the National Curriculum and inservice priorities, and monitored the achievement of targets.

Supportive: about 35 per cent of the LEAs were in this category

The LEA recognised the value of development plans and planning processes for effective management in schools. In the early stages it frequently emphasised the plan itself. Later it tended to focus more on improving the planning processes rather than the end product. It developed guidelines, inservice materials and a strategy to promote an understanding of planning as a management tool, both for the school and the LEA.

Proactive: approximately a quarter of the LEAs were in this category

The LEA promoted the linking of professional issues with other pressures on management, such as LMS and close involvement of governors, parents and support staff. Networking with inspectors, curriculum advisers, officers, other schools, local employers and other services had become an integral part of determining planning priorities.

Systematic: approximately 30 per cent of the LEAs were in this category

The LEA encouraged schools to incorporate internal analysis, target setting and review. It related the prioritisation of policies and resources at LEA and at school levels. It incorporated short, medium and longer-term planning cycles into a structure that was economical in its use of time, was supported by those involved and was flexible but firm enough to direct activity that achieved desired outcomes.

CONCLUSIONS

This typology deliberately uses 'characteristics' rather than watertight boundaries. In some cases evidence about the same LEA suggested that it would be misleading to equate certain characteristics with every area of the LEA – individual officers and inspectors did not necessarily all display the same characteristics or reflect an agreed style. In other cases the changes to the LEAs were forcing changes which were in conflict with a previous style of working. Inevitably the data themselves comprise a variety of snapshots, but the range of evidence on each LEA does combine into a montage. The typology is intended as a sketch to convey an impression rather than as a technical drawing from which a measured artefact could be built.

7

THE HEADTEACHERS' STORY

There were two stages to the analysis of the data obtained from the semi-structured interviews of the headteachers and the classteachers. The first stage was to describe the two stories and compare and contrast them. This chapter summarises the headteachers' accounts. It begins with a description of the steps taken to analyse the responses and then tells the story which emerged. The story is in five parts which, combined, represent the five aspects of development planning – context, purpose, process, content and outcomes – identified from our literature review. Each of these will be examined in turn, drawing, as appropriate, on the responses to questions in our three headteacher interview schedules.

THE ANALYSIS OF THE RESPONSES

Four steps were taken to analyse the headteacher and classteacher responses.

Step one

The five key aspects of development planning derived from our examination of the planning process in Chapter 3 were used to structure the analysis. The five themes – *context, purpose, process, content* and *outcomes* – were taken in turn. For each theme, the relevant questions from the six instruments were identified and listed. Then, using our SPSS coding framework, data in respect of each of the questions identified were extracted and recorded. The data obtained from the interviews held in the 1992/3 academic year were used as the basis for the analysis. The range of responses for each item was noted, as was the number of headteachers out of the nine and the number of class-teachers out of the 18 who responded to each item.

Step two

The next step was to look for patterns in the data in respect of the similarities and differences of the responses across the five themes. Patterns were explored from the following perspectives:

- Those responses where all nine headteachers or the 18 classteachers were in agreement.
- Those responses where at least two-thirds of the headteachers or class-teachers were in agreement.
- Those responses which were mixed in that four or five headteachers or seven to eleven classteachers were in agreement.
- Those responses where one-third or less of the headteachers or the class-teachers were in agreement.
- Those responses where one headteacher or one classteacher was in the minority in that the reply was different from all the others.
- In addition, omissions and processes and procedures not mentioned were noted, although caution was exercised because of the difficulty of making inferences related to issues not mentioned (Gray and Wilcox, 1993).

For each theme the responses were categorised under these six headings. For some questions there were multiple responses and we had to re-examine these in more detail. For example, when asked what their role was in development planning, between them, the headteachers mentioned 29 different roles. A re-examination of the original responses revealed a combination of a range of leadership and management responsibilities. It was then possible to analyse the key roles each headteacher had identified. Once the categorisation was completed, similarities and differences within the accounts, and then between the two accounts, were studied in detail.

Step three

The data analysis was cross-checked by the research team from several perspectives. Some points of accuracy in respect of the preliminary coding were clarified and agreement was reached about the interpretation of the data. Where data had been reanalysed, as in the example provided in step two, the accuracy of this reanalysis was checked and the overall validity of the analysis was confirmed by cross-checking the 1992/3 data with the data obtained from the interviews conducted in 1993/4.

Step four

To facilitate the writing of the two accounts, the structure of the interview schedules – in relation to each of the five key themes – was used. What follows is the story which emerged from the headteachers, which is told in five parts.

PART ONE: THE CONTEXT FOR DEVELOPMENT PLANNING

General background factors

The teaching experience and qualifications of the headteachers

In the last ten years all nine schools had experienced at least two changes of headteacher and in two of the schools there had been three such changes. Two of the headteachers had taken up their appointment in the last year and, for one, this was a second headship. Two-thirds of the headteachers had been in post in their present school more than seven terms and one headteacher was in the sixth year of headship. Eight of the headteachers were female and ages ranged from 36 to 53. All but two had taught across the primary-age range, although none had taught nursery-aged pupils. Without exception, each head-teacher's experience was relevant to the statutory age range of the school. The amount of teaching experience prior to headship tended to be extensive: only one had taught less than ten years; five had 16 to 20 years' experience; and one, more than 20 years. All but one had been a deputy head which, for one respondent, was in the same school where she was now the headteacher. Three of the headteachers had taught abroad and two had other work experience. The subject expertise of the headteachers was relatively narrow. For example, during initial training, no headteacher had specialised in mathematics or science; three had studied English; and five, a humanities subject. Two-thirds of the headteachers had obtained additional inservice qualifications, three at diploma level and one at BEd and MA level. One headteacher had studied for a management diploma, two had experience of teaching on management courses and four had been seconded previously as an adviser in their LEA.

Staffing changes in the schools

Two-thirds of the headteachers reported that in the last ten years their school had increased in size and almost all cited staffing changes. Apart from the small rural school which had no deputy head, the other eight schools had experienced at least two changes in deputy head in the last ten years. There had been three deputies in one school, four in another and, for a third school, there had been six deputy heads in the same time period. In the two terms prior to the headteacher interviews, seven of the schools had experienced at least two teaching staff changes and for one school there had been four changes. In the same time period, however, no changes in support staff were reported.

School aims and general management procedures

Apart from the newest headteacher in post, all the schools had a written set of aims and in the majority of cases these had been updated in the year prior to the research interview. The majority of headteachers (more than six) said they involved the teaching staff in important decisions and, at the time of the interviews, in all but one school the headteachers had established a formal

were given which indicates that the content of the plans appeared to corres-
pond not only with external demands but also with the particular purposes of
each school. For the eight headteachers with previous experience of development planning, these purposes had come into sharper focus as a result of the
impact of earlier development plans.

Significant changes in the formulation and implementation of plans

In response to the question about any significant changes they had made in the
way present plans were formulated and implemented, all the headteachers said
they now recognised the importance of involving all the teaching staff and
others and that inservice training to implement plans was essential. The majority of headteachers claimed that support staff and governors were now involved in the school development planning process.

The majority of headteachers with previous experience of development planning reported on the significant changes in roles and responsibilities and job
descriptions for teachers which had occurred as a result of formulating and
implementing plans. Similarly, the majority of headteachers also reported that
they now linked resource management with school development and that the
content of their plans had changed to include, for example, management (five)
and building and premises (five). The headteachers appeared to be recognising
the interface between the requirements of local management and SDPs.

All the headteachers stated that they now communicated about the plan and
its outcomes with a wider audience and that this had led to changes in reporting procedures. For example, once the plan had been agreed, all said they
communicated the content with governors, five with LEA inspectors, and four
with parents and support staff. One-third of the headteachers said they formally communicated with staff and two said they did so with pupils. Although
all the headteachers saw a relationship between SDPs and accountability, four
of them said they were not formally required to communicate with anyone
about the content of the plan. A similar number said they were uncertain as to
whether or not this was an LEA requirement. A third felt obliged, or assumed
it was necessary, to communicate the content of the plan with governors and
two felt the same in respect of LEA inspectors. All the headteachers said they
reported to their governors on the outcomes of the SDP at the end of the
planning cycle. Six said they also reported to parents and seven said they
would do so with the LEA via the local adviser or inspector. Interestingly,
whilst all the headteachers cited the importance of staff involvement in school
development planning, only one-third said that they would formally communicate the outcome of the plan to staff.

All but one of the eight headteachers with previous experience of development planning reported that they had made significant changes to the way
plans were now evaluated. By implication, the headteachers were identifying
another purpose for development planning, namely, as a means of monitoring

planned development over a period of time. This is despite the fact that only one-third of the headteachers identified the gathering of evidence about outcomes as a benefit of development planning.

The perceived benefits of development planning

Four of the headteachers with previous experience of development planning commented that initially SDPs were externally imposed. From subsequent answers, however, it seemed to us that, whilst the idea of school development planning was generated from outside, the majority of headteachers had identified ways in which school development planning could further their own purposes and, as such, they appeared to have a sense of ownership over the process. Two-thirds saw staff discussion as a particular benefit of development planning. Four of the headteachers said that SDPs had led to the documentation of plans which were previously 'held in the head'. The process was said to provide a structure and a coherence to planning which was logical and 'common sense' and which led to a more efficient use of time. Some of the headteachers talked about how SDPs 'empowered' the staff to have control over their own development. The procedures of development planning, particularly the audit, review and evaluation processes, were found to be beneficial. Five of the headteachers with previous experience of development planning identified the importance of shared ownership, common agreement and shared beliefs as some of the key lessons learned from this approach to planning.

Changes in understanding about school development planning

When asked about the extent to which their understanding of development planning had changed in any way, it would appear that the headteachers were at different stages in their understanding about the purpose of development planning. A particularly interesting point made by two of the headteachers with previous experience of SDPs was that they now recognised the need to embed the planning process into the culture of the school for it to be most effective.

Answers which were individual in nature

Five of the headteachers gave answers to some questions which were different from those given by the other headteachers. A close examination of these answers revealed a few interesting issues. Two headteachers gave very individual responses as to why they had decided to have an SDP. One headteacher gave staff involvement as the sole reason. The other headteacher gave only an external purpose for introducing development planning, namely, an LEA requirement. This was the only headteacher who said she involved the local inspector in the early stages. Two headteachers gave different answers about the reasons for determining priorities. One cited external reasons only and talked about national and LEA demands. The other said the purpose of the plan was, in part, to fulfil the needs of the local cluster group to which the school belonged. When it came to describing to whom the outcomes of the plan would be communicated, only one headteacher said that the pupils would be informed.

Omissions

It is clear from the range of responses that the headteachers perceived SDPs to be multipurpose in nature. However, when considering any omissions – any issues which no headteacher raised – one in particular emerged. None of the headteachers identified improving the pupils' achievement and the quality of their learning as the central purpose of development planning. We came to the conclusion that, in all probability, because the headteachers had identified staff involvement in SDPs and staff development as two out of the three key purposes of development planning, they were making an assumption that this would have a positive impact on pupils' learning.

PART THREE: THE PROCESS OF DEVELOPMENT PLANNING

Introduction

As described earlier, all but one of the headteachers had previous experience of development planning and all teachers were said to be involved in the process. In response to a general question about school development planning when initially providing information about themselves, the headteachers mentioned others who were also involved. Two-thirds said they involved support staff; seven, the governors; four, the pupils; five, LEA inspectors and advisers; and one-third, the parents. In subsequent answers to specific questions about who was involved in formulating and implementing SDPs there was a mismatch with what had been said earlier. Only a third of the headteachers reported any involvement of pupils, support staff, governors and parents in some of the stages in the process. Only one headteacher appeared to involve the LEA at the formulation stage, whilst two-thirds said they intended to look for external support from the LEA in monitoring the implementation of the plan. It could be that the headteachers' definition of 'involvement' included communication about the plan with others. Although, again, as described in the section on the purpose of development planning, there were considerable differences between the headteachers in relation to whom they felt accountable at both the formulation and implementation stages.

This section is in two parts. The first part describes the planning processes said to be used currently in the nine schools. The second describes the impact of previous plans and the subsequent changes which were said to have occurred in the planning process.

Current planning processes

Introducing SDPs into the school

All headteachers said they knew what to do when introducing SDPs as a result of attending an LEA course. This was despite the fact that three of the head-teachers had said earlier that they had not been on a specific school development planning course prior to introducing the idea into their school. Two headteachers said they found the DES guides helpful and two headteachers said the LEA inspectorate had also been of assistance. When describing the origins of SDPs in their schools, some of the headteachers said they had been selective about whom to involve in the process initially.

In three cases the headteachers chose not to introduce the idea to all the staff and did not involve the whole staff in the early stages. Three headteachers involved the deputy head only, two the INSET co-ordinator, and two the chair of governors. One headteacher said the idea of SDPs was introduced through informal discussion and one involved the local inspector. By way of contrast, three headteachers introduced the idea of SDPs to all the teaching staff through an INSET session and, in addition, one of these headteachers also introduced the idea to pupils, governors and parents. This headteacher was the only one who used a wide range of strategies – six in all – at this early stage. Interestingly, however, this headteacher, along with all the others, did not see a need to introduce SDPs to the support staff.

The length of the planning cycle

The length of the planning cycle varied. Two-thirds of the schools had a two- or three-year cycle, two schools had a one-year cycle and for one school the length of the cycle was four years. For the latter school this was the first experience of development planning and it is worth noting that of those headteachers with previous experience, five said that the planning cycle was now longer, whereas two said that they had shortened the length of the cycle compared with earlier plans. Two-thirds of the headteachers said the cycle began in the summer term in preparation for the coming academic year. For two schools the cycle began in the autumn term. For one school the cycle began in the spring because of the timing of DFE Grants for Education Support and Training (GEST).

Formulating the plan

The answers the headteachers gave about the processes used to formulate the plan were mixed and there was very little unanimous or even majority agreement about the steps taken. Apart from the common strategy of involving the teaching staff, different approaches were used to identify priorities for development. The following strategies were used by at least three schools: discussion with the deputy head; meetings with individual staff; a staff meeting; an inservice training day; a review of last year's priorities; and an examination of outside priorities and the prioritisation of new initiatives. One school mentioned the impetus of the visit from our research officer. One met with the senior management team. One discussed informally with governors and one used a questionnaire for pupils, support staff, parents and governors.

There was only one process to establish and agree the priorities for development which was common to all nine schools, namely, whole-staff discussion. Beyond that, four headteachers also used the senior management team and a third of the headteachers mentioned a list they made themselves, governor discussion and a training day. Two headteachers did an audit, one had an input from the local community, one involved support staff, one mentioned discussion with parents and one used GRIDS. When asked who was involved in establishing priorities, a third of the headteachers said pupils, support staff and governors, which did not reflect entirely the previous strategies described.

A third of the headteachers said that at this early stage in the planning process they did not select any ways in which they could assess the subsequent effectiveness of the plan. Four headteachers said they had built in review procedures, including departmental reviews, individual teacher reviews and follow-up staff meetings. These procedures were more to do with monitoring than evaluation. A third described how they had identified aims, targets, tasks and timelines to assist with evaluation. Only two schools referred to the identification of success criteria and performance indicators linked to final outcomes.

All the headteachers said that they would communicate the content of the plan to the governors once it had been agreed. When asked if they intended to make any changes to the content of the plan, eight of the headteachers said that they did. The description of the changes, however, was more to do with processes than content. For example, four said they would probably change strategies, such as altering the timescales and review procedures, and one-third anticipated changes in relation to the involvement of others, such as parents and the local community. The one headteacher who did not anticipate that changes would be made said that she did recognise the need to be flexible.

Implementing the plan

When the headteachers were asked about the implementation process, a different picture emerged. Whilst the responses were varied they were more evenly spread. There was much more total, or at least, majority agreement about some of the procedures used. At the other extreme, there were more instances in which the answers given by individuals about this phase of the planning cycle were different from the rest. For some responses there was mixed agreement which revealed some interesting issues.

Strategies for putting plans into action   All the headteachers indicated that inservice training had been provided for the implementation of the plan. The training was either school based or involved attendance on an LEA course and, in some cases, it was not just concerned with the content of the plan. For example, five headteachers said staff needed training on the development planning process itself and three headteachers arranged for key members of staff to attend management or curriculum leadership courses.

All but one headteacher identified target setting and the allocation of tasks as common procedures for putting plans into action. Two-thirds of the headteachers said they built in timescales and the majority allocated roles and responsibilities to members of the teaching staff. All the headteachers said financial resources had been allocated towards the implementation of the plan, whereas only five said they had allocated time as a necessary resource for implementation. One-third of the headteachers drew on the LEA and cluster group as another resource and two headteachers said they used governor and parental expertise.

When asked if any of these procedures were new to staff, five headteachers said at least some of the following were: delegation; working groups; access to resources; and working in a structured way. In addition, a third of the headteachers identified target setting as another new strategy. Only one headteacher felt that the procedures used were not new to staff.

Roles and responsibilities   All the headteachers identified specific roles and responsibilities for themselves and others in the implementation of the plan.

Between them the nine *headteachers* described 29 different jobs they performed. An analysis of the answers revealed a balance between leadership and management activities. Four leadership roles emerged:

1. An *overview* role (four out of nine).
2. An *initiator* role (four out of nine).
3. A *support* role (seven out of nine).
4. A *pressure* role (six out of nine).

The overview role was described by one headteacher as 'being responsible for the vision'. The others talked about the importance of 'standing back', 'seeing things coming' and 'being realistic'. In the role of initiator, headteachers described how they initiated discussion, 'planted ideas', 'acted as a catalyst' and 'started things off'. The support role involved a range of actions, such as facilitating development, recognising achievement, giving praise, being positive and, as two headteachers described it, 'empowering staff'. By way of contrast, the pressure role was described as 'steering, leading, pushing, delegating and keeping staff interested and involved'. No headteacher adopted all four roles. A third of the headteachers assumed three roles and the remaining two-thirds undertook at least two of the roles. The support and pressure roles were adopted by the majority of the headteachers.

From the 14 management activities identified by the headteachers, four specific roles emerged:

1. General *staff management* (two out of nine).
1. Specific *management of the implementation of the plan* (eight out of nine).
3. *Monitoring* (six out of nine).
4. *Communication/liaison* (four out of nine).

The general management role included professional development interviews, arranging team meetings and redefining job descriptions. The description of the specific management of the SDP process revealed that some of the eight headteachers concerned were much more heavily involved than others in the implementation of the plan. One took responsibility for putting the plan into action and three took an overall co-ordinating responsibility. A few kept staff on task and checked that nothing had been missed out and one headteacher assigned herself a specific responsibility for implementing an aspect of the plan. The monitoring role assumed by only two-thirds of the headteachers included the identification of weak areas. The fourth role involved communication and liaison between groups, including parents, governors and the LEA. In relation to these four management roles two headteachers were in the minority of one for very different reasons. One of the headteachers adopted all four roles. In the case of the other headteacher, she did not identify a role for herself in the management of the SDP process. This particular headteacher only assumed a monitoring role.

The eight headteachers who had a *deputy head* all identified a role for their deputy in implementing the plan. Fourteen jobs were mentioned. Four could be described as concerned with leadership and ten were concerned with management. Unlike the headteachers, a leadership role was only identified for five of the deputies. This included leading staff meetings, being objective, taking a whole-school view, steering, 'chivvying up' and facilitating and supporting other members of staff. Management responsibilities for all the deputy heads were outlined and these could be classified into three main roles and responsibilities:

1. General *staff management* (three out of eight).
2. Specific *management of the implementation of the plan* (eight).
3. *Monitoring* progress (one out of eight).

Three of the deputies were said to be involved in general staff management. This concerned arranging and informing staff about general duties. A role for all the deputy heads in the management of the implementation of the plan was identified. This included such tasks as putting plans into action, assisting staff with target setting, working with individual co-ordinators and curriculum leaders, advising teams, discussing with staff, organising inservice training and disseminating information about courses. When it came to monitoring the implementation of the plan, however, a different picture emerged. Only one deputy head was described as having a formal monitoring role. This deputy was responsible for managing the implementation of the plan including the establishment of review charts and discussion of these at staff meetings. These responsibilities formed part of this particular deputy's job description. Two other headteachers mentioned a much more informal monitoring role for the deputy head. One described how, apart from meeting on a weekly basis with the deputy which provided an opportunity to review the plan more often, the deputy also had informal discussion with staff. The other headteacher said the deputy head had a similar role to herself and implied, therefore, that monitoring was a shared responsibility although no specific examples were given.

Eight of the headteachers identified other *senior staff* who had a specific role in implementing the plan. Of the six responsibilities named, in the case of six schools the post-holders were said to be involved in overseeing the implementation of the plan. Beyond that, only three of the headteachers mentioned other tasks, each of which were performed by no more than two of the senior teachers. These tasks concerned writing documents, providing training, planning staff meetings, supporting individual teachers and reviewing and monitoring. One of the headteachers was alone in expecting her senior staff to perform all six tasks named.

In relation to the involvement of *others* one-third of the headteachers said that all the teachers had a role in implementing the plan and in five cases governors were mentioned. Despite earlier comments about the range of people involved in development planning, only three commented on support staff, no headteacher identified a role for pupils and only one headteacher mentioned parents as having a particular responsibility.

Overcoming difficulties   Eight of the headteachers said they were experiencing some difficulties in implementing their present plan and six of them said they were having four or more specific problems. Interestingly, for the headteacher who said she was not experiencing any difficulties, this was her first plan. Five of the headteachers said there was insufficient time for the SDP and that there was too much to do. A similar number said they had been too ambitious, had set too many targets and that they needed tighter implementation strategies which included the identification of success criteria. A third of the headteachers cited problems caused by staff changes, job specifications and the introduction of appraisal. The introduction of other new developments, such as statutory assessment, was also mentioned by two headteachers. Additional difficulties experienced by at least two of the headteachers concerned: initial aims which were insufficient in detail; the change in focus from individual teachers to whole-school issues; and lack of external support. All the eight headteachers described the ways in which they were trying to overcome these difficulties. Two-thirds said that one of the strategies was to improve the process by, for example, making the structure tighter, creating more time, releasing staff and reducing the number of priorities. Five headteachers said they had improved communication and review procedures with staff and governors and four mentioned the use of appraisal and outsiders, in particular, LEA inspectors and advisers.

Monitoring the implementation of the plan   Although only two-thirds of the headteachers identified a monitoring role for themselves, they all said that the implementation of the plan would be monitored. Despite the fact that two of the headteachers expressed uncertainty about how to do the monitoring, they all described the procedures they were using or intended to use. Four main ways in which to monitor the plan emerged. Eight headteachers said they would monitor the plan, in part, by the use of their own judgement, walking about, 'gut reaction' and talking to people. Seven used whole-staff and team meetings to review and monitor the process. Two-thirds said that they used aspects of the planning process itself to monitor implementation, such as the timeline, 'ticking off achievements and individual targets' and referring to criteria established at the outset. They also mentioned the use of curriculum co-ordinators in the exercise. The same six headteachers said they looked for external support for monitoring from their LEA inspector. One headteacher was not satisfied with the extent to which the plan was being monitored, and another reported that the procedures for monitoring and reviewing the plan were new to staff.

Evaluating the outcomes   All the headteachers referred to the quantitative and the qualitative evidence which they intended to gather to evaluate the plan. Three kinds of evidence which could be quantified were identified:

1. Documentary.
2. Pupils' progress.
3. Test results.

Two-thirds cited documentary evidence such as policy documents, teachers' plans, new job descriptions and inspection reports. A third of the headteachers intended to use pupils' progress, in particular, work samples, records of achievement and reading records. A third of the headteachers mentioned the use of test results, both LEA tests and SATs. Five of the headteachers were using pupil evidence as an indication of successful implementation. Only one school was using all three types of data.

We categorised the evidence which could be defined as qualitative in nature in two ways:

1. Observable evidence.
2. Evidence gleaned from discussion.

Seven of the headteachers said they intended to use 'looking around the school' and 'using their own judgement' as sources of evidence. Two-thirds also said they would talk with staff either individually or at meetings. Discussion with parents and governors was mentioned by two of the headteachers. Despite the range of evidence cited, two headteachers said they were still not sure how they would know whether or not they had achieved their aims.

Reporting outcomes   All the headteachers said that at the end of the planning cycle they would communicate the outcomes of the plan with governors. Seven headteachers intended to communicate the outcomes to the LEA adviser or inspector and two-thirds said they would inform the parents. Only one head-teacher said outcomes would be communicated to the pupils.

Sustaining developments   Eight of the headteachers described the ways in which they would sustain the changes being worked on beyond the life of the present plan. One headteacher was uncertain about this issue. Seven said they would adopt the strategy of regular reviews and the examination of teachers' plans. Four had decided to allocate time and money and to build the need to sustain present developments into the next cycle through, for example, inser-vice training sessions.

The impact of previous plans on the development planning process

Formulating the plan

All the headteachers with previous experience of development planning said they had made two significant changes in the way plans were now formulated. The changes concerned:

- the procedures used to establish priorities; and
- the involvement of staff and others.

Some of the headteachers identified specific examples of procedural changes. Three said they now used more inservice training and two commented on the fact that the process was now more structured. Seven indicated that they had made changes in the identification of success criteria, and two headteachers now used LEA inspectors to help with this process. Five reported that they had recognised the need to build in evaluation as a means of identifying success. The publication of the document was new to one of the headteachers.

Seven headteachers commented on how they had made the formulation process more open and consultative and two-thirds said they now involved all teaching staff and that they delegated more responsibility to them. The same number claimed there was more structured discussion and communication with staff and five said there was greater governor involvement. Two head-teachers noted that they now included parents, one mentioned that support staff was now involved, and one said the same of pupils. Three of the head-teachers said they now communicated with the LEA adviser at this stage in the planning process.

Implementing the plan

Seven of the headteachers identified significant changes in this phase of the planning cycle. All of them identified five aspects of planning which had altered:

1. Roles and responsibilities.
2. Financial support.
3. INSET support.
4. Monitoring procedures.
5. Evaluation procedures.

Roles and responsibilities   Six of the headteachers said they now designated specific responsibility for implementing the development plan to staff, and three delegated more to working groups. Three of the headteachers also felt that governors now had 'a voice' in the process and two headteachers identified increased roles and responsibilities for LEA inspectors and parents. One headteacher noted that support staff were now included and another, the pupils.

Financial support   Seven of the headteachers said they now allocated some financial resources to facilitate the implementation of the plan.

INSET support   Five headteachers had increased the amount of school-based inservice training provision.

Monitoring procedures   Five of the headteachers said they now had more open whole-school discussion and review meetings. A similar number reported that more people within and outside the school were now involved in monitoring the plan and that targets and success criteria had been introduced.

Evaluation procedures   Two headteachers said they now gathered both qualitative and quantitative evidence during the implementation phase and two said they went round classes more systematically.

When asked if they had made any other significant changes, four of the headteachers emphasised that they felt more people now had 'a sense of ownership' of the plan. Two headteachers said they were taking a longer-term view of development for their school.

Sustaining development

Six of the headteachers claimed that major areas of previous development had been sustained and all of them offered explanations as to how they had ensured this continuation. They gave examples, such as specific monitoring by themselves (three); the use of INSET (three); communication, sharing and the delegation of responsibility (three); and the use of outside support (two).

Three of the headteachers did not identify the reasons for some developments not being sustained. The remainder identified a range of internal problems, such as: lack of time, expertise and money; insufficient planning and unrealistic expectations; loss of enthusiasm; and the difficulties involved in getting people to change beliefs. One school gave external reasons which were a combination of National Curriculum and assessment demands and lack of LEA support.

Main lessons learned

All the headteachers involved in school development planning before, as well as the headteacher new to the process, said they had learned lessons although, as described in the previous section, one headteacher did not explain in what ways these lessons had influenced subsequent planning procedures. Twenty-three lessons were identified which could be classified in three ways.

Lessons about the leadership and management of people   Between them, five of the nine headteachers gave a range of examples about the lessons they had learned. These concerned the importance of ownership, shared beliefs and common agreement; the way people were used and empowered and had their skills and experience increased; and the need for a combination of support and pressure.

Lessons about general management practices   Five of the headteachers commented on the need to use time efficiently and the importance of staff meetings and communication.

Lessons about the management of planning itself   Eight of the headteachers identified issues concerned with all aspects of planning. They talked about the lessons they had learned about the need to identify aims and objectives which were broad but not overambitious and unmanageable. They described the importance of documenting the plan and of having a structure. They mentioned the necessity for monitoring, building in regular review checks and setting criteria for evaluation at the outset.

The headteachers were then asked in what ways these lessons had influenced subsequent planning procedures and their own role and understanding about development planning.

The impact of previous plans on the leadership and management of people   Seven of the headteachers mentioned how they now extended roles and responsibilities, developed individual strengths and expertise, and provided additional inservice training for staff to give them more confidence. Reference was also made to the wider involvement of support staff.

The impact of previous plans on general management strategies   Five headteachers commented on this aspect. New management strategies were described, particularly those concerned with the organisation of meetings, communication procedures and the creation of time for observing in classrooms.

The impact of previous plans on approaches to planning   Five headteachers identified changes they had made. Between them, they mentioned that they now had a longer-term view of planning which encouraged them to start small but think big and to identify priorities which represented a balance between 'easy and hard things'. Several commented that the documentation of the plan was now more detailed.

The impact of previous plans on specific planning processes   All eight headteachers said they now drew up action plans, established timescales and built in monitoring and evaluation procedures. It was claimed by some that they now had more refined success criteria.

The impact of previous plans on the headteacher's role   The headteachers were asked about the impact of past experience of planning on their general role as a headteacher. Seven of the headteachers identified ways in which their approach to leadership and management had changed. Two of them described the considerable impact of planning on them personally. They felt they now had a greater sense of vision and credibility and an ability to oversee and to review the school as a whole. They felt their past experience had challenged the way they had been operating and they were now considering such issues as the balance between responsibility and delegation. Five of the headteachers cited ways in which their leadership style had changed. They talked about 'opening up and letting go', working alongside teachers, being part of a team and moving in and out of different styles more than they did before. Two of the headteachers who described the impact of planning on their leadership also mentioned the impact of planning on their management practices. They described how the process provided a feedback on their management style and how public relations with parents and governors had improved.

The impact of previous plans on the headteacher's understanding of the development planning process   Finally, the headteachers were asked if their understanding of development planning had changed in any way. All responded in the affirmative. From their answers, seven made it clear that they now recognised that the planning process is much more complex than they had originally thought and that it is not a 'one off'. There was a recognition of the importance of the management of planning and the problem of lack of time. Four of the headteachers talked about how their understanding of people had changed. The importance of staff confidence and involvement and of the headteacher working with staff were all mentioned. As described in the section on the purpose of planning, two of the headteachers said they now understood the need to embed development planning into the culture of the school.

PART FOUR: THE CONTENT OF SDPS

The present plan

The number of components

A curriculum component was common to all nine SDPs but, beyond that, there was wide variation in the number and type of content areas. Eight out of the nine headteachers listed two or more components in their present plan. One headteacher named nine and two named seven or more. Five headteachers named six or more components and four, four or less. Components concerned with premises, INSET, whole-school management, teaching and learning, and curriculum continuity, progression and consistency were mentioned by five headteachers and four said they had a finance and resource component. A third of the headteachers identified staffing as a component, and sections on governors, parents and the community were mentioned by two headteachers. Individual headteachers identified one of the following components: image/ethos; appraisal; LMS; and the local cluster group.

The priorities in the plan

When asked about the priorities in the present plan, the curriculum featured substantially in the answers given by every headteacher. Every plan included two or more National Curriculum subjects; two-thirds had four or more. Eight headteachers identified one or more National Curriculum core subjects; two had all three. Science was the least represented (two out of nine), whereas two-thirds of the headteachers said they were working on mathematics and computing. Other National Curriculum subjects which featured in plans were: art and music (five); history and geography (four); and technology (two). No school had religious education in the present plan.

In addition to the basic curriculum, other curriculum subjects and dimensions were mentioned by four of the headteachers. Four said special educational needs and equal opportunities were a priority and three noted sex education. One headteacher included school journey and cooking as additional priorities.

Appraisal, record-keeping and assessment were priorities identified by seven headteachers and two-thirds had priorities concerned with management and teamwork. Five mentioned priorities related to teaching and learning. A similar number identified curriculum continuity, consistency and progression as a focus for attention. Four headteachers had premises issues as a priority and three identified parents, governors, community and cross-phase links. For one headteacher, resources were a specific priority.

Why the priorities were chosen

From the answers given as to why particular priorities were chosen, it was clear that every school had a combination of internally and externally determined priorities. It could be argued that some of the internal priorities, such as the development of policies and changes in management arrangements, were indirectly initiated from outside because of, for example, the requirements of the National Curriculum and LMS. Every school's plan reflected one or more central government initiatives and eight of the headteachers cited national policies as one of the reasons for choosing priorities. The ninth headteacher insisted that the staff alone determined priorities for development. Two-thirds of the headteachers anticipated having to make changes to the content of the plan to accommodate unforeseen national changes, particularly in relation to the National Curriculum and SATs. Five headteachers said preparation for appraisal was a necessary priority and four said they needed to develop record-keeping and assessment.

Other reasons given for selecting priorities for development included the need to establish, complete or review policies (five out of nine) and the need to define staff roles and responsibilities (five out of nine). Additional reasons mentioned by at least two headteachers included: the need to improve communication with parents; a response to a governor request or requirement; and a response to an LEA policy directive. One headteacher said the content of her plan was, in part, determined by the priorities of the cluster group. Overall, two headteachers gave 11 or more reasons for choosing priorities. One headteacher gave two reasons only, both of which were external ones, namely, the National Curriculum and LEA policy.

The content of previous plans

The impact of previous plans on the number of components

Seven of the eight headteachers with previous experience of SDPs said there had been significant changes in the number and range of components in the plan. In the case of six plans, finance, resources and LMS had been added and five headteachers mentioned management roles and responsibilities as well as premises and image as new content areas. Three headteachers referred to inservice training and professional development. Interestingly, seven of the headteachers specifically mentioned the impact of LMS on the components.

Previous priorities for development

All the schools with previous plans included National Curriculum subjects as a priority for development. Five of the headteachers said they had worked on one or more core National Curriculum subjects. Other subjects noted were history and geography (two) and art and music (one). Technology was not identified. In addition to National Curriculum subjects, one headteacher mentioned one of the following: religious education; sex education; and personal, social and health education. Other major areas for development identified by five headteachers were assessment and record-keeping, management, teamwork and staffing. Curriculum continuity, progression and consistency were mentioned by four headteachers as were teaching and learning activities and appraisal. Between them, three headteachers mentioned special educational needs and equal opportunities; premises; parents; governors; and cross-phase links.

Sustaining previous priorities

As described in the section on the development planning process, six of the headteachers said previous major areas of development had been sustained. When commenting on content issues, one headteacher talked about the identification of themes as a way of achieving continuity and sustaining development.

The impact of previous plans on the content of present plans

Five headteachers said they now recognised the need for broader content over a longer time period. Two headteachers said they had learned to make the content more specific and to have fewer priorities for development at any one time.

PART FIVE: OUTCOMES OF SCHOOL DEVELOPMENT PLANNING

Threaded through the four previous sections on the headteachers' story have been issues concerned with the outcomes of school development planning. This section will focus on an analysis of some of these issues. The headteachers were able to identify the perceived benefits of introducing SDPs into their school. The considerable agreement about some of the central purposes of development planning revealed aims and objectives shared by the majority and, in some instances, all the headteachers. When describing the priorities for development in their present plan, the headteachers gave an indication of some of the intended outcomes they were seeking. The types of evidence to be used to evaluate the outcomes of the plan were outlined although, as described, at least two headteachers said they were unsure about the extent to which they would know whether or not they had achieved their aims. The headteachers with some experience of development planning were able to identify the outcomes of earlier plans and the impact of previous SDPs on subsequent plans and the planning process.

Different kinds of outcomes concerned with different aspects of the life and work of each school were identified. There were outcomes concerned with the planning process itself as well as the content of the plan. There were outcomes for particular groups, not least the headteachers themselves, who described the lessons they had learned and the subsequent changes they had made in their approaches to leadership and management. There were also outcomes for the school as a whole, including governors, parents and the community; for classroom practice; and for pupils.

The wide range of outcomes reflects the multipurpose nature of development planning identified by the headteachers and confirmed in the literature. There was a consistency between the range of outcomes identified by the headteachers and the three key purposes for planning agreed by all of them. The more specific outcomes described by individual headteachers revealed considerable variation between the schools. Such variation was reflected in the range of leadership and management roles adopted by each of the headteachers, and the range of specific strategies used to involve others in the process.

The next chapter examines the classteachers' story and compares it with that of the headteachers. It provides an indication of the extent to which there was a relationship between the rhetoric and the reality about the outcomes of school development planning as described by the headteachers.

8

THE CLASSTEACHERS' STORY

This chapter summarises the classteachers' accounts. It is structured in the same way as Chapter 7 except that, threaded throughout the analysis, is a commentary on how the classteachers' accounts compare with those of the headteachers.

PART ONE: THE CONTEXT FOR DEVELOPMENT PLANNING

General background factors

The initial training of the classteachers

All the classteachers had attended a full-time training course. Three had obtained a teachers' certificate and one had also completed a one-year degree course. Eight had a post-graduate certificate and seven had a BEd degree. A third of the teachers had trained in London, whereas others had trained as far away as Portsmouth, Exmouth and Manchester. A third were junior trained, seven were infant trained, four had taken a general primary course and one had trained for the middle-school age group. Like the headteachers, the subject expertise of the classteachers was relatively narrow with two out of the three core National Curriculum subjects noticeably under-represented. During initial training, whilst four had specialised in English, only one teacher had specialised in science and one in mathematics combined with physical education. In addition, five teachers had studied a humanities subject. Other subjects mentioned by individual teachers were music, art and religious education.

The classteachers' work history

The 18 classteachers, two men and 16 women, were first interviewed in 1992: 17 in the summer term and one in the autumn term after she had taken up her new post. At that time, a third of them had two or less year's teaching experience and for five they were nearing the end of their first year of teaching. Between them, the teachers represented a wide age group which ranged from 23 to 59 years of age. Four teachers were under 25, eight were aged 25–30,

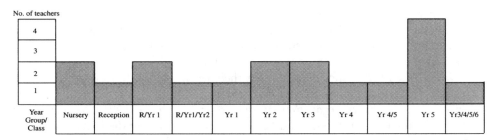

Figure 8.1   The spread of classes taught by the classteachers

three were between 39 and 45 years of age and three were aged 50 and over. Overall, half of the teachers had been in the profession for four or less years, four had been teaching between 5 and 8 years and the remaining five had 14 or more years' experience. The two teachers with the most experience had taught for 19 years and almost 30 years respectively.

All the teachers were teaching an age group for which they had been trained or had previously experienced. Figure 8.1 indicates the spread of classes taught by the teachers. The previous teaching experience of the classteachers was mixed and was as follows: nursery, two teachers; Key Stage I, 12 teachers; and Key Stage II, 12 teachers. Figure 8.2 indicates the range of this experience. In addition, one teacher had taught for a year in a special school, one had

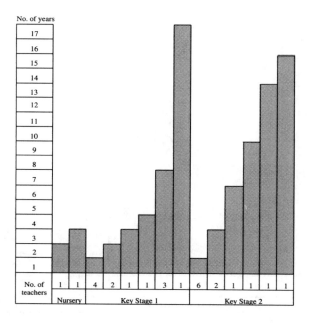

Figure 8.2   The previous teaching experience of the classteachers

secondary experience, one had some experience of teaching adults for whom English was a second language and four teachers had taught abroad. Before joining the profession, half the teachers had been engaged in other work experience. For example, one had spent ten years as a cartographer, another nine years in secretarial work and one, six years in banking.

When asked for further details about their work history, for a third of the teachers this was the first post they had held in their present school. In all, two-thirds of the teachers began their present post during the 1991/2 academic year. The three teachers who had been in their current post the longest were appointed in September 1989. Four teachers had held a responsibility post in another school.

Roles and responsibilities, curriculum interests and areas of expertise

Eleven teachers identified an aspect of the school's work for which they had a particular responsibility, although only nine teachers were receiving a responsibility allowance (four Bs, four As and one acting A allowance). Ten teachers named a curriculum responsibility and, of these, four were responsible for two curriculum subjects and three also had additional school-wide co-ordinating responsibilities. The eleventh teacher had a range of management responsibilities. The teachers were then asked about their present curriculum interests and areas of expertise. Figure 8.3 illustrates the range of responses given and the number of teachers who mentioned particular subjects and areas of interest.

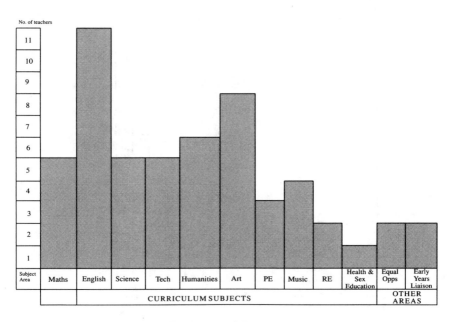

Figure 8.3 Subject interest and expertise of the classteachers

Classroom practice

The teachers were asked to describe the main ways in which they organised the pupils' learning. Two approaches were common to the majority, namely, the use of an integrated day and the teaching of subjects through topic work. Eleven teachers described how they planned an integrated day. Fifteen teachers said they used topic work as a medium for planning learning activities, although all but one of these teachers said they taught mathematics separately and nine of them described how they taught language work as a discrete activity. Eight teachers also said they used a mathematics scheme and three a scheme for reading. Seven said they were involved in whole-school or team planning and two said music was taught separately. When asked how they grouped the pupils the responses were more varied. Three types of group work were mentioned. Ten teachers said they grouped the pupils by ability, seven used mixed-ability groups and nine mentioned friendship groups. Four teachers said they used all three types of pupil grouping, five mentioned a combination of ability and friendship groups, one a combination of ability and mixed ability and two teachers said they used mixed-ability grouping only. Ten teachers in all mentioned that they used a mixture of teaching methods including whole-class reading.

Only four teachers had total responsibility for their class. For the other 14, members of staff either taught the class on occasions or provided learning support for particular groups of pupils. For example, seven teachers had Section Eleven teaching support, five had help for pupils with special educational needs and three teachers mentioned the role of the nursery nurse. In the four schools where the deputy head was free of class responsibility, a teacher from each of these schools mentioned the role of the deputy in teaching their class. Two teachers mentioned teaching support from the headteacher and specialist support for physical education was referred to by one teacher, as was music.

Seventeen of the teachers described how they used other learning support in the classroom. This took the form of primary helpers (11 teachers), parents (12 teachers) and students (three teachers). The involvement of other adults, such as governors, was mentioned by seven teachers. The type of support varied from general classroom organisational tasks (ten teachers), to help with reading and writing (seven teachers) and practical activities (six teachers), through to specific help with art and craft (four teachers) and mathematical games (three teachers).

Professional development

Since initial teacher training a third of the teachers had obtained additional qualifications: one at diploma level; one a higher degree; and four a certificated course. One other teacher was in the process of studying for a higher degree. When asked about any management courses, three teachers said that they had attended at least one such course. Every teacher was able to describe inservice training courses they had attended and the significant influence of such courses on their classroom practice. Fifteen mentioned courses they had attended off-site, with LEA professional development opportunities singled out by seven teachers. Seven teachers also talked about the influence of the induction programme. When asked about any other significant influences on their practice, 16 teachers cited members of the teaching staff in their present or previous schools. Of these, 14 mentioned other teachers, four the deputy head and two the headteacher. Three teachers also commented on the significant influence of the National Curriculum and a couple mentioned publications.

The teachers' understanding of educational change, management and leadership

The teachers were asked what they thought were the main factors which influenced successful change in schools and they identified three key issues. Seventeen teachers mentioned the importance of staff involvement and collaboration and 14 teachers from eight schools talked about the need for effective management strategies. Eight teachers from two-thirds of the schools described the need for strong leadership. The teachers were questioned further about what the terms 'management' and 'leadership' meant to them. Two teachers drew a distinction between teaching and management and said they required different skills. One teacher differentiated between classroom management and whole-school management. Two teachers saw management as the responsibility of the headteacher and senior management team and a further six were explicit in their view that management was a concern of the headteacher, deputy head and senior experienced staff. The management of staff was identified as the most significant management activity and was mentioned by 16 teachers from all nine schools.

Between them, the teachers commented on 29 different aspects of leadership. Of these responses, 26 gave the impression that the teachers considered leadership to be vested in the headteacher. By way of contrast, the answers given by two teachers implied that they thought there were others in the school who could also exercise leadership responsibility. From an analysis of the responses the same four leadership roles emerged as had been identified by the headteachers:

1. An *overview* role (11 teachers from eight schools).
2. An *initiator* role (11 teachers from eight schools).
3. A *support* role (11 teachers from seven schools).
4. A *pressure* role (three teachers from three schools).

The ability of the headteacher to delegate fairly emerged as the most significant factor in the overview role. Six teachers from five schools mentioned this particular issue. In the initiator role, the importance of the leader having definite ideas and involving everyone was identified by seven teachers. In the support role, teachers said they would look to the leader to provide cohesion and advice and to display such qualities as enthusiasm, respect and a sense of calm. Interestingly, whilst these three roles were identified by more than half the teachers, only one-sixth of the teachers mentioned the pressure aspect of the leadership role. These three teachers talked about the need for the leader to 'move things on' and to see that 'deadlines were met'. One teacher commented that if 'left alone I won't do it'. All 18 teachers said they had formed these opinions from experience of working in school. Four teachers also mentioned the influence of friends and other teachers, three drew on their own ideas and one mentioned the influence of the LEA.

Factors concerned with SDPs

The range of experience of development planning

The teachers were asked some general questions about school development planning to establish how much experience they had of the process and their overall attitude towards it. Only one teacher had been involved in a nominal way in school development planning in another school. One other teacher had experienced a curriculum development plan elsewhere. When questioned about the origins of school development planning in their present school, 15 teachers said there had been SDPs in the past, two did not know and one teacher said there had not been an SDP until the new headteacher introduced the idea. Two teachers were uncertain as to how formal these past plans were, whereas six teachers from three schools said that, like the present plan, previous plans were formal, detailed documents. By way of contrast, two teachers noted that plans were now less formal and more simplified.

The perceived benefits and drawbacks of school development planning

When asked for their views about the benefits and drawbacks of development plans and the planning process an interesting range of responses emerged. Seventeen teachers identified some benefits in having a plan. An analysis of these answers revealed the teachers' views about the purposes of SDPs (see below). There was one teacher who was consistently negative about development planning. She was of the view that her own planning was more important and, unlike her other colleague in the same school, could not see why there was a need to become involved in whole-school planning issues. Six other teachers identified some disbenefits of SDPs. Three teachers from two schools commented on the problem of overload, although the two from the same school said this problem had now been overcome. The other three teachers from two schools talked about the lack of staff involvement and two teachers from the same school described the problem of plans made which were not implemented.

The attitude of the classteachers towards development plans

In response to the question about how they felt about SDPs in their present school, seven teachers from six schools had only positive comments to make. They talked about how the plan provided a focus to work towards and was a means of sharing tasks and 'getting things done'. Of the six schools, two teachers from the same school were both positive. In two of the other schools, whilst one teacher was positive, the second teacher was new in post and so was unable to comment. In three of the schools, whilst one teacher was totally positive, the second teacher expressed negative views. In one of these schools, the second teacher was not critical about the principle of SDPs, rather, the fact that external demands generated by the LEA and the DES had led to a sense of loss of ownership over the priorities in the plan. There was a resentment that the plan no longer served the school's own purposes. This was in stark contrast to the noticeable enthusiasm and support for SDPs by the other teacher in the same school.

There were three schools in which both teachers had negative feelings about the introduction of SDPs. Two teachers claimed that it was the headteacher's plan not theirs and that it had therefore had no impact on them. Similarly, the other four teachers felt a lack of ownership because they were not involved in the formulation of the plan. Two teachers from the same school felt the plan had been too general and lacked specific targets and therefore had not been used by the staff.

Once they had described their feelings about the introduction of SDPs, the teachers were asked if most people in their school felt as they did. Some interesting comments emerged. Of the seven teachers who felt very positive about SDPs, four said yes, one thought so, one did not know and one said only some of the teachers. Of the nine teachers who had expressed some negative feelings, seven said yes, one no and one did not know.

From this analysis of the teachers' attitude towards development planning, it is possible to classify the responses in four different ways:

1. In one school the two teachers had nothing but a positive attitude towards SDPs.
2. In two schools one of the teachers was very positive, the other teacher was new in post.
3. In three schools teachers had mixed feelings about SDPs, although only one teacher expressed a consistently negative view.
4. In three schools previous experience of SDPs had caused teachers to have negative feelings about them, although all six teachers spoken to were able to anticipate potential benefits of development planning.

PART TWO: THE PURPOSE OF DEVELOPMENT PLANNING

The main purposes identified

Unlike the headteachers, the classteachers were not unanimous in their views about the main purposes of development planning. No one purpose was identified by all the teachers and it would appear that teachers' personal views about

SDPs were influenced by the context in which they worked. When asked what they understood about development plans and the planning process three main purposes emerged which were identified by at least half the teachers. These purposes did not entirely match those identified by the headteachers. It was said school development planning provides

- a sense of direction for the school as a whole (14 teachers from seven schools);
- a focus for staff discussion and involvement (13 teachers from eight schools); and
- a planned approach to inservice training (9 teachers from six schools).

Teachers described how SDPs provided a framework for their work in the form of an overall plan which details areas to be covered and enables achievements to be reviewed. The use of training days to enable staff to discuss the plan was described and three teachers felt that such discussions led to a shared sense of ownership by staff. The relationship between the development plan and the staff development plan was identified by four teachers. Others talked about how the plan could incorporate school-wide inservice training needs as well as personal ones.

Unlike the headteachers, the classteachers did not explicitly identify an external accountability purpose for SDPs. This was confirmed in their uncertain answers about who would be informed about the outcomes of the plan at the end of the planning cycle (see p. 108). It could be argued, however, that in identifying the role of SDPs in providing a sense of direction for the school, underlying this purpose is a different kind of accountability. As one teacher put it, 'you know what you have to do'. Another talked about 'a list of things to cover in the year'. The implication is that SDPs make teachers feel more accountable for whole-school development. If this is the case, then it is not surprising that teachers identified staff discussion and inservice training as important elements of school development planning. For headteachers, accountability was to the outside community. For classteachers accountability was in relation to the development of the school itself.

The responses to the question, 'What do you anticipate getting out of the implementation of the plan?', confirmed the three main purposes already identified. Ten teachers from eight schools said more discussion and whole-school involvement. Nine teachers from five schools identified increased inservice training. Seven teachers from five schools anticipated improvements in the way the school was structured and organised, especially staff meetings. Some of them felt they would have a wider view of the school and would be able to participate in the writing of policies.

From a further analysis of the responses to this question a fourth purpose for development planning emerged. The teachers not only identified the contributions they could make to the school, and the impact the plan was likely to have on them, they were also concerned about the benefits for them in terms of supporting their own practice in the classroom. In other words, the extent to which the plan met their own purposes. For example, nine teachers from seven schools felt they would be better informed about the curriculum and anticipated improvements in topic planning and progression. Individual teachers mentioned the benefits of additional classroom resources and of more time to observe other teachers at work.

The need for the plan to support teachers' own work in the classroom appeared to be an important issue and there were examples in the answers given by some teachers of a mismatch between school-wide purposes and teachers' own purposes in the classroom and their own professional needs. For example, one teacher described how SDPs had been used by the staff for their own purposes for some time but that she now resented the way external demands had changed the purpose and nature of the plan in such a way that it no longer met her needs. There were examples of teachers, eight in all, who did not entirely agree with the priorities set; some felt there were too many, others would have liked more curriculum subjects to be included. The teachers were of the opinion that their own curriculum priorities and classroom needs were not being met sufficiently. There were two teachers who complained that the plan had 'fizzled out' and made no impact and two others said previous plans had been written by the headteacher and that for them they had been of little benefit. Despite this mismatch between the plan and teachers' own purposes, what is interesting to note is that, as has already been established, all but one of the teachers in the sample could identify potential benefits of development planning for them and the school. The perceived ownership of the plan and the extent to which it satisfies a range of purposes would appear to be important factors. Like the headteachers, the classteachers considered SDPs to be multipurpose in nature.

PART THREE: THE PROCESS OF DEVELOPMENT PLANNING

Introduction

In responding to questions about the origins of development planning in their present school, it was established at the beginning of this chapter that 15 teachers from all nine schools said that there had been SDPs in the past. Two-thirds of the teachers from seven schools said that all the teaching staff were involved with these earlier plans. Five teachers, including all four from two schools, said only the headteacher or the headteacher and the deputy head were involved. The involvement of others was mentioned by six teachers and included: governors (three teachers); support staff (two teachers); and parents and the research team (one teacher). No role for the LEA was mentioned. These answers differed noticeably from those given by the headteachers.

Like Chapter 6, this section is in two parts. The first part describes the planning processes currently in use in the nine schools. The second describes the impact of previous plans and the subsequent changes which were said to have occurred in the planning process.

Current planning processes

The length of the planning cycle

The classteachers, like the headteachers, indicated that the length of the planning cycle varied between schools but, beyond that, the answers in some cases not only differed from the headteachers but also between the two teachers in the same school. In all, six pairs of teachers agreed with one another about the length of the cycle. From their answers five schools emerged as having a planning cycle of two to three years in length and for the sixth school the cycle was a year. The answers given by the two teachers from one of the five schools provided an example of incompatibility with the response of the headteacher from the same school. In the previous chapter it was noted that in the school where the headteacher was engaged in development planning for the first time, it was said the cycle lasted four years. By way of contrast, the two teachers from that school said it only lasted two years. Of the three pairs of teachers whose answers differed from one another, in the case of one pair there was a noticeable difference of opinion. One said the cycle lasted for a year, the other, four years. The headteacher's answer agreed with the former teacher.

Seventeen teachers said the cycle commenced at the beginning of the academic year and one was not sure. Whilst five did not offer a reason for this timing, nine said it began after a summer term review. Two teachers from two schools in the same LEA said the plans had to be submitted to the LEA in June.

Formulating the plan

Seventeen teachers concurred with the headteachers that staff discussion had been used to establish agreed priorities for development. The one exception said the headteacher decided. Like the headteachers, the classteachers described a range of different strategies to identify priorities. Only two strategies were mentioned by more than two teachers. Seven teachers from four schools talked about the use of a training day and four teachers mentioned the specific role of those with a co-ordinating responsibility. Individual teachers mentioned that attention was given to personal needs, national priorities or outside opinions. One said there was governor involvement and one that there was a discussion with the school's inspector. No mention was made, unlike the headteachers, of the involvement of pupils and support staff in the process.

Whereas a third of the headteachers said that at this early stage in the planning process they did not select any ways in which they could assess the subsequent effectiveness of the plan, 15 teachers from eight out of the nine schools said this did happen. For example, one teacher mentioned performance indicators, but did not go into any detail. Two described how success criteria linked with staff meetings would be used. One teacher said that evidence would be sought that both policy and practice were in place and two teachers identified specific outcomes in relation to pupils which were linked to the priorities in the present plan, such as improvements in pupil behaviour and pupils' increased use of books.

The teachers were unanimous in their agreement that, once written, the plan would be shown to them (a point overlooked by the headteachers). Unlike the headteachers, however, they were not unanimous about whether or not the governors would see the plan. Fourteen teachers from eight schools said they would, whereas four teachers were not sure who else, apart from themselves, would see the plan. Seven teachers said the LEA would be sent the plan, although it is worth noting that six of these came from the same local authority. Three others thought the inspector would see the plan, four said support staff would, three the parents and three teachers commented on the fact that the plan was open to everybody.

Implementing the plan

Strategies for putting plans into action Two main strategies emerged for putting plans into action. Like the headteachers, there was considerable agreement that aspects of the process itself, mentioned by 15 teachers from eight schools, would be used. All 15 agreed that roles and responsibilities were designated, 12 mentioned the use of timescales and 10 the use of targets. Two teachers from the same school mentioned success criteria. The other strategy concerned the use of inservice training and staff discussion. Whereas all 9 headteachers said training had been provided to help implement the plan, only 12 teachers from seven schools either specifically mentioned inservice activities or coupled these with staff discussion. Thirteen teachers from all the schools said some of the procedures were new to them. This was despite one headteacher saying this was not the case.

Roles and responsibilities The teachers were asked what their role was in implementing the plan. Some 33 different roles were mentioned. Whilst only a third of the headteachers said that all their staff had a role, it is interesting that the classteachers were unanimous in identifying at least one role for themselves in implementing the plan. Seven teachers from four schools identified between four and six roles for themselves. Two teachers from one school identified seven roles between them and two teachers from another school identified a total of nine roles. Five main roles were noted:

1. Leadership and management of the plan (seven teachers from five schools).
2. Curriculum and assessment responsibilities (eight teachers from six schools).
3. INSET-related activities (seven teachers from five schools).
4. General school-wide responsibilities (five teachers from four schools).
5. Writing policy documents (four teachers from three schools).

Teachers described how they led staff meetings, co-ordinated the plan and supported other teachers. Specific subject responsibilities linked with assessment were identified, such as science, humanities and technology. In relation to inservice training, answers ranged from providing training, persuading others to participate in courses, through to participating in inservice activities themselves. School-wide responsibilities included health and safety, the environment, liaising with parents and others and responsibility for the nursery. It was noticeable that no teacher identified a monitoring or evaluation responsibility for themselves.

When asked if there were others who had particular roles and responsibilities, two-thirds of the teachers repeated that all staff had a role. In addition, specific members of staff were singled out as having a particular role. Only six teachers from four schools identified the headteacher. This was in stark contrast to the headteachers who all identified multiple roles for themselves. Seven teachers from four schools mentioned the deputy head. Again, there was a noticeable mismatch with the headteachers who identified multiple roles for all eight deputy heads in the sample schools. Ten teachers from six schools cited roles for teachers with responsibility allowances. Like the headteachers, only a few classteachers mentioned others who had a role. Four teachers mentioned support staff, one referred to governors and three mentioned a role for the LEA in the provision of either advisory support or inservice training. No role for pupils or parents was identified. The teachers were asked how financial and other resources were allocated for the implementation of the plan. Two teachers said they were not. Six said that the headteacher controlled the budget, although half these teachers were then able to identify resource issues. Nine teachers talked about how money was made available for resources, specific equipment and inservice training, two mentioned fund raising by parents and two the allocation of class budgets. The other two resources mentioned concerned time and INSET. Nine teachers from six schools described different kinds of time allocation. Seven mentioned time for inservice training and six, time for staff meetings. Individual teachers mentioned time for advisory support for post-holders, for visits and for sorting out resources. In response to the question about whether or not they needed any training to implement the plan, a total of 14 teachers said that they did. These answers were slightly at variance with the earlier responses to the question about strategies for putting plans into action and again there was a mismatch with the headteachers' story. Twelve teachers mentioned inservice training related to the curriculum and two described a management course related to the plan itself.

Overcoming difficulties   Eight headteachers said they were experiencing some difficulty in implementing the present plan and this was borne out in the teachers' answers. Although only 12 teachers said they too were having difficulties they did represent the same eight schools. Two teachers said they were not experiencing any difficulty, three said it was too soon to say and one said not yet. Like the headteachers, the main problem identified by ten teachers was related to issues to do with time and the lack of it. The remaining responses were individual in nature but the problems identified were important, and between them the teachers raised some significant issues. They talked about the gap between policy and practice; lack of consistency in follow-through by the headteacher; lack of enthusiasm and involvement; lack of meetings and reviews; lack of clarity about targets and how to implement them; lack of money; the unmanageable nature of the plan; and the demands of the classroom.

The 12 teachers who said there were difficulties described three ways in which they were overcoming these. The main ones, mentioned by ten teachers, concerned staff attitudes and the better use of staff and others in and out of school. The need to be positive, take initiative and offer encouragement was commented upon, as was the sharing of ideas, discussion and review. The use of support staff and parents was mentioned and one teacher referred to the use of an LEA adviser. A third strategy, mentioned by two teachers from the same school, concerned ways of creating more time through, for example, using the headteacher and parents, being more flexible and using supply cover for record-keeping. One teacher said they had been unable to overcome this problem. The fourth strategy was also mentioned by two teachers from the same school. It involved the acquisition of additional financial resources from parents.

Monitoring the implementation of the plan   Fifteen teachers from eight schools said the plan would be monitored. Contrary to their headteacher, the two teachers from the ninth school said it would not. Three monitoring strategies were identified. Thirteen teachers from eight schools described the use of whole-staff and team meetings and discussion to review progress. Seven teachers from five schools identified an overview role for senior staff. For example, six teachers from four schools said the headteacher and deputy head monitored the plan. This was in contrast to twice the number of headteachers who identified such a role for themselves. Two teachers mentioned specific monitoring roles for curriculum and INSET co-ordinators. The third strategy was referred to by four teachers from two schools and concerned their own personal monitoring responsibility through, for example, keeping a diary and engaging in an individual review of progress. Unlike the headteachers, no mention was made of using the planning process itself as a means of monitoring the plan and no mention was made of the use of any external support.

Evaluating the outcomes   Apart from three teachers, two of whom said no evidence about the implementation of the plan would be gathered and one who was uncertain (these were the same three teachers who said there would be no monitoring), 15 teachers referred to evidence which could be described as either quantitative or qualitative in nature, or both, which would be used to evaluate the plan and the extent to which aims had been achieved. When asked how they would know if the aims had been achieved, the same three teachers said they did not know and one other teacher also fell into this category. When asked how the school itself would know if aims had been achieved, the same two teachers from the one school said they did not know, along with one other teacher.

Three main kinds of evidence which could be quantified were identified, the first two of which had also been identified by the headteachers:

1. Documentary
2. Pupils' progress
3. INSET completed

Nine teachers from six schools described a variety of documentary evidence, such as written policies, teachers' plans, new schemes of work and an SDP review sheet of tasks completed. Pupils' progress was also mentioned by nine teachers, this time from seven schools. The evidence ranged from samples of pupils' work and records of achievement, through to increased numbers of pupils taking books home, increased parental involvement in reading and the results of reading tests. Four teachers from three schools talked of keeping a record about INSET sessions completed and in two cases linking this with success criteria.

Three kinds of evidence which could be defined as qualitative in nature were described by the classteachers, some of which were similar to the headteachers' story. There was

1. observable evidence;
2. evidence gleaned from discussion; and
3. evidence concerned with attitudes and feelings.

Thirteen teachers from eight schools described the kinds of evidence they would look for themselves and that the staff as a whole would use. The evidence concerned three levels of change. School-wide changes were referred to. This evidence related to physical changes in the look of the school and improvements in the environment (five teachers from three schools). There were changes in classroom practice. Eight teachers from four schools described evidence such as teachers' plans, and the extent to which these provided evidence of a wider curriculum being offered. Changes in practice were mentioned, such as the use of a new scheme, the use of resources, the influence of inservice training and the presence of a new record-keeping system. The third level of change concerned the pupils themselves. Eight teachers from six schools identified pupils as a source of evidence. They mentioned looking at pupils' work, both in their books and on the wall; pupils' use of and increased enthusiasm for books; the content of what they were being taught; and whether or not individual pupils 'had got the support they needed'.

Fourteen teachers from eight schools identified discussion as a means of evaluating the planning process and outcomes. Ten of the teachers mentioned staff meetings, review meetings and whole-staff discussion. Nine also noted discussion amongst the staff including joint planning, informal chats and an appraisal discussion with the headteacher. Two teachers mentioned talking to visitors and representatives of outside agencies, such as the educational psychologist. Only one teacher described talking with pupils.

In respect of the third kind of evidence, three teachers from three schools referred to people's feelings. They talked about changes in attitude and evidence of the extent to which staff felt relaxed, happy and confident.

Reporting outcomes

The teachers had very different views from the headteachers concerning whom the school would communicate with about the outcomes of the plan at the end of the planning cycle. Amongst them, no two teachers from the same school were in total agreement with one another. Four teachers said they did not know to whom outcomes would be reported although one of these said the staff would be informed. One teacher said the outcomes would be made known to the senior management team only and seven teachers referred to the governors. Of these teachers, one presumed the governors would be informed, but did not really know, and another teacher said governors should be informed but it did not happen; she was certain about this because she was the teacher representative on the governing body. Four teachers mentioned the LEA, although for one of these teachers it was only a presumption and she did not know if it actually happened. The other three teachers mentioned discussion with LEA inspectors and advisers about either the plan itself or specific aspects of the plan.

A small number of teachers mentioned other groups who would be informed about the outcomes of the plan. Two teachers referred to parents; one thought a letter would be sent; the other noted the intention by the school to make available a book of policies for parents to see. Two teachers mentioned other schools, four, friends and other teachers met on courses, one said an initial teacher trainer linked to the school, and one our research officer. These varied and, in some cases, uncertain answers would appear to reflect in some respects the earlier non-identification by teachers of an external accountability purpose for SDPs.

Sustaining developments

Seventeen teachers described ways in which they, and the staff, would sustain the changes being worked on beyond the life of the plan. The responses were more detailed and wide ranging than those of the headteachers. Twelve teachers mentioned the use of discussion and the planning process itself, for example building in time for review and modification and designating specific responsibility to teachers. Seven teachers from four schools talked about how present developments would become part of the work of the school as a whole in subsequent years through, for example, whole-school timetabling, policies, schemes of work and practice in the classroom. Individual teachers noted attendance on courses, increased resources, the use of a parents' evening and the need to 'slow down and not take on new things'. Three teachers from three schools said it would not be possible to sustain all the current developments because of, for example, loss of initiative, changes in staff and because a present priority had not brought about the changes anticipated.

The impact of previous plans on the development planning process

Formulating the plan

In contrast to the headteachers who were unanimous in saying they had made significant changes in the way plans were now formulated, only ten teachers from seven schools identified changes in practice. Of those ten, there were three pairs of teachers. For the other four, there was a mismatch between what they said and the comments of their other colleague. Seven teachers, with one pair amongst them, said there had been no changes and one teacher, who was new, said she did not know.

Like the headteachers, the classteachers identified the same two changes: the procedures used to establish priorities and the involvement of staff and others. Eight teachers from five schools described new procedures concerned with the format of the plan and the number of components; the timetable; roles; and target setting. Two teachers noted the impact of increased external directives. Seven teachers from six schools described how the procedure was now more democratic because all or at least more staff were now involved and there was more discussion. One teacher noted that there was now governor involvement at this stage.

Implementing the plan

Thirteen teachers from eight schools, including both teachers from five schools, identified significant changes in the way plans were now implemented, whereas only seven headteachers commented on such changes. Four teachers said there had been no changes and one teacher, who was a new member of staff, said she did not know. It was possible to classify the teachers' responses in almost the same way as those of the headteachers. They commented on changes in four aspects of planning:

1. Roles and responsibilities
2. Financial support
3. INSET support
4. Monitoring procedures

Roles and responsibilities   Ten teachers from seven schools described a range of changes, such as more discussion and extended team planning; increased involvement of support staff; more clearly defined roles and responsibilities; more delegation; and more clearly defined tasks. As one teacher put it, 'things now get done'.

Financial support   Only two teachers from the same school commented on this aspect. They talked about budgeting for the future and how resources and their effective use were now linked into the plan.

INSET support   Four teachers from three schools described how inservice training was now planned ahead and how staff meetings were used for professional development. One teacher noted that inservice activities were now 'more highbrow'.

Monitoring procedures   Five teachers from five schools had something to say about changes in monitoring procedures. They described an increase in review meetings and how monitoring was now more structured. However, unlike the headteachers, the classteachers made no reference to any changes in evaluation procedures. Two teachers identified changes which had resulted in a negative impact for them: one was critical that plans were now more complicated; the other complained that there was now less time to implement the curriculum, less non-contact time and less money for implementation.

Sustaining development   The teachers were asked if past major areas for development had been sustained. Their answers were not as clear cut as the headteachers and of those teachers who responded, there was considerable disagreement amongst them. Also, the reasons given for developments not being sustained were different in a number of respects from those given by the headteachers. Nine teachers from seven schools said previous major developments had been sustained, seven said they had not and one new teacher did not know. Of those whose answers were in the affirmative, there were only two pairs of teachers from the same school who were in agreement. As with the headteachers, lack of time was identified as one of the reasons for not continuing with earlier priorities. Four teachers said time to revisit past developments had not been built into the SDP and that time had not been spent valuably on inservice training. Another reason identified by four teachers was the addition of new priorities in the present plan. Other problems concerned staff changes; larger class sizes; lack of resources; a policy written but not shared; lack of clarity about aims and definitions; the inappropriateness of the previous development for younger pupils; and the headteacher out of school too much. In many respects, the classteachers were giving reasons why problems identified by the headteachers had occurred, such as loss of enthusiasm and the difficulty in getting staff to change beliefs. Only two teachers specifically mentioned an external problem, namely, the National Curriculum.

The teachers who said previous developments had been sustained offered an interesting range of reasons as to how this had been achieved, which included: building in time for staff discussion; making past developments part of the current plan; monitoring by the headteacher and deputy head; responding to National Curriculum imperatives; incorporating new ideas into everyday practice including the use of resources; and using the impetus of whole-school projects.

Main lessons learned

At the end of the academic year the teachers were asked what lessons they had learned. All but one of the classteachers were able to identify lessons they had learned which were specifically related to previous plans. In the main, the lessons focused on the management of the development planning process itself. The comments made by the teachers indirectly indicated lessons for the head-teacher and senior management team about the leadership and management of people and about general management practices. The lessons were twofold in nature; some concerned school-wide planning issues, some, unlike those cited by the headteachers, concerned practical issues in the classroom. It was notice-able from the responses that, understandably, the teachers were identifying lessons from their perspective as a classteacher. As such, there were examples of where teachers' purposes and headteachers' purposes were at variance.

The lessons described by the classteachers built on their earlier comments about the impact of previous plans. The teachers focused on two aspects of the development planning process:

1. Identifying priorities
2. Putting plans into action

Identifying priorities　　Seven teachers from five schools commented on this aspect of the process. Positive lessons concerned how the SDP acted as a focus for concentrating on priorities and for being aware of what needed to be done. The process provided a formal opportunity to contribute ideas and teachers com-mented that it felt good when ideas identified by the staff were seen to be written into the plan. Warning lessons were also identified. Some teachers noted that there was a need for better consultation to achieve agreement and clarity about aims. It was felt by one teacher that priorities in the past were too long term and vague and that, instead, there was a need for more short-term practical priorities. Another teacher described how the headteacher and senior management team looked at priorities differently from the staff and cited an example of a priority decided by the senior management team which the teachers thought was irrelevant. Instead, the classteachers wanted a practical focus on a curriculum area with inservice training and guidance on how to use new resources and equipment in the class-room. Another teacher felt that in the past there was an imbalance in priorities which had led to too much time being spent on some aspects of the curriculum at the expense of other curriculum subjects thought to be more important.

Putting plans into action　　Fifteen teachers from all nine schools commented on this aspect of the planning process. General points were raised about the need for a clearer implementation structure and about the importance of work-ing together to establish a common policy which was understood and im-plemented by everybody. Particular lessons to do with time, staff meetings, progress reviews and classroom practice were identified. Two teachers from the same school talked about the need for more time and about how time should be built into the process to enable teachers to be better prepared in advance to consider policy issues. Two teachers from another school noted that, in the future, the pace of development should be slowed down in order to ensure that the staff can 'do things properly'. They said that new ideas should be introduced to staff early in the term to create time to introduce these in the classroom.

The importance of regular staff meetings planned in advance was recognised by several teachers. It was said that regular discussion enabled ideas and experiences to be shared and one teacher suggested that at these meetings the headteacher should remind staff throughout the year of the aims they were seeking to achieve. Another teacher noted that using the meetings for sharing practice as well as forward planning was important.

Linked with meetings were lessons about the need for regular reviews. Review meetings were seen as a means of 'keeping the momentum going'. Learning how to put policy into practice was a lesson referred to by at least three teachers. One teacher felt strongly that inservice training needed to be more practical to ensure it had an impact on classroom practice. Another teacher had recognised that previous developments did not stop the following year, rather, they needed to be worked on continuously if they were to be sustained. Only one teacher referred to any lessons about the evaluation of outcomes. She saw a need to analyse outcomes to see if the original goals set had been met. This was in noticeable contrast to the eight headteachers who described how the impact of past plans had influenced the introduction of new evaluation procedures.

PART FOUR: THE CONTENT OF SDPs

The present plan

The number of components

In common with the headteachers, the classteachers revealed variation in practice between the schools. The teachers identified 12 different components. Surprisingly, unlike the headteachers, the classteachers were not unanimous that a curriculum component was common to all plans. Only 15 teachers from eight schools mentioned the curriculum. Twelve teachers from seven schools said there was a whole-school management component which, for some, included specific implementation timetables, targets and tasks. Other components identified by five or more teachers concerned governors; finance and resources; premises and the school environment; staff development; and a general section providing information and a review of the previous plan. At least two teachers identified parents, special needs, appraisal and the LEA. One teacher mentioned the community.

There was a mismatch between the answers given by the headteacher and the classteachers from the same school about the number of components. For example, three headteachers named seven or more components, two named six or more. In contrast, the highest number of components identified by classteachers was six (four teachers from three schools). There was also disagreement amongst the teachers themselves. For example, five pairs of teachers named the same number of components but, of these, only three pairs named the same components. The remaining teachers gave different answers from one another and there was a noticeable discrepancy between two teachers from the same school; one teacher named six components in the plan, the other only two.

The priorities in the plan

The teachers were asked if priorities for the different components had been agreed. Fifteen teachers said they had, although one said it was the headteacher, not the staff, who had made the decision. Two teachers were unsure and one said the content of the plan was still to be formalised. The most noticeable feature of the description of the priorities chosen was the absence of information about curriculum priorities. Only five teachers from four schools specifically mentioned the following curriculum areas: mathematics (two teachers); language development (two teachers); art, music and physical education (one teacher). This was in stark contrast to the detailed responses given by the headteachers about the range and the number of curriculum priorities, in particular, those concerned with the National Curriculum. Three teachers identified priorities concerned with the school environment and its image and two mentioned reviewing and writing policies. A number of priorities were mentioned by only one teacher: appraisal; teaching and learning; induction for new staff; special needs; child abuse; and the playgroup. This raised a question for us about the teachers' sense of ownership of the SDP in their school and some of the comments about the priorities chosen confirmed that this was an issue.

Teachers' views about the priorities chosen

In the section on the purpose of development planning it was noted that nearly half the teachers were not entirely happy about the content of the present plan. In answer to a specific question about whether or not they agreed about the components and priorities in the plan, initially 13 teachers said they did. Another teacher agreed with the priorities but said there were too many in the plan and two other teachers said they only agreed with part of the plan. A teacher who was new to the school said she would have liked a review of areas already covered to be included in the plan. The remaining teacher could not understand how the school could plan so far ahead. Five teachers, three of whom had earlier said they had agreed with the plan, went on to identify other priorities which they thought should have been included in the plan. These priorities concerned the curriculum, for example, new National Curriculum subjects and a review of two of the National Curriculum core subjects.

The content of previous plans

Previous priorities for development

Fourteen teachers were able to recall major areas of development in previous plans. Two teachers did not know of any previous priorities or could not remember and two teachers, not from the same school, said there had been no previous SDP. Twelve teachers from seven schools identified areas of the curriculum of which all but one was a National Curriculum subject. Nine teachers from five schools identified the core subjects of English, mathematics and science. Other subjects noted were information technology (two teachers); humanities (two teachers); the creative arts (one teacher); and sex education (two teachers). In ten cases, only one teacher from a school named a particular curriculum area. In relation to five subjects, two teachers from the same school were in agreement with one another. Two other previous priorities were named by four teachers; one concerned record-keeping and assessment, the other, special needs and the behaviour policy. In the case of the latter priorities, two teachers from the same school were in agreement with one another. Appraisal was mentioned by two teachers, otherwise the remaining five priorities were identified by individual teachers with four named by the same teacher. These priorities were continuity and progression (one teacher); cluster group, home/school and community liaison, early years and the playgroup, and policy documents (one teacher).

Sustaining previous priorities

The teachers' responses about the extent to which previous priorities had been sustained have already been described in detail. However, it is worth drawing attention in this section to one particular response which was a specific comment about the content of plans. Four teachers from four different schools noted that new priorities added to the next plan had prevented previous priorities from being sustained. One teacher said that the attitude in the school was that 'we have done it so now we go on to something else'. The responses of the headteachers in relation to lessons learned about the content of plans indicated a growing awareness of this issue.

PART FIVE: THE OUTCOMES OF DEVELOPMENT PLANNING

General outcomes

Like the headteachers' story, issues concerned with the outcomes of school development planning have been threaded through the teachers' story in the previous four sections. The following are some of the key issues which have emerged so far. All but one teacher was able to identify the benefits of SDPs. This was despite the fact that half the teachers had something negative to say about them as a result of past experience. Although the teachers were not unanimous in their views about the purposes of development planning they were able to identify four main purposes. The answers the teachers gave about the gains anticipated from implementing the plan confirmed these purposes. When reflecting on the main lessons they had learned from previous plans the classteachers were also able to identify the impact of the outcomes of previous plans on the plan itself and the planning process. For example, three teachers described the introduction of a new planning sheet and a format for planning which was more detailed and which had more components. By way of contrast, three teachers described how the plan had now been simplified and had fewer components. Eight teachers from six schools commented on a range of changes in relation to the planning process. These changes included the increased involvement of staff; the way priorities were identified; a new form of staff meeting; a new timetable for action which was more manageable and realistic; the 'setting of targets and naming of names'; new kinds of inservice training; and new review procedures.

Fifteen teachers from eight of the schools were able to identify strategies which would be used to assess the subsequent effectiveness of the plan. In common with the headteachers, the teachers' answers reflected outcomes at three different levels: for the school as a whole; for classroom practice; and for pupils. A wide range of evidence in relation to these outcomes was also identified.

Not all the teachers said the implementation of the plan would be monitored and not all the teachers said outcomes and the achievement of aims would be evaluated. Only four teachers identified a personal monitoring role for themselves and no teacher identified a role in evaluating the impact of the plan. When it came to reporting the outcomes of the plan, the teachers were very uncertain in their answers and demonstrated a limited view of the use of SDPs for external accountability purposes.

Specific outcomes

To glean more information about the outcomes of development planning, the teachers were asked, in the first set of instruments, about the impact of past and present experiences of planning on their general role and philosophy. Seventeen teachers were able to identify outcomes which, like their answers about evidence, concerned three levels of change.

School-wide changes

Eleven teachers from seven schools identified the impact of school-wide changes. Some teachers reported that they now had a whole-school perspective and that as a staff they were more focused and there was a more caring atmosphere in the school. The teachers talked about being part of a whole-school plan and one noted, for example, that the process had provided a means whereby she could assume school-wide responsibilities. Others cited increased management responsibilities, such as leading teams and leading staff meetings. Teachers talked about the benefits of inservice training and of working with others. Opportunities for team and year-group planning were described; so, too, were observing in one another's classrooms, linking with another school and working with specialists from outside. Improved progression and continuity were appreciated by some teachers, as was the usefulness of school policy documents.

Changes in classroom practice

Six teachers from five schools referred to outcomes for them in the classroom. They mentioned using the SDP as a planning framework in the classroom; applying lessons from inservice training sessions and from examples of other practices; being better organised and able to take on more; being more confident and enthusiastic; and questioning their role with pupils. As one teacher put it, 'it changes the way you look at what you are doing'.

Changes for pupils

Three teachers from three different schools identified changes for pupils. One felt she was now 'less dictatorial'. Another talked about how the pupils had been able to benefit from an LEA adviser working with the class. One teacher could identify the positive benefits of the preparation of pupils for school because stronger links had been achieved with a preschool playgroup. Interestingly, this was the teacher who was identified earlier as being consistently negative about SDPs, yet she was one of the few teachers who was able to identify specific benefits for pupils.

When asked if they had any further comments to make, one teacher did express concern about the impact of development planning. In the context of her own school she wondered 'how much does filter down to the pupils'. Another teacher commented that 'SDPs are not a tablet of stone. If you don't do something the world won't end'. These answers reflected the teachers' growing understanding of development plans and the planning process. It could well have been that the teachers' responses were not just influenced by their previous experiences of planning but also by the stage of understanding they were at in relation to the process. To explore this issue further the teachers were asked at the end of the 1992/3 academic year about the impact of that year's plan and the planning process on the school as a whole, their role as a classteacher and the pupils. They were asked to express the outcomes in terms of benefits and drawbacks. The answers revealed a growing awareness of the complexity of the development planning process.

A similar range of attitudes towards SDPs as expressed a year earlier emerged although, on this occasion, three teachers, as opposed to only one before, were unable to identify any benefits that had been experienced. In contrast, four teachers were very positive about the outcomes and did not name any disbenefits. The responses of the remaining ten teachers were mixed, but more benefits than drawbacks were identified. In all, 12 teachers were able to identify benefits for the school as a whole, for them and, to some extent, for the pupils.

In many respects, the kinds of benefits described were similar to those commented on previously, although there were some noticeable additions. At the level of the whole school, the beneficial increase in confidence and expertise in respect of the curriculum was particularly noticeable and this was also reflected in the benefits classteachers identified for themselves. Nine classteachers commented very favourably on specific curriculum support which they had received. In turn, these curriculum benefits were reflected in answers about the outcomes for pupils.

In respect of the drawbacks identified, concerns about the impact of SDPs were expressed, the majority of which were to do with the content of the plan and the way the plan had been mismanaged. One teacher, for example, complained that the plan 'was not linked to teaching' and another that it 'took attention away from planning for pupils'. The concerns identified previously about the lack of time for the implementation of priorities and about the nature of the priorities were repeated. One teacher noted that because of the pressure to implement new curriculum priorities and because inservice training was fully timetabled, she had much less time for day-to-day classroom maintenance and display. On the benefits side, however, this same teacher explained how, because of the provision of good training opportunities, she was now much more confident in her mathematics teaching which had been one of the curriculum priorities for development, and that this, in turn, had led to a positive outcome for the pupils. She also described how, as a result of special needs being a priority, she had attended very useful inservice sessions which had resulted in direct benefits for the pupils in her class. Examples such as these reveal the differential impact that school development planning can have on the school as a whole and on teachers and pupils in the classroom.

9

THE EMERGENCE OF DIFFERENT TYPES OF PLANS

Chapter 7 provided a description of the headteachers' story from an initial analysis of the data. Chapter 8 concentrated on the classteachers' story and how it compared with that of the headteachers. This chapter describes the second stage in the analysis of the data and the formulation of the two stories. It reveals how, as a result of examining the agreements and disagreements and the similarities and differences between the two accounts, four different types of development plans were found to be in use across the nine schools.

THE EMERGENCE OF A NEW HYPOTHESIS ABOUT SDPs

Sorting the data

We began the analysis with a consideration of the agreements and disagreements, and the similarities and differences, between the perceptions of the headteachers and classteachers in an attempt to identify key issues and common themes. A framework was needed within which to do this and a decision was made to use the four aspects of development planning – context, purpose, process and content – derived from Chapter 3 in the re-examination of the data, because they had already proved to be useful during the first stage of the analysis. The two accounts subsumed a complex set of data and a systematic process was established to relook at the evidence available so far. The four aspects of development planning were lettered (a) to (d) respectively. Then, each aspect of the headteachers' and classteachers' accounts was recorded on a separate piece of paper. Also recorded separately were comments and questions as a result of cross-referencing back to the issues identified in Chapters 3 and 4. Each item was given a letter to indicate which aspect of development planning it related to and a number. Also, the source of the data or comment was identified. The result was 418 separate items grouped under the four general headings, rather like individual pieces of a jigsaw. It proved necessary to move some of the items around to ensure they were nested under the most appropriate heading.

Looking for patterns and identifying issues

It was then possible to look for patterns by grouping the items together. The most revealing data concerned the perceived benefits and disbenefits of planning, the difficulties experienced in sustaining developments, the lessons learned from engaging in the process and how subsequent understandings about the process had changed. What became clear was that the majority of difficulties and lessons concerned internal school matters not, somewhat surprisingly, difficulties in coping with externally imposed change. They concerned, in the main, planning issues which were within the control of the school. Five particular issues emerged in relation to SDPs and the planning process. These concerned

1. the *ownership* of the plan;
2. the *purpose* of the plan;
3. the *leadership* of the process;
4. the *management* of the process; and
5. the extent to which these four aspects of development planning were *shared* by those involved.

From the data, it appeared that there was a relationship between the degree of shared ownership, purpose, leadership and management across the nine schools and the nature and depth of the impact of SDPs on the three dimensions of the culture of the school identified in Chapter 4. For example, SDPs have had a negative impact on professional relationships in one school because of the gap between the rhetoric of the plan, as described by the headteacher, and the reality as experienced by the classteachers. In another school, the SDP appeared to be being used predominantly as a management and accountability tool by the headteacher to improve efficiency. The teachers cited few, if any, benefits for them and for the pupils. In some schools, however, teachers felt a strong sense of ownership and involvement in the process and could cite significant improvements not just for the school as a whole in relation to general organisational and management arrangements but also for their own teaching and the learning opportunities for pupils in the classroom.

From this preliminary analysis, therefore, there appeared to be evidence that development planning had a differential impact on schools and that this was related to the issues identified. What was not clear at this stage was whether or not there was any relationship between the content of plans and the subsequent impact they might have. We made a particular note of the need to investigate this further.

The identification of a new hypothesis

It was at this point in the analysis that we decided to consider the data from a different perspective. Until now attention had been concentrated on contextual

Table 9.1   A summary of the characteristics of the four types of plans

Type one	Type two	Type three	Type four
• No ownership either by the headteacher or the teaching staff	• Owned by headteacher only	• Partial ownership by the teaching staff but willingness to participate	• Shared ownership and involvement of all teaching staff and of some others connected with the school
• Lack of clarity of purpose	• Used as a management tool by the headteacher	• Used to improve both efficiency and effectiveness	• Shared sense of purpose to improve efficiency and effectiveness
• No leadership or management of the process	• Limited leadership and management of the process	• Led by head-teacher but management of process shared amongst some teaching staff	• Shared leadership and management of the process by the teaching staff
• Negative impact	• Limited impact	• Positive impact across the school and in classrooms	• Significant impact on school development, teacher develop-ment and pupil learning

factors and on the planning process itself, in particular, strategies for formulating and implementing plans. The format of the semi-structured interviews had facilitated this approach. What was needed was a further examination of the data to ascertain what could be learned about the nature of the plans themselves. The question to be answered was: Does each school have the same kind of plan? It soon became clear from relooking at the disaggregated data that, just as there were different approaches to planning across the nine schools, so, too, were different types of plans in evidence. From these data, it was possible to discern a relationship between the extent to which there was a shared sense of ownership, purpose, leadership and management of the planning process and the type of plan that had resulted. It was this finding that led us to a new hypothesis. The hypothesis was that there were different types of development plans in use across the nine schools. In the light of this hypothesis the items under each heading were re-examined and four types of plans were distinguished. Each type appeared to have a particular set of characteristics and corresponding outcomes. Table 9.1 provides a summary of these characteristics.

In consideration of these characteristics we gave each type of plan a name:

- *Type one:* the rhetorical plan
- *Type two:* the singular plan

- *Type three:* the co-operative plan
- *Type four:* the corporate plan

Then, each school was classified tentatively under one of the four types.

It was at this stage that the hypothesis was refined. We surmised that as there were at least four types of plans in use it was possible to classify the schools in relation to these plans. We then tested the validity of this hypothesis through a detailed reanalysis of the data. The outcome of this analysis was confirmation that there were different types of plans in use and that the type of plan could be identified. The tentative classification of the schools at the outset of the analysis was found to be valid for eight out of the nine schools. One school had to be reclassified as it was found to have a different type of plan from the one surmised originally. The final classification of the schools was as follows:

- A rhetorical plan – one school - School A
- A singular plan – one school – School B
- A co-operative plan – five schools – Schools C–G
- A corporate plan – two schools – Schools H and I

What follows is a detailed description of our findings in relation to each type of plan after this final classification of the schools. The outcomes described follow the order in which the analysis was conducted and are accompanied by a commentary. The majority of anomalies and surprises are incorporated in the commentaries.

AN ANALYSIS OF THE TYPOLOGY

A combination of quantitative and qualitative techniques was used to examine the characteristics of each type of plan. By moving between techniques we found that it was possible to confirm and extend the numerical classification of responses and to learn more about what was happening in each of the schools. We decided to use direct quotations from headteachers and classteachers to capture the nuances of the data. The size of the sample made this possible. For each type of plan every response to the semi-structured interview questions by the headteachers and classteachers was recorded in full for each of the schools listed under a particular type. The responses were then examined from five perspectives:

1. For each type of plan where there was more than one school listed, the headteachers' responses were cross-checked for agreements and disagreements and for similarities and differences.
2. Similarly, the classteachers' answers in each school were cross-checked and then compared across schools where appropriate.
3. Then the headteachers' and classteachers' responses were compared within and between schools as necessary. A distinction was made between answers that were in agreement or very similar; similar but also had some differences; different but not in disagreement; in disagreement.

4. This was followed by an examination of the quality and nature of the answers and the extent to which these matched the typology. This was carried out using answers about the content of plans; the planning process; and the impact of previous plans and lessons learned.
5. Finally, any anomalies and surprises were identified in detail and checked.

During this analysis attention was also paid to some contextual issues, in particular, the number of previous plans, the range of experience of planning and the length of experience of planning of the headteachers.

The outcome of our analysis of agreements and similarities, differences and disagreements between the classteachers' responses and between the classteachers' and headteachers' accounts

The reason for focusing on these aspects of the classteachers' and head-teachers' accounts to begin with was that it was anticipated that, if the typology had any validity, there would be significant variations in the comparison of the answers across the different types. We surmised, for example, that there was likely to be substantial disagreement between the classteachers and the headteacher in a school with a rhetorical plan, whereas a corporate plan was likely to produce agreement.

For the classteachers, two instruments were examined in detail: the one which had gathered information about each school's previous and present development plans and planning processes and their impact; and the one which reviewed the impact of the 1992/3 SDP from the classteachers' perspective. Responses to a total of 41 questions that were relevant to the analysis were examined for agreement (A), similarity (S), difference (Df) and disagreement (Dis).

To compare the headteachers' responses with those of the classteachers, the three instruments described in Chapter 5 were used: the one which had collected background information about the headteacher; the one which had focused on each school's present development plan and planning processes; and the one which had provided information about the headteachers' estimation of the impact of previous plans. Those items that cross-referenced to the classteachers' interviews in that the same question was asked of both groups

Table 9.2 The spread of the two classteachers' responses to the 41 questions, expressed as a percentage

	Total no. of responses	%
No. of responses in agreement and similar (A + S)	21	51
No. of similar but also different responses (S + Df)	4	10
No. of different responses (Df)	9	22
No. of responses in disagreement (Dis)	7	17
Total	41	100

were marked. Thirty-six common items were identified and coded and then compared to ascertain which were in agreement or very similar, which had some similarities but also some differences, which were different and which demonstrated disagreement. The findings of this twofold analysis of schools in relation to the different types of plans. The Tables provide a graphical representation of the analysis.

Table 9.3 A comparison between the two classteachers' responses and the headteacher's responses to the same 36 questions asked of both groups, expressed as a percentage

	Total no. of responses	%
No. of responses in agreement and similar (A + S)	4	11
No. of similar but also different responses (S + Df)	0	0
No. of different responses (Df)	0	0
No. of responses in disagreement (Dis)	32	89
Total	36	100

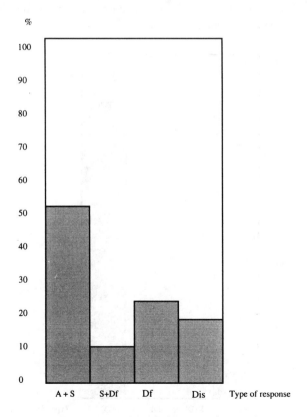

Figure 9.1 A graphical representation of the two classteachers' responses to the 41 questions

The rhetorical plan: School A

Commentary   Figure 9.2 reveals the essence of a rhetorical plan. The amount of disagreement between the classteachers and the headteacher was substantial and indicated a lack of any kind of shared sense of ownership and purpose. What was interesting was the level of agreement and similarity between the two classteachers in Table 9.2 and Figure 9.1. An examination of the actual responses revealed that what the teachers were agreeing about was the negative outcome of the SDP. Whilst they could both identify the benefits of development planning, they were totally dissatisfied with the way in which the process had been led and managed. As a result of this experience, 54 per cent of their answers were negative. Some typical comments from teachers were 'there was no overall plan, classteachers were not involved and were unsupported and undirected . . . and it fizzled out'; 'there was a lot of discussion but no outcomes'; 'I anticipated that the SDP would make me more informed about the curriculum, instead, it has led nowhere'. Clearly, the teachers felt frustrated and disillusioned and were distanced from the headteacher. This type of plan exposed not just a gap between the rhetoric and reality of the plan itself but also between the headteacher and staff.

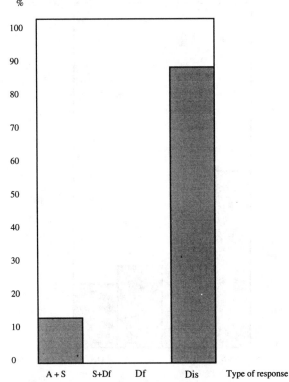

Figure 9.2   A graphical representation of the comparison between the two class-teachers' and headteacher's responses

The singular plan: School B

Commentary The graph of the classteachers' responses (Figure 9.3) represents a lack of shared ownership and sense of purpose between the two teachers, with a fairly even balance between answers that were in agreement or similar and those where there was disagreement. By way of contrast, the imbalance in consensus between the classteachers and the headteacher is

Table 9.4 The spread of the two classteachers' responses to the 41 questions, expressed as a percentage

	Total no. of responses	%
No. of responses in agreement and similar (A + S)	13	32
No. of similar but also different responses (S + Df)	9	22
No. of different responses (Df)	6	15
No. of responses in disagreement (Dis)	13	31
Total	41	100

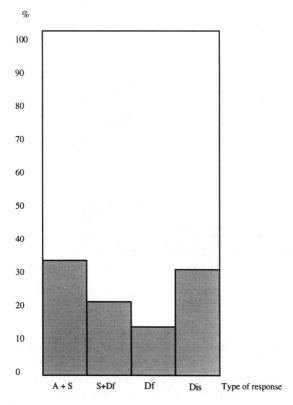

Figure 9.3 A graphical representation of the two classteachers' responses to the 41 questions

Table 9.5 A comparison between the two classteachers' responses and the head-teacher's responses to the same 36 questions asked of both groups, expressed as a percentage

	Total no. of responses	%
No. of responses in agreement and similar (A + S)	5	14
No. of similar but also different responses (S + Df)	2	6
No. of different responses (Df)	6	17
No. of responses in disagreement (Dis)	23	63
Total	36	100

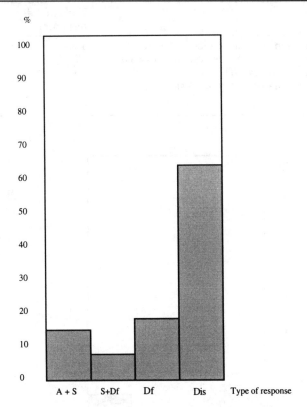

Figure 9.4 A graphical representation of the comparison between the two class-teachers' and headteacher's responses

noticeable (Figure 9.4) and reveals considerable disagreement. Compared with the rhetorical plan, however, the reasons for this disagreement were different. In this school, the headteacher did have ownership of the plan but was using it as a management tool and, in some respects, for accountability purposes for the governors. For example, the headteacher said of school development planning: 'It is important for good management of the school. It makes change manageable and helps with forward planning.' In contrast, one of the classteachers thought her 'own planning was more important' and that 'you are either a teacher or a manager' and placed the headteacher in the latter category. The singular plan was one-dimensional in character in that it was only owned by the headteacher and had one main purpose, namely, to improve efficiency. The teachers appeared not to be engaged with the process.

The co-operative plan: Schools C to G

Commentary   The graph of the classteachers' responses (Figure 9.5) reveals a distinct change in pattern from the previous two types of plans. For the classteachers, the percentage of answers which are in agreement or similar, if only in some respects, was noticeably higher, although the percentages range from 44 per cent in School D to 69 per cent in School F. The responses revealed that this trend reflected an increasing sense of ownership and purpose on behalf of the teachers. When talking about SDPs, for example, typical comments from the teachers were 'the headteacher knows where she wants to go' but 'there is staff discussion and ownership'; 'SDPs provide a framework for what you should be doing, a sense of direction and purpose . . . a list of things to cover in a year . . . a way of reviewing what has been achieved'.

A further reflection of this trend was the low average percentage of disagreement between the teachers, although, for School D, it was twice the average. What was interesting, however, was that the percentage of answers that were different was relatively high; higher than the other three types of plans. In some

Table 9.6   The spread of the ten classteachers' responses to the 41 questions, expressed as a percentage for each school

	School C		School D		School E		School F		School G	
	Total no. of resp.	%	Total no. of resp.	%	Total no. of resp.	%	Total no. of resp.	%	Total no. of resp.	%
No. of responses in agreement and similar (A + S)	17	43	10	24	16	38	22	54	14	34
No. of similar but also different responses (S + Df)	7	17	8	20	11	27	6	15	6	15
No. of different responses (Df)	15	36	15	36	8	20	11	27	18	44
No. of responses in disagreement (Dis)	2	4	8	20	6	15	2	4	3	7
Total	41	100	41	100	41	100	41	100	41	100

Table 9.7　The average percentage of the ten classteachers' responses

	%
Av. % of responses in agreement and similar (A + S)	39
Av. % of similar but also different responses (S + Df)	19
Av. % of different responses (Df)	32
Av. % of responses in disagreement (Dis)	10
Total	100

instances, this appeared to be due, in part, to some teachers being very new to the school. For example, both the teachers in School G were new to the school and one was in her induction year. However, what was noticeable was that an examination of the responses revealed that some teachers, in the main those holding a post of responsibility, although this was not always the case, had a much greater sense of ownership of the plan. They provided very detailed responses to questions about their particular role and responsibility in relation to the management and implementation of the plan. This issue of differential involvement is discussed further in a subsequent section.

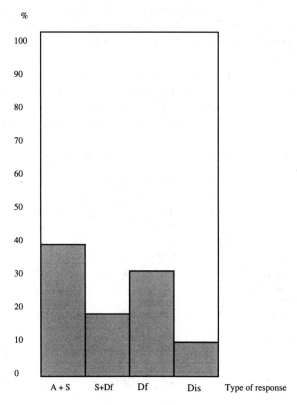

Figure 9.5　A graphical representation of the average percentage of the ten class-teachers' responses

Table 9.8 A comparison between the ten classteachers' and the five headteachers' responses to the same 36 questions asked of both groups, expressed as a percentage for each school

	School C		School D		School E		School F		School G	
	Total no. of resp.	%	Total no. of resp.	%	Total no. of resp.	%	Total no. of resp.	%	Total no. of resp.	%
No. of responses in agreement and similar (A + S)	15	42	8	22	14	39	10	28	10	28
No. of similar but also different responses (S + Df)	12	34	13	36	13	36	17	47	15	42
No. of different responses (Df)	6	16	10	28	5	14	4	11	3	8
No. of responses in disagreement (Dis)	3	8	5	14	4	11	5	14	8	22
Total	36	100	36	100	36	100	36	100	36	100

Table 9.9 The average percentage of the comparison between the ten classteachers' and the five headteachers' responses across the five schools

	%
Av. % of responses in agreement and similar (A + S)	32
Av. % of similar but also different responses (S + Df)	39
Av. % of different responses (Df)	15
Av. % of responses in disagreement (Dis)	14
Total	100

The comparison between the classteachers' and headteachers' responses also demonstrated a noticeable change in pattern. The graph (Figure 9.6) revealed considerable agreement and similarity in the replies. There was an average of 71 per cent, although, for School D, the percentage was noticeably lower (58 per cent) compared with the other four schools. School D's context revealed the possible reasons for this apparent anomaly. The headteacher was new yet the school itself was not new to development planning. There had been six previous SDPs but, according to the accounts, these had been rhetorical in nature. The semi-structured interviews took place at a time when the new headteacher was in the early stages of seeking to engage the co-operation and involvement of previously, according to the teachers' comments, disillusioned, sceptical staff in a new type of plan.

One of the other five schools, G, is also worthy of further comment at this stage in the analysis. What was surprising was that this was the school's first development plan and the headteacher was only in the second year of head-ship, yet the percentage of answers where the classteachers and the head-teacher were in agreement, or provided similar responses, was high (70 per cent). Possible reasons for the rapid achievement of this high degree of co-operation are suggested in subsequent sections of the analysis.

Unlike the singular plan, the co-operative plan appeared to be multi-dimensional in nature with headteachers and classteachers developing a shared sense of agreement about the adoption of a planned approach to improvement.

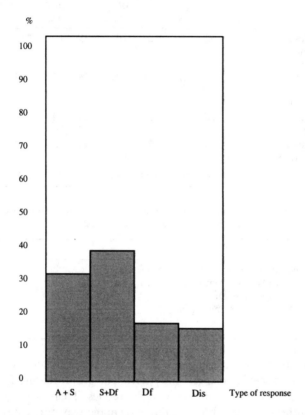

Figure 9.6 A graphical representation of the average percentage of the comparison between the ten classteachers' and the five headteachers' responses

The corporate plan: Schools H and I

Commentary   The graph (Figure 9.7) of the collective classteachers' responses reveals some very important findings. The percentage of answers that are in agreement or similar, if only in some respects, was extremely high, the average being 81 per cent. Similarly, the 3 per cent average of disagreement between them was very low. This pattern reflects an even greater sense of ownership and sense of purpose in relation to SDPs compared with the co-operative plan. This shared involvement in development planning was confirmed in the graph (Figure 9.8) of the comparison of the classteachers' and headteachers'

Table 9.10 The spread of the four classteachers' responses to the 41 questions, expressed as a percentage for each school

	School H		School I	
	Total no. of resp.	%	Total no. of resp.	%
No. of responses in agreement and similar (A + S)	20	50	22	54
No. of similar but also different responses (S + Df)	15	36	9	22
No. of different responses (Df)	5	12	8	20
No. of responses in disagreement (Dis)	1	2	2	4
Total	41	100	41	100

Table 9.11 The average percentage of the four classteachers' responses

	%
Av. % of responses in agreement and similar (A + S)	52
Av. % of similar but also different responses (S + Df)	29
Av. % of different responses (Df)	16
Av. % of responses in disagreement (Dis)	3
Total	100

responses. It illustrates an exceptionally high level of agreement and similarity between the two groups; an average of 86 per cent. It also shows an equally exceptionally low level of disagreement, with none at all in one of the schools. The contrast between this graph and the one for the rhetorical plan (Figure 9.2) summed up the very noticeable differences between these two types of plans. Some typical comments from classteachers involved in a corporate plan illustrated this difference: 'SDPs are helpful as a new member of staff, everyone shares, is involved and does a little, I'm impressed'; 'all the teaching staff, support staff, governors and the local authority adviser are involved.' These, and other comments, demonstrated a high degree of confidence among the teachers and a very strong sense of shared purpose in the plan and the planning process; a sense of unity that went beyond the teaching staff to include others who worked in and with the schools.

What was interesting was that the two schools that were found to have a corporate plan were very different. The school where there was no disagreement at all (School I) had been involved in five previous SDPs. By way of contrast, surprisingly, the other school had only commenced school development planning in 1990, the year after the present headteacher took up her appointment. The school was part way through the second year of planning at the time of the interviews. This raised a number of questions that needed to be answered, not least, how had School H been able to achieve such a high degree of shared ownership, purpose and involvement in school development planning in such a short space of time? Was it something about the context and

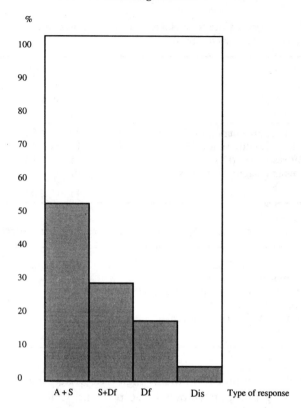

Figure 9.7 A graphical representation of the average percentage of the four class-teachers' responses

content of the plan and the strategies used to formulate and implement it that had contributed to the differences between corporate planning and the other three types of plan? The next two phases of the analysis address these questions in turn.

Table 9.12 A comparison between the four classteachers' and the two headteachers' responses to the same 36 questions asked of both groups, expressed as a percentage for each school

	School H		School I	
	Total no. of resp.	%	Total no. of resp.	%
No. of responses in agreement and similar (A + S)	18	50	18	50
No. of similar but also different responses (S + Df)	13	36	13	36
No. of different responses (Df)	4	11	5	14
No. of responses in disagreement (Dis)	1	3	0	0
Total	36	100	36	100

Table 9.13 The average percentage of the comparison between the four classteachers' and the two headteachers' responses across the two schools

	%
Av. % of responses in agreement and similar (A + S)	50.0
Av. % of similar but also different responses (S + Df)	36.0
Av. % of different responses (Df)	12.5
Av. % of responses in disagreement (Dis)	1.5
Total	100.0

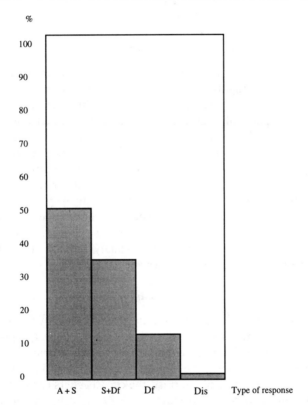

Figure 9.8 A graphical representation of the average percentage of the comparison between the four classteachers' and the two headteachers' responses

The outcome of our analysis of the context and the content of the plans across the typology

The examination of the content of SDPs revealed differences across the schools, not just in relation to the content of present plans but also to changes that had taken place in the type of content from one plan to the next. We decided, therefore, at this stage in the analysis to include contextual information about the range of experience of development planning across the schools along with the range of headship experience represented in each type of plan.

Six questions asked of headteachers and classteachers focused on the content of SDPs. The questions concerned the number and nature of the components and priorities in the present plan and why the latter were chosen; whether any new components had been added more recently; the content of the previous plans where one had existed; and the extent to which any lessons learned from previous experience of SDPs had influenced the subsequent content of plans. Our findings were as follows for each type of plan. They are summed up in a commentary at the end of the chapter.

The rhetorical plan: School A

The headteacher, appointed a year prior to the interviews, was responsible for the current plan. For this headteacher it was a second headship after seven years in another school. It was reported by the headteacher that the school had had two previous plans although the classteachers said this was not the case. According to the headteacher the present plan had one component, the curriculum, and six priorities. The reasons given for choosing the priorities were a combination of internal and external imperatives. Despite this apparent simplicity, the classteachers' answers about the number of components and priorities conflicted with one another and neither answers were in agreement with the answers given by the headteacher. Neither the headteacher nor the classteachers were able to comment on any changes that may have occurred in the content of the plan. As with the previous analysis, a total lack of ownership and involvement by the classteachers was evident.

The singular plan: School B

It was the fourth year of headship for the headteacher of School B and the school's second plan, the first having commenced in 1989. The plan was said, by the headteacher, to have six components and nine priorities, chosen for internal and external reasons, the latter a combination of local initiatives and national legislation. By way of contrast, the classteachers each cited only three components, only two of which matched those cited by the headteacher. In relation to the priorities, one teacher did not know which they were and the other listed a totally different set of priorities from the headteacher. In respect of any changes as a result of lessons learned, the answers were again contradictory. The headteacher said the number of components had increased and that the content was now broader. The influence of LMS and national priorities, such as appraisal, was noticeable. However, the one classteacher who did comment said that the plan now had fewer components and, as a result, it was simpler. This analysis confirmed that there was very little evidence of any sense of ownership of the plan by the classteachers.

The co-operative plan: Schools C to G

All the headteachers were in their first headship and the length of experience ranged from a headteacher in the first year in post to one in the sixth year. The schools also represented a wide range of experience of development planning from no prior experience through to a school that had been planning in this way for eight years. Consequently, the number of previous plans across the five schools ranged from none to six.

Similarly, there were marked differences across the schools in terms of the number of components and priorities in the present plan. School D, with a new headteacher, and School G which was new to planning as well as having a relatively new headteacher, both had only two components, the curriculum and inservice training. In addition to these same two components, two schools each had four other components and one, School C, had a further seven. With regard to the number of priorities, these ranged from eight in School E to 20 in School C. In four out of five cases the reasons given by the headteacher for the choice of priorities were a combination of internal development needs and external requirements. These latter included requirements from governors, LEA policy initiatives and national policies. The influence of the National Curriculum and assessment requirements was particularly evident across all the schools. One school said the priorities reflected staff needs only although these, in turn, were heavily influenced by national imperatives.

The four schools with previous experience of development planning had increased the number of components and, like School B, now included resources, whole-school management and buildings and premises; a clear indication of the influence of LMS on SDPs. Two schools now included a component on governors and one on parents as a reflection of their respective increased involvement in the process. Two headteachers said they now made the content longer term and one said the content had been reduced to make it more manageable.

In contrast to both the previous types of plans, the classteachers had more to say about the content of plans, confirming their greater sense of ownership of the process. However, their answers to questions about the actual priorities were 'different rather than similar' in relation to the responses of their respective headteachers. Judging from the responses, this was possibly because those mentioned were ones which had impinged directly on the classroom; priorities that they felt a sense of responsibility for, and that they could relate to, in their everyday work.

The corporate plan: Schools H and I

Like the schools in the previous type of plan, the circumstances of these two schools were very different. One headteacher was in the third year of headship, the other the fifth year. School H had had one previous plan, School I, five. Therefore, the experience of development planning ranged from one to six years. The number of components and priorities also varied. In addition to the curriculum and inservice training, School H had two other components and a total of 14 priorities. School I had an additional four components and ten priorities in all. Both headteachers said they had increased the number of components and both now included, for example, governors and resources. One headteacher said the content had been broadened, the other said the plan now had less in it to make it more specific and manageable.

An examination of classteachers' responses revealed not only their high level of awareness about the components and priorities in the present plan but also their noticeable agreement about these with one another, and with their head-teacher. This added further confirmation about their considerable sense of ownership and involvement in development planning. What was interesting was that the sense of ownership appeared to be so strong in School I that the teachers described a potential conflict that was emerging in respect of the choice of priorities for next year's plan. Classteachers had very clear ideas about what should be in the plan that would best meet their needs. It was said that these ideas did not coincide with views being expressed by members of the senior management team. The teachers were aware that a corporate decision would have to be taken to resolve this difference of opinion.

Commentary on all four types of plans   A range of issues emerged from this analysis of the context and content of plans including some anomalies and surprises. For example, no relationship was established between the length of headship experience of development planning and the type of plan. There was a clear indication, therefore, that the quality of leadership and management of the plan was a key factor. This issue was one of the focuses of attention in the next stage of the analysis. This finding also raised a question about whether or not there was a relationship between the number of previous plans in the school and the type of plan. It seemed likely, for example, that where a rhetori-cal plan had been in place for some time, as was the case with School D, a new headteacher would find this a very different and potentially difficult starting point, compared with a new headteacher of a school that had been engaged previously in either a co-operative or a corporate type of plan, although the latter could be equally challenging for a new headteacher for different reasons.

There was one common component and priority across all types of plans and all schools, namely, the curriculum. It was also noticeable that both the co-operative and corporate plans had an inservice training component. All the schools with these types of plans linked staff development with school develop-ment, which may have been one of the reasons why School H had been able to achieve a corporate approach very quickly. Beyond this, it was difficult to discern any relationship between the number of components and priorities and the type of plan, except that simplicity clearly did not equal efficacy. The rhetorical plan was the simplest in that it had the smallest number of compo-nents and priorities, yet there was no link between this and the classteachers' sense of involvement and ownership. With the exception of the rhetorical plan, the other three types had all increased the number of components, particularly in relation to whole-school management, premises and resource management. This indicated the increased use of school development planning to aid self-management and to combine both internal and external developmental requirements. There was also evidence in these three types of plans of involvement in planning being extended to include support staff, governors, parents and LEA personnel to varying degrees across the schools. Only four schools, C and F and both schools with corporate planning, noted any pupil involvement. The definition of involvement, however, was an issue, given that it was only the classteachers engaged in corporate planning whose answers correlated most closely with those of the headteachers.

This analysis helped to confirm some of the characteristics of the different types of plans already identified. It also opened up other issues to be explored. It seemed likely, for example, that the way in which priorities were established and implemented was a significant factor and that the interrelationship among priorities, particularly those concerned with the curriculum, staff development and whole-school and resource management, was important. More also needed to be known about the actual nature and focus of the priorities. For example, whether they were focused on school-wide policy development or more directly concerned with practice in the classroom. To explore these issues it was necessary to go beyond the content to an examination of the processes of planning across each type of plan.

The outcome of our analysis of the planning processes across the typology

The rhetorical plan: School A

Weaknesses emerged in relation to all aspects of the planning process when the headteacher's and classteachers' responses were compared. There was disagreement about the extent to which the teachers were involved in establishing priorities, with one classteacher stating that 'the headteacher decided'. Both teachers then went on to say that at the formulation stage no procedures were put in place to assess the subsequent effectiveness of the plan. There was disagreement between the headteacher and classteachers about processes used to put the plan into action and neither teacher said they had any specific responsibility. The headteacher did not identify a leadership or management role in respect of monitoring the plan and there appeared to be no resource allocation targeted at the plan. No specific INSET was said to be provided to support the plan, yet the headteacher and classteachers described difficulties in implementing the plan, albeit for different reasons. The headteacher blamed the culture of the school and lack of governor support. The classteachers blamed weak leadership and management. For example, one teacher complained about 'lack of enthusiasm, lack of involvement, lack of regular meetings'. The other talked about the 'lack of clear targets and timescales'. A lack of confidence and any sense of control over the process by both the headteacher and the classteachers emerged from the answers. When it came to procedures for gathering evidence and evaluating the plan, there was little or no reference to pupils and the classteachers said that no evidence was being gathered. They expressed a total lack of confidence either that the plan would be evaluated or that present priorities would be sustained in the next planning cycle.

The singular plan: School B

Like the rhetorical plan, there were weaknesses at all stages in the planning process but these were somewhat different in nature. The headteacher expressed more confidence in the process. The classteachers were less confident but agreed that staff discussion was used to establish priorities and, unlike the headteacher, they were able to describe some processes for assessing the subsequent effectiveness of the plan. There was some agreement between the classteachers and the headteacher about processes for implementing the plan, although only one teacher, an allowance holder, identified a particular responsibility. There was only limited evidence of the use of financial resources and INSET to support the implementation of the plan. In addition, classteachers looked to the headteacher to fulfil leadership and management responsibilities in respect of monitoring the plan; a role not identified by the headteacher.

Both the headteacher and the classteachers reported that they were having difficulties in implementing the plan. Although the reasons given were different, what they did have in common was the type of pressures cited, some of which were external in nature and were seen to be beyond their control. For example, the headteacher said 'the environment, time, SATs, LMS and appraisal'. A classteacher talked about problems with 'non-contact time, time for record-keeping and lack of money'. The need to improve the leadership and management of the development planning process itself was not identified as a possible means of overcoming some of these difficulties, although the headteacher did recognise the need to achieve 'more staff ownership and involvement'. The types of evidence to be used to evaluate the effectiveness of the plan were limited and consisted mainly of 'ticking off achievements'. The headteacher made no reference to a focus on the work of classteachers or pupils when describing evaluation procedures. It was the headteacher who took personal responsibility for endeavouring to sustain the changes made beyond the present planning cycle.

The co-operative plan: Schools C to G

The nature and quality of the answers about the planning process were noticeably different from the previous two types of plans. Staff discussion, involving all teaching staff, was again cited as a principal means of formulating priorities but, for this type of plan, subsequent answers indicated a greater sense of ownership and involvement in the overall processes of development planning by both the headteachers and the classteachers. At the formulation stage some weaknesses emerged in respect of the identification of ways of assessing the subsequent effectiveness of the plan. Two headteachers said no strategies had been identified, the other three said they would use the planning process itself. Interestingly, all five pairs of classteachers cited at least some practical strategies that, as far as they were concerned, would be used.

With the exception of the headteacher of School D, whose answer was rather limited, the headteachers of the other four schools identified a wide range of strategies to implement the plan. For example, eight procedures for putting the plan into action were described by the headteacher of School E: 'targets, tasks, timescales, allocation of roles and responsibilities, school-based INSET, money for supply cover, staff meetings, and senior management team monitoring and review.' The classteachers' answers, on the whole, confirmed this increase in implementation strategies and much emphasis was placed on the role of the headteacher, the deputy head and staff with allowances, in particular, for those with co-ordination responsibilities for the curriculum and inservice training.

Common to all five schools was the use of this training, supply cover and other financial resources to support the implementation of the plan. Training took many forms and was frequently a combination of school-based sessions, attendance at LEA courses and the use, in school, of LEA advisory services. Two types of professional development were discerned. There was training specifically related to priorities in the plan itself, for example, to increase knowledge and improve practice in an area of the curriculum. There was training for members of the senior management team to enable them to enhance their knowledge and skills in relation to the management of the development planning process itself.

All the headteachers had clear views about their leadership and management responsibilities. Four out of five said that one of their leadership responsibilities was that of initiating ideas. Four out of five specifically identified a monitoring role for themselves and the remaining headteacher of School G took full responsibility for the overall management of the process including monitoring. All five headteachers identified roles and responsibilities for the deputy head. Three described a combination of leadership and management responsibilities but only the headteacher of School F identified a monitoring role for the deputy. Apart from School G, some management responsibilities were also identified for other members of the senior management team but none of these concerned monitoring the plan. The answers about who else had responsibility for the management of the process were less clear and differences emerged between the headteachers and classteachers. Whilst all the teachers claimed to have some general responsibility as a classteacher for implementing the plan, which was an indication of their level of involvement and willingness to co-operate with the plan, two headteachers said that there were no others who had particular roles and responsibilities.

A further analysis of classteachers' answers concerning their views about SDPs and their role revealed three kinds of responses. There were those who clearly welcomed the strong leadership and management provided by the head-teacher and senior staff. For example, a teacher from School G, when talking about the benefits of development planning, said 'we all know what we're doing, the SDP provides a framework, a systematic organised sense of direction for the school'. There were those, particularly post-holders, who commented on how their responsibility in relation to the plan had enhanced their own professional development. One classteacher described how she had developed her management role through 'leading staff meetings and by providing leadership and management for a team of teachers'. There were some teachers, however, who felt there was still insufficient whole-staff involvement in the identification of priorities and one teacher complained that 'only certain people have contributed'. Another described how there was a need for all staff to be involved in a regular review of the plan because at the moment 'only post-holders tend to do this'.

Apart from School G, which was new to planning, the other headteachers and classteachers described difficulties they were experiencing in the implementation of the plan. The majority of comments were about school factors, not least the lack of time and how this valuable resource could be used better. A number were to do with the planning process itself. One headteacher said, for example, 'aims were not clear enough and there is a need for tighter implementation strategies'. All the headteachers, and the majority of class-teachers, identified practical ways in which they could improve the process. In general, a sense of confidence and control over the planning process emerged from the answers. This was further confirmed in the responses provided about the evaluation of the plans. A wide range of quantitative and qualitative evidence was described by all the headteachers and the majority of the class-teachers. The headteachers tended to concentrate on school-wide evidence, such as inspection reports, test results and policy documents, although all said they would look around the school and talk with teachers. Classteachers tended to concentrate on evidence concerned with their own professional development as well as school-wide discussion and the production of policies and schemes of work. Only two teachers specifically mentioned the use of evidence of pupils' actual work. Similarly, only one headteacher focused on pupils as a specific source of evidence. The range of evidence cited, however, indicated that the co-operative plan was perceived to be multipurpose in nature in that it was concerned with improving both efficiency and effectiveness.

Finally, when it came to the question about how present developments would be sustained, in some instances the headteachers were more confident than the classteachers that this would happen. Although classteachers described how the planning process could be used to sustain changes beyond the life of the present plan, some teachers were perhaps being more realistic than their headteachers in stating that probably not all priorities would be sustained. One of the teachers from School D was still very sceptical. It was the headteachers who appeared to assume the major leadership and management responsibility for this aspect of planning.

The corporate plan: Schools H and I

Our initial analysis had revealed a high level of agreement between head-teachers and classteachers engaged in corporate planning. The subsequent analysis of the quality and nature of this agreement revealed distinctive patterns, not least the sense of corporate working relationships between teachers and others. This was a common thread throughout. Whole-staff involvement in the identification of priorities was stressed by all respondents, and class-teachers from the two schools described how both school-wide and personal professional needs were incorporated into the plan. A strong sense of involvement and ownership was evident, so much so that one experienced teacher in School I felt a sense of resentment that the school no longer had total ownership of development planning, as was once the case, because of the recent increase in external demands, both local and national. It was noticeable that all the answers to the question about whether the school selected ways of assessing the subsequent effectiveness of the plan at the formulation stage were strong and a range of strategies was identified. One headteacher talked about how they had 'set targets, success criteria and individual teacher review and target sheets'. The two teachers from the same school echoed the same response. It was the same story with the other school. One classteacher said 'yes, through teachers' plans and evaluations, timed priorities and staff review of the plan'. The other said 'yes, through targets, performance indicators, and policy and practice in place'.

This shared sense of ownership and purpose was further illustrated in the responses concerned with the implementation of plans; so, too, was a notice-able shared sense of leadership and management of the planning process. Both headteachers assumed support and overview leadership roles and, likewise, when describing their role in the management of the planning process, they both stressed communication and liaison as well as monitoring. Roles and responsibilities for members of the senior management team, all other teachers and also governors were identified. The classteachers' answers confirmed this sense of shared responsibility.

Like the co-operative plan, resources were specifically allocated to support the implementation of the plan, in particular, money for classroom resources and for inservice training for management development and for workshops and courses connected with curriculum priorities. The classteachers' description of the training revealed that it was seen to be important and was very practical and focused on teachers and pupils in the classroom. One teacher, for example, described inservice activities as being 'more highbrow', another said that 'the INSET linked with curriculum priorities was superb'.

When asked about any difficulties in implementing the present plan, the headteachers were very self-critical and focused on ways in which they could improve the process. For example, the headteacher of School H said difficulties had arisen because 'too many targets had been taken on and fewer were needed'. The solution to overcoming these difficulties was 'to communicate, talk, involve everyone in what's going on, become more efficient, release teachers, use advisory support and expert outsiders'. The classteachers from this school talked about difficulties in finding 'time to work with others' and 'to go on courses'. They too had positive, practical ideas about how to resolve these difficulties, such as 'to discuss individual needs with the headteacher'. They had creative solutions for enabling teacher release, such as the better use of supply cover.

Answers about monitoring and evaluating the effectiveness of the plan revealed a similar sense of confidence and control over the process. All were agreed that the plan would be monitored and all the classteachers appeared to be very involved. Their answers portrayed a definite sense of responsibility. A typical answer from one teacher about how the implementation of the plan would be monitored was 'headteacher and deputy headteacher overview, personal diary, personal responsibility, individual teacher review, INSET and curriculum co-ordinator review and staff review meetings'. Both headteachers emphasised the specific monitoring of samples of pupils' work. They also both talked about discussion with governors.

When it came to gathering evidence to evaluate the outcome of the plan, it was noticeable that quantitative and qualitative evidence in three main areas were described by both schools, namely, whole-school policies, teachers' work and pupils' output. What was particularly evident was the strong emphasis on evidence related to teachers and pupils in the classroom. For example, headteachers talked about 'reading records, records of achievement, teachers' plans, test results and samples of pupils' work'. Teachers from both schools talked about 'joint planning, classroom observation, pupils' work and records of achievement including samples and portfolios of pupils' work'. The focus on pupils by all respondents was a marked characteristic of the corporate plan. It was also interesting that headteachers and classteachers said they would seek the views of others as a source of evidence, for example, governors, parents and visitors. Like the co-operative plan, the corporate plan was also seen as multipurpose in nature but, with this plan, the focus on improving the quality of teaching and learning was particularly noticeable.

When asked about sustaining changes beyond the present plan, the classteachers gave confident, practical solutions indicating that they saw development planning as a continuous process. The headteacher relatively new to planning provided an equally confident answer. The headteacher of School I expressed uncertainty and stressed the importance of staff motivation, involvement and reflection on the process if present changes were to be sustained.

Commentary on all four types of plans   Five key issues emerged from this analysis of the use of the planning process in relation to each type of plan. These concerned the nature of the leadership and management of both the process itself and the implementation of the plan; the integrated nature of the process; the extent to which the plan was monitored and evaluated; the focus of the process; and its purpose.

The contrast across the four types of plans in respect of leadership and management was considerable. It ranged from the rhetorical plan, which totally lacked leadership and management, to the corporate plan, which was characterised by a high degree of shared leadership by the headteacher and senior staff and shared management of the process itself, as well as the implementation of the plan, by all the teaching staff and others. For the singular plan, leadership and management were vested almost entirely in the headteacher. For the co-operative plan, strong leadership was provided by the headteacher but the management of the process was shared by some staff, most of whom were members of the senior management team, although there was a willingness on behalf of other teachers to be involved and to co-operate. As leadership and management became more widely shared, answers appeared to indicate a growing sense of confidence and control over the process.

The varying degree to which different aspects of the management of the school were incorporated into the plan and interrelated with the implementation of priorities for development was a noticeable feature. Unlike the rhetorical and the singular plans, both the co-operative and corporate plans were supported by financial resources and linked with a staff development programme; teachers' own learning was seen to be important.

When it came to specific aspects of the planning process, the most noticeable weakness was in relation to monitoring and evaluating the plan. It was the corporate plan which demonstrated the most comprehensive range of monitoring and evaluation strategies, with the answers from the classteachers indicating a considerable sense of personal responsibility for the implementation of the plan. A limited approach to monitoring and evaluation characterised both the rhetorical and singular plans, whereas in the case of the co-operative plan, demonstrable steps were being taken, particularly by the headteacher and senior management team, to improve monitoring procedures and to evaluate a range of outcomes.

It was the range of outcomes that revealed the focus and purpose of the plans which, in turn, revealed major differences between the types of plans. The rhetorical plan lacked both focus and a sense of purpose. The focus of the singular plan was improved efficiency. It was seen as a means of enabling the headteacher to have greater control over the management of the school. The focus of the co-operative plan was an improvement in both efficiency and effectiveness. Particular attention was paid to school-wide improvements and the professional development of teachers. Like the co-operative plan, the corporate plan was also multipurpose in nature and it too focused on both school-wide and teacher development. However, there was an added dimension to the focus. This was a distinct emphasis on bringing about improvements in pupils' learning. This focus, along with the quality of leadership and management of the plan and the process, could well have accounted for the high level of teacher ownership and shared responsibility for the plan.

It was noticeable that those involved in the co-operative and corporate types of plans were self-critical and were using the process to overcome difficulties and bring about improvements. Our final analysis of the data, therefore, concentrates on the impact of the plan and the planning process to assess the lessons learned and the extent to which the improvements sought had been achieved.

The outcome of our analysis of the impact of school development planning across the typology

The impact of SDPs was examined from a range of perspectives. Significant changes in the way plans were now formulated and implemented as a result of past experience of the planning process were looked at closely, as was the personal impact of these experiences. Answers concerned with the outcomes of the plan were scrutinised in terms of the impact priorities for development had on school-wide management and other organisational arrangements; professional relationships; professional development; classroom practice; and pupils' learning. The analysis revealed significant differences in the quality and nature of the impact of SDPs across the typology.

The rhetorical plan: School A

There was very little agreement about any significant changes that had taken place in planning procedures. The main lesson learned by the headteacher was the need to achieve staff involvement and ownership. This need for ownership was echoed by the classteachers, as was the need for leadership. As one teacher put it, 'morale is low, we have been stumbling along and operating as individuals'. The headteacher was dissatisfied with the outcome of the plan. When the classteachers were asked about the impact of the present plan, it was said to have had no positive impact at the level of the whole school or in classrooms, for either teachers or pupils. One teacher said 'the plan didn't happen, I didn't know where I was and this led to stress'. The other complained that 'I had no praise, I didn't know if I was doing the right thing'. The negative impact as a result of the way the plan had been poorly led and managed was evident.

The singular plan: School B

The classteachers could not agree about the impact the development plan had on present planning procedures despite the fact that the headteacher said that there was now more staff and governor involvement. For the headteacher, past experience of planning had had a positive impact on the efficient management of the school. The need to 'prioritise, give things a timescale, identify roles and responsibilities and draw up an action plan' were emphasised. For the classteachers, 'having a plan at all and being part of it' and 'the production of policy documents and new organisational arrangements' were seen as noticeable benefits. Beyond that, the classteachers were unable to identify any impact that the present plan had had on them as teachers and on the pupils in the classroom.

This type of plan had a limited impact. It increased the efficiency of the school but appeared to have had no effect on classroom practice.

The co-operative plan: Schools C to G

There was general agreement among the headteachers and classteachers that past experience of development planning had had a significant impact on the way plans were now formulated and implemented, although there were some disagreements and differences when it came to specific details. The headteachers talked about increased consultation and involvement of teachers, more delegation, clearer roles and responsibilities and targets. Particular mention was made of the introduction of more structured inservice training. They were aware of the need to monitor the process and they described improvements which had been made in relation to evaluation procedures. All the headteachers said that the audience for the plan had widened. Reports to governors were now more detailed and parents were now informed about the outcomes. For them personally, all the headteachers with previous experience of development planning said they had learned that the process was more complex than originally anticipated and now appreciated that planning was a continuous process. As two headteachers put it, 'the planning process is cyclical but continuous and not a one-off'. It was noticeable that three headteachers had increased the length of the planning cycle in contrast to the headteachers of the previous two types of plans who had both shortened the cycle. It was also interesting to note that the same two headteachers quoted earlier, both of whom had had more experience of planning than the other three, reported they were aware that what was needed now was to 'spend time in classrooms to observe the actual effect of the plan on the pupils'.

Classteachers identified changes in the management of the process including new approaches to inservice training. It was interesting that both teachers from School D had much to say that was positive about changes in the way the plan was now formulated and implemented under the leadership of the new headteacher. For example, when commenting on any significant changes at the formulation stage, one teacher said 'all staff are now involved, it is more democratic, there is more discussion, there is a new and detailed format with more components, there is a timetable and new staff meetings with agendas'. The other teacher talked about 'setting more specific, manageable and realistic targets and naming names, review by the deputy head and governors and staff review'. Both agreed that to aid implementation there were 'more clearly defined roles and responsibilities, and resources and their effective use were linked in, as were INSET and staff meetings'.

Lessons learned by the classteachers concerned the need to keep the process going by the headteacher and deputy head and the importance of increasing the involvement of all staff. Their views about the drawbacks of planning were realistic and they focused, as described earlier, on insufficient time to implement all the priorities.

Headteachers and classteachers agreed that school development planning had had a positive impact on the school as a whole and in classrooms for both teachers and pupils. For the headteachers there was mixed satisfaction with the outcomes, and their answers reflected the multipurpose nature of the plan and a desire to keep on learning and improving. All the headteachers, with the exception of School D, described the impact of previous plans or, in the case of School G, of the present one. They talked about improvements in whole-school planning; staff attitudes and expectations; classroom management and organisation; teaching content and methods; pupil behaviour; continuity in learning; and access for pupils to new areas of the curriculum. It was established in the previous section that the headteachers tended not to focus on pupils as a source of evidence of improvement and it was interesting that, whilst the classteachers were also able to identify a range of benefits for the school as a whole and for them in the classroom, particularly in relation to their own professional development, there was concern expressed about the actual impact on pupils. One teacher could not identify any such benefits. One did not think the plan had had enough impact on them and one said the pupils had not been affected at all. This type of plan had a positive impact on whole-school management and organisation and on professional relationships. It led to improvements in teachers' work in the classroom. Specific improvements for pupils were not so easily discernible. The teachers' willingness to co-operate and to be involved in the process, and their practical suggestions as to how future plans could be improved, indicated that for the majority of them they had found, as the headteachers had done, that development planning had been a positive learning experience.

The corporate plan: Schools H and I

Those involved in this type of plan all agreed that significant lessons had been learned from past experience of development planning. Both headteachers, when describing changes in the way plans were now formulated, placed emphasis on 'increased whole-school open consultation and the involvement of others'. They described how there was now more delegated decision-making through, for example, the use of working groups. The need to build in regular review and evaluation procedures at this stage was recognised and both headteachers talked about how communication about the plan was now more structured in relation to governors and the LEA. As with the co-operative plan, the headteachers both said the planning cycle was now 'longer and ongoing'.

When it came to significant changes in the way plans were now implemented, again there was noticeable agreement between the headteachers. They stressed that there was now 'a whole-school approach, there were more specific individual responsibilities and job descriptions had changed'. They both referred to the influence of LMS. Like the headteachers concerned with co-operative planning, they stressed improvements in whole-school management and in the approach to inservice training. It was clear that they were now using the development planning process to monitor progress and included more precise success criteria, the involvement of governors and, in their words, 'the use of outside experts'. There was a noticeable increase in the range and use of quantitative and qualitative evidence to evaluate the plan and reference was also made to external moderation. Like the co-operative plan, the audience for the SDP had broadened to include governors and parents.

The classteachers agreed with the headteachers about many of the changes that had occurred. They confirmed that they thought the process was now 'more democratic with shared responsibility' and they described how roles and responsibilities had changed.

The quality and depth of the answers about personal lessons learned by both the headteachers and classteachers were noticeable. The headteacher of School H focused on 'communication about the plan, the use of time, the breadth of the plan and the integration of the curriculum, the use of past experience and the importance of worthwhile staff meetings'. She also said she had learned 'the positive benefits of something imposed originally from outside'. The headteacher of School I talked about 'ownership and the empowerment of all staff; the importance of communication and of the headteacher encouraging but also imposing a bit; the need to share common beliefs and check them regularly; and the importance of structures to cope with new things'. Both headteachers mentioned how they had learned the need to create 'a balance between being positive and critical'. As a result of these lessons, they described how they had increased in efficiency and how staff development had been restructured to 'increase staff skills, use individual strengths and expertise and to improve confidence'.

Although the classteachers' answers were different, they too had all learned positive lessons and were able to identify practical ways, from their perspective, in which the process could be improved further. One teacher from School H talked about the importance of 'the everyday maintenance of the plan, keeping it all going so that a priority is put into practice' and how 'it happens sometimes not how you thought it would'. The other teacher talked about how she was 'much more aware now of what needs to be done and that the process doesn't finish. You can't leave one core curriculum subject just because you now have a different priority, you need to include review meetings in the next plan'. The two teachers from School I stressed the importance of curriculum balance within the plan and talked about decision-making in relation to the identification of priorities and how classteachers, particularly less experienced staff, can have different perspectives from the headteacher and members of the senior management team. As described in the analysis of the content of plans, one teacher referred to a potential conflict of views in respect of next year's priorities for development. Such conflict could well be interpreted as a healthy sign of this teacher's commitment to, and involvement in, the process and that there was a sense of shared leadership. Such an interpretation found support when considering this same teacher's positive answers about the impact past and present experiences of planning had had on her personally. In her response, she talked about 'team planning for topic work; using specialists in school; INSET, working with others and the enthusiasm to try out ideas in the classroom; and leading staff meetings and being able to take on more responsibility. The SDP helps to clarify thoughts and be more organised'. A response to the same question from a teacher in School H also revealed the considerable impact the SDP had had on her. She identified the following: 'It has made me question my role with pupils, I'm now less dictatorial; the importance of whole-staff communication; and time to observe in one another's classrooms which has improved progression and continuity and provided a whole-school perspective.'

The extent of the impact of development planning was a feature of both the headteachers' and classteachers' answers. Both the headteachers said they were only fairly satisfied with the outcome of previous plans and both had a range of ideas about how to sustain changes already achieved including, for example, 'embracing themes across plans to allow you to revisit past developments'. They were able to describe how previous developments had had an impact on the school as a whole, in classrooms and on pupils' learning in particular. One headteacher was now encouraging pupils to look for evidence of improvement themselves. Pupils' increased access to the curriculum and to practical activities, improvements in independence as learners and greater indepth work were described. Similarly, the classteachers talked about benefits for the school as a whole, such as new policy documents; year planning; schemes of work; very good inservice training; and a review of resources. Benefits for them in the classroom concerned an increase in curriculum knowledge, expertise and confidence; changes in teaching methods; and improvements in resources. All four teachers identified benefits for pupils. These included improvements in curriculum provision; better quality learning experiences; greater awareness of work in hand; an increased independence; and more opportunities to work with experts brought in from outside. From the teachers' answers it was easy to trace how professional development opportunities structured at whole-school level had had a direct impact, not just on them but also on the pupils themselves.

This type of plan had had a significant impact on the schools. It appeared to foster a community of learners as exemplified by the ability of both headteachers and classteachers to learn from their positive experiences of planning. As the headteacher of School I said when asked if her understanding of development planning had changed in any way, 'the process is now embedded as part of the culture of the school'.

Commentary on all four types of plans In many respects, the quotations used to illustrate the differential impact of SDPs exemplify some of the key characteristics of each type of plan. Two main issues emerged from the analysis. One concerned the range of the impact of SDPs from a negative one, as a result of the rhetorical type of plan, through to a very significant, positive impact on both the efficiency and effectiveness of the school as found with the corporate plan. The other concerned the extent to which the different types of plans provided professional development opportunities for headteachers and class-teachers. It was only the co-operative and corporate plans which noticeably built professional development into the plan. There was evidence that the corporate plan, in particular, enabled all those involved to learn from experience and to put that learning to positive effect. For this type of plan it was possible to perceive a link among school development, teacher development and pupil development.

CHECKING THE VALIDITY OF THE TYPOLOGY AGAINST OTHER DATA SOURCES

On conclusion of the analysis of the data derived from the semi-structured interviews, further steps were taken to confirm or disconfirm the validity of the typology. To begin with we scrutinised the written plans to see if there was any correlation between the type of plan in use and the written documentation. Then the outcomes of the classroom observations were examined for any evidence of the typology. Similarly, the responses from the governors were analysed along with those from the inspectors and officers in the LEAs of the nine schools. The next four chapters describe what we found.

10

THE WRITTEN PLANS

In this chapter we describe the written plans of each of the nine schools in detail and identify similarities and differences between the documents themselves and the manner in which they appear to have been constructed. We then compare the plans with the typology which emerged in Chapter 9.

Documentation relating SDPs in the academic years 1992/3 and 1993/4 was collected from all nine of our sample schools. Where there was relevant documentation that preceded the academic year 1992/3, this was also collected. In the first instance we examined the 1992/3 documents and created a framework to analyse the plans. The ten questions which formed this framework were as follows:

1. Who wrote the plan?
2. Who is the audience?
3. What is the nature of the document?
4. What is its format? (Length/layout/structure.)
5. What components are included?
6. Are priorities or targets expressed and, if so, at what level?
7. Is there a length of cycle?
8. What is the focus of planning?
9. What are the review arrangements?
10. What are the reporting procedures?

The purpose of these ten questions was to interrogate the documentary evidence relating to the plans themselves and the planning processes which had been used to put the plans together. The questions were devised to provide a simple but cohesive framework to analyse the plans and provide further information on the ownership, involvement, audience, use, format, components, structure and processes that were being employed in the schools. We found that the plans varied enormously, the evidence indicating a wide range of practice taking place in the nine sample schools and differing developments in

150

individual schools over the two academic years. The following sections summarise our analyses of the documents.

THE 1992/3 PLANS

School A

This school did not have the documentation to support the claim of having a written SDP. The documentation that was available suggested that there was an agenda for staff development and that there was some attempt to identify strategies and processes to support this. From this documentation, there was no evidence of the LEA playing a role in influencing any stage of the development plan, the planning processes or playing a role in monitoring the activities of the school.

School B

There was evidence of the involvement of parents and governors in consultations about issues in the plan. However, the reliance on an annual cycle, the clear focus on the primary ownership by the headteacher and the lack of detailed targets and ongoing review procedures were causes for concern.

School C

This was a plan with many strengths. A mission statement had been incorporated into the plan. Discussions with non-teaching staff, parents, governors and pupils, as well as teaching staff, were well documented. There was evidence of regular review, staff with named responsibilities and the LEA format was partially used. There appeared to be an unresolved tension between the formats used by the LEA and the school and further support appeared to be needed in structuring targets and priorities.

School D

This plan was detailed but was lacking in cohesion. Links between past, present and future developments and priorities were difficult to trace. The involvement of teaching staff and other members of the school community was unclear. Although there was evidence of the LEA having a role in some reviewing procedures, these processes were not made explicit. The lack of emphasis on maintaining developments was of concern.

School E

This was the second school, but the first from this particular LEA, to mention the involvement of their local cluster group in the development planning process. This plan was clearly devised by members of staff apart from the headteacher and deputy headteacher and also involved the governors. However, in common with other schools, the structuring of targets and priorities was underdeveloped.

School F

There was a lack of cohesion in the documents which meant that many of the positive initiatives, such as involving parental views, were structurally weak. Since most of the documentation was generated by the headteacher who kept the sole copy, this raised questions about the wider ownership of the plan.

School G

This plan made the school development planning process explicit. It was well structured and easily accessible. Targets were weak due to the subjective manner in which they had been structured, for example, 'Teachers to be happier about . . .'

School H

This plan used an LEA format which was clear and incorporated some school aims. The evidence appeared to be limited in relation to the ongoing nature of the reviews, the involvement of members of the school community and the reporting arrangements. Again targets and priorities, while present in some cases, needed further development.

School I

This was a cohesive, detailed and well-structured working document which explicitly addressed many of the main issues and clearly described a supportive process relating to the school's development, management and aims. There was evidence of a management structure involving many levels within the school.

An overview of the 1992/3 plans

Several clear patterns emerged from this analysis of the documentation of the 1992/3 plans. School A was of particular concern because not only did a formal plan not exist but there also appeared to be very little evidence of LEA involvement. Of the other eight plans the main lead had been taken by the headteacher in five cases. In three schools (two from the same LEA), there was clearer evidence of a wider involvement of teaching staff.

A general area of weakness which applied to most of the plans was the lack of structure in, and the subjectivity of, targets and priorities. The absence of evidence in relation to ongoing reviews and the implicit limited audience of the documents also suggested that the exercise had not been thoroughly thought through.

In three of the eight schools (two from the same LEA) only one set of documents existed. This must have hindered access to, familiarity with and involvement in the plan and its associated planning processes by all members of the school community, but particularly by the teaching staff. The involvement of any pupils in the planning process was only made explicit in one set of plan documents.

THE 1993/4 PLANS

We adopted the same procedures in order to examine the following year's plans.

School A

The lack of documentation that was available for long periods of time was a matter of considerable concern. The lack of continuity in the leadership of the school (three headteachers during the course of the two academic years), the wide-ranging nature of the improvements that were urgently required and the limited role of the LEA in ongoing monitoring of the school were important factors. The plan was detailed but lacked a realistic structure, particularly in terms of timescales, processes such as review and monitoring and the spread of areas to be covered. No other documentation was made available by the headteacher during the course of the academic year 1993/4.

School B

While there was continued evidence of the involvement of parents and governors in sharing information about the SDP, the document primarily remained as a management tool for use by the headteacher. A considerable number of loose-leaf papers and documents were made available to the research team. These included a number of policy documents on, for example, pupils' welfare, English, handwriting, science, art and religious education; inspection reports by the LEA; booklets for parents; and new methods of record-keeping. This was the most extensive list of documents made available by any of the schools in the research project. Some of the documents were poorly presented, however, and it was unclear to us how frequently they were reviewed or updated.

School C

There did appear to be a lack of development in the documentation of the plan in 1993/4. This coincided with the bulk of the time that the headteacher was away on leave. There was, however, a considerable generation of well-produced documents which related to previous priority areas. Copies made available to the research team included the following: multilingual admissions information for parents: *Help Your Child to Spell* and *Help Your Child to Read* booklets; policies for equal opportunities, language and appraisal; and parents' monthly newsletters.

School D

The substantial documentation lacked clarity and specific detail in areas relating to individual responsibility and targets. It also lacked a clear structure. Additional documentation supplied by the school included a school brochure; job descriptions; sex education, behaviour, health and safety and whole-school pay policies; an appraisal statement of practice; and LEA specific review reports.

School E

Although there was clear evidence of a shared approach to the formulation of the documentation, the main cause for concern was the lack of detail relating to 1993/4 and the lack of evidence of any further development in this academic year since the new headteacher took up the post. There was evidence to suggest that the headteacher who left the school at the end of the academic year 1992/3 had tried to leave a detailed summative plan with enough flexibility for continued development by the new headteacher. There was no documentary evidence to indicate that this continued development occurred. The headteacher also supplied a number of additional documents, including an evaluation of inservice experiences; policies on teaching and learning, staff development, finance and resource management, review, monitoring and evaluation, and health and safety; an LEA review; the identification of individual professional development needs; and a draft curriculum booklet for parents.

School F

This plan had a very brief summative format. Whilst this may have been more realistic in terms of its aims and more reasonable in terms of the amount of time needed to produce it, it was, nevertheless, lacking in some detail and was clearly focused primarily for the use of the headteacher. Additional available documentation included a newsletter to parents and the community; various school booklets; a school report form; parent and governor questionnaires; individual management responsibilities; and policies for discipline, display and mathematics. There was evidence of considerable collaboration in this school but many of the documents and the plan continued to be presented poorly.

School G

This was a clearly and simply structured document that worked for the staff and was being widened to include participation from other groups. The main weaknesses were the almost exclusive focus on whole-school priorities and the lack of clarity of the success criteria. This document was, however, the one with the most clearly defined participation of individual members of the teaching staff. Additional documents available to the research team were a parents' questionnaire and a governor *aide-mémoire* about building priorities; policies for behaviour and discipline, home/school relationships, special educational needs and writing; a booklet for parent helpers; and an action plan for assessment. All these documents were produced to a uniformly high standard. The evidence of updating an existing document and signalling this clearly was unique to this school.

School H

There was clear evidence of increased participation by school staff. Several other documents based on priorities were made available. These provided evidence of considerable collaboration and activity and included special needs, language awareness, mathematics and health and safety policies; detailed breakdown relating to the mathematics National Curriculum attainment targets; language and science post-holder job descriptions; and a variety of new school brochures and leaflets.

School I

This was an impressive, detailed document. It provided evidence of a shared approach and detailed, systematic ways of working. Additional documentation provided included a *Music in the Making* document; policy statements for music, art and design, mathematics, handwriting, geography, history and appraisal.

An overview of the 1993/4 plans

The plans and documentation for the academic year 1993/4 showed evidence that in a number of schools headteachers and their staffs were becoming more detailed and structured in the recording of their planning processes and priorities. An example of this was the breaking down of timescales into termly blocks from the annual cycle. There was also some evidence to suggest that the involvement in the planning processes and the plan itself was becoming wider. More references were made to parents and governors and there was some individualisation of roles for teaching staff. Explicit evidence, however, of the detailed involvement of individual members of the school community, particularly classteachers, apart from when they operate as a whole-staff group, was limited; it appeared in the documentation of only four schools. This had clear implications for the impact of planning processes and priorities for classteachers and pupils in individual classrooms.

The documentation for 1992/3 and 1993/4 suggested that schools may need specific support in the setting of targets or priorities in ways that will facilitate achievable and measurable outcomes and in the implementation and review of detailed procedures, including individual and collective responsibility for reviewing, monitoring and evaluating planning processes and priorities. Further areas that appeared to need specific support included ensuring that the audience for the plan is considered and made explicit; incorporating within the development plan classroom and child-focused aims; and stating the explicit components of the plan and its associated processes.

The role of the LEA, beyond supplying the schools with a voluntary framework or set of guidance for development plans and the planning process, appeared to be unclear. The links between supporting and reviewing the school and its plan were only made partially explicit in the documentation of one school.

The participation of members of the school teaching staff was clearer in the plans relating to 1993/4. It was made explicit in the plans of four schools. The lack of clearly defined roles and responsibilities, however, coupled with the main responsibility for the plan and its associated planning processes resting on the headteacher was a matter of concern. Three of the sample schools experienced at least one change of headteacher during the course of the two academic years studied. This appeared to have a detrimental effect on the plan, the planning process and the development of both. There are clear messages here concerning the need to ensure wider involvement and ownership. Many schools produced documents and policies in addition to or as part of their SDP. The efforts that went into these initiatives could be more widely recognised, celebrated and given status. These documents were only sometimes dated and the names of the participants rarely included. This was a missed opportunity to make participation and involvement explicit.

In four of the schools there was only one set of documents. One LEA encouraged schools to publish their plan more widely and the result was a high-quality, organised document from the three sample schools involved. In three of the schools where there was only one set of documents, the quality of presentation and the organisation of the documents themselves were also poor. These factors must play a part in hindering participation and ownership of the plan and the planning processes by anyone apart from the headteacher.

Two of the schools in their 1993/4 plans made parental and governor involvement explicit. Only one school included a direct reference to the involvement of the pupils in decisions relating to priorities in the plan.

In summary, the schools in our project appeared to need further support in developing and using a framework which is sufficiently detailed and structured to enable participation of all members of the school community. Classteachers did not seem to have a clearly defined or individualised role in the majority of cases. Arising from our perusal of the documentation are serious concerns about potential weaknesses in the processes of reviewing, monitoring and communicating to the whole-school audience.

We then compared the written plans with the typology which had emerged. We found that there was a noticeable correlation between the different types of plans and the planning documents produced. The following relationship was found.

The rhetorical plan: School A

There was no written plan; instead the SDP had to be culled from the general report to governors and it was the governors who appeared to be the main audience. The plan, which was more like a curriculum development plan, lacked focus. It was difficult to discern how it was to be managed, given that targets, success criteria and review and evaluation arrangements were not identified explicitly.

The singular plan: School B

The headteacher wrote the plan although there was some reference to consultation with staff and governors. The plan comprised a collection of papers. It was not a working document and it was not written in a form that could be used by staff. The main audience of at least some of the papers appeared to be the governors. The plan lacked a clear management strategy. Targets were general in nature and concerned school-wide issues. No review procedures were built in although arrangements for reporting to governors were evident.

The co-operative plan: Schools C to G

The plans were all said to be written following staff discussion and there was evidence of staff involvement in writing the plan in two of the schools, although the audience was unclear across all five schools. For four out of five of the schools it was a working document. For the fifth school, it took the form of a published report. Management of the process was in evidence but, with the exception of one school, there was a noticeable lack of success criteria, and the targets for improvement were rather general. Review procedures were incorporated into all the plans but in some cases these were limited in nature. In four plans, reporting arrangements were difficult to assess and governors were not mentioned. In the fifth plan there was evidence that the SDP was reported to the LEA.

The corporate plan: Schools H and I

There was considerable similarity between the two school plans. There was clear evidence that the plans had been written as a result of staff discussion and agreement. They had been written for a wide audience including teaching and support staff, governors and LEA inspectors and advisory teachers. They were both open, working documents and it was significant that both schools had a clear policy statement about the aims and purposes of the development plan and that these guided the format and content of the plans. The management of the process was clearly identified and included targets, success criteria and regular review and evaluation procedures. For both plans, reporting arrangements involved staff, governors and the LEA. In one school, parents were also included.

Commentary on the relationship between the written plans and the typology

This analysis provided further confirmatory evidence about the typology. Weaknesses in the management of the rhetorical and singular plans were self-evident and some aspects of the management of the co-operative plans were limited, especially the review and evaluation procedures. What was particularly noticeable was the distinct similarity between the two schools engaged in corporate planning, yet these schools were in different LEAs and were of a contrasting size and type. The sense of involvement of staff and others was noticeable, as was the fact that both schools had a written policy statement on the aims and purposes of development planning.

11

THE CLASSROOM STORY

This chapter describes the findings of the classroom observation schedules used in the project. It begins with an overview of the use of the SCOTS schedule followed by an analysis of the data it gathered. The relationship between the data and the typology is subsequently explored. The findings of the second classroom instrument are then described together with an analysis of those main issues which emerged in relation to the typology.

Two instruments were used to gather evidence about the impact of planning in classrooms on both teachers and pupils: the SCOTS schedule, and our specially prepared observation instrument. The development and content of these two schedules were described in Chapter 5. Four observations took place in the academic year 1992/3 and a further two observations were completed during 1993/4. As explained in Chapter 5, because one of the main intentions of the research project was to track the impact of the SDP and its planning processes on the teaching and learning experiences of the pupils, it was decided to follow the pupils through into the second academic year of the study. On the whole, class groups remained the same and, where there was some remixing of class groups, the class with the majority of the 1992/3 pupils in 1993/4 was studied.

The research project's aim of observing pupils from the nursery to year six was achieved. For example, in 1993/4 observations took place in the following types of classes:

1. One reception class of pupils in a primary school.
2. One combined reception and year-one class in an infant school.
3. One combined class of reception, year-one and year-two pupils in a primary school.
4. One combined class of year-one and year-two pupils in a primary school.
5. One year-one class in an infant school.
6. Three year-two classes in two infant schools and a primary school.
7. One year-three class in a primary school.
8. One combined class of year-three, four, five and six pupils in a primary school.

9. Three year-four classes of pupils in two primary and one junior school.
10. One year-six class of pupils in a junior school.

Class sizes over the course of the research project ranged from 9 to 32 pupils and the ethnic composition of the classes and the schools was very mixed. Care was taken to select classteachers with both wide-ranging and differing experiences and to work with pupils from the full primary-age phase. What became clear was that other than the predominantly female nature of the adults working with the pupils, other factors such as class size, ethnic mix and the different numbers of adults working in the classroom varied considerably. There did not appear to be any patterns which related these factors to particular forms of classroom planning practice.

THE SCOTS DATA ANALYSIS

Before describing the data which we collected using this instrument it is useful to consider some of the main similarities and differences in the way it was used between this research project and the projects conducted by Powell (1985) and Mortimore *et al.* (1988).

Similarities

1. The same 15 categories (listed on p. 54) were used as in the Junior School Project (Mortimore *et al.*, 1988).
2. Observations using the other classroom instrument, for example, counting the number of adults and pupils in the classroom and drawing a plan of the classroom, were carried out before the modified SCOTS schedule was used. This was to enable the research officer to collect less subjective data first and to give all participants time to settle and relax, and thus act normally. This was a similar methodology to that which had been previously used in the Mortimore *et al.* (1988) and Powell (1985) projects.
3. The research officer was a non-participant observer wherever this was possible. Like the observers in the 1985 (Powell) study, she attempted to be quiet and unobtrusive and to move as little as possible. In common with observers in the two previous projects every effort was made to find an optimum position from which to observe as much of the classroom as possible. Sitting at the edge of the classroom, by a table or desk which was isolated or was not being used and attempting to sit out of, or on the periphery of, the classteacher's range of vision all appeared to be successful strategies to employ. Whilst being pleasant to the pupils, further approaches, particularly concerning help with work in progress, were not encouraged. (It was a source of some surprise to us that classteachers were not more interested in exactly what it was the research officer was doing.)

Despite the fact that the research officer was never formally introduced to some of the classes, with the exception of the very youngest involved in the project, pupils were not very curious either.

Differences

1. The instrument was only used once during the course of each visit to the sample school classrooms. The Powell (1985) and Mortimore *et al.* (1988) studies used the SCOTS schedule on five occasions during each visit.
2. Observer fatigue was reported after three observations a day in the 1985 Powell study. In this research project there were only ever two classrooms observed on the same day.
3. All observations were carried out by one observer. There was no use of paired or shared observers and observations.
4. No additional observer's notes were made although additional notes were added to the instrument. There was therefore no measure of observer reliability.
5. There was no attempt to cluster teacher behaviour and no enquiries were addressed to the classteacher to confirm or rectify the observations.

As a team we were conscious of the limitations of an instrument such as the modified SCOTS and we attempted to minimise some of its risks. We focused on the collection of 'hard' evidence. The research officer made every effort to visit the schools on different days of the week and during different weeks in each half-term in order to minimise timetabling similarities. It was also decided that where possible the research officer would be present from the very outset of the period of teaching in order to observe how activities were introduced and organised.

Each of the 15 categories was coded along a 1–5 scale. As noted in Chapter 5, these numbers matched detailed statements which provided the 'best match' to the specific category being observed. Most of the statements which corresponded to 1 were negative or would not be considered to be 'good practice' but this was not always the case. Many were also context specific, for example category 8 'pupil talk' had the following statements:

1. Class works silently except for communication with teacher.
2. Class works silently though some talking may develop towards the end of an assignment or a period of work.
3. Talking occurs though not when teacher is addressing class or when it is necessary for pupils to work alone (e.g. during test).
4. Talking occurs almost all the time though not necessarily at unrestricted volume. Occasionally, however, there may be complete silence for a special purpose.
5. Talking occurs almost always although not necessarily at unrestricted volume.

Although these statements are detailed, many codings could be affected by the age of the pupils concerned, and there could be variation according to the particular tasks or activities being undertaken and the general atmosphere in the class. In cases such as these, cross-referencing with other categories was necessary in order to obtain a clearer picture of teacher behaviour and teacher/pupil interaction.

Other categories where the scoring was particularly context – and task – dependent were

1. control of pupil learning activities;
2. pupil responsibility for managing own work;
3. Pupil choice of work activities; and
9. pupil movement.

The following lists give a more detailed breakdown of specific categories which could be expected to have high or mixed scores.

Categories where high scores would be desirable were as follows:

4. Teaching situation:

    1 = teaching/teaching situation dull and unstimulating
    5 = teaching/teaching situation is outstandingly bright, interesting and challenging.

5. Organisation of work:

    1 = much pupil time is wasted
    5 = pupils always have plenty to do.

6. Industry:

    1 = lack of application to work
    5 = general air of industry.

7. Interpupil co-operation:

    1 = teacher seeks to prevent co-operation among pupils
    5 = teacher encourages implicitly and/or explicitly.

10. Pupil motivation:

    1 = incentives to work provided by the teacher are all extrinsic
    5 = extrinsic incentives are not more than a formality.

11. Reinforcement:

    1 = teacher emphasises error and wrongdoing
    5 = teacher seeks opportunities to praise good or improved work/conduct.

13. Pupil self-discipline:

    1 = teacher coerces pupils; control is almost entirely by deterrence
    5 = teacher encourages self-control by pupils.

15. Apparent teacher attitude to class:

   1 = teacher usually shows a strong dislike for class
   5 = teacher usually shows an ebullient enthusiasm for teaching class.

Categories where a range of scores, depending on the classroom context, would be desirable are as follows:

1. Control of pupils' learning activities:

   1 = control of pupils by teacher entirely direct
   5 = few signs of direct teacher control of pupils' work.

2. Pupil responsibility for managing own work:

   1 = pupil has no control of own work
   5 = teacher intervention infrequent and different in type.

3. Pupil choice of work activities:

   1 = teacher totally authoritarian
   5 = pupils make suggestions that are taken up by the teacher.

8. Pupil talk:

   1 = class works silently
   5 = talking occurs almost always.

9. Pupil movement:

   1 = pupils not allowed to leave seats
   5 = most pupils free to visit areas out of classroom.

12. Teacher audibility:

   1 = teacher's voice heard loudly in all parts of the room
   5 = all speech to class at extremely low level.

14. Pupil/teacher social relationship:

   1 = teacher is reserved
   5 = teacher very friendly with pupils.

For the purposes of this book, the data are used to provide more detailed background information and to describe individual classes and the similarities between the two classes in each of the sample schools. In all cases there was considerable variation of scores across the six visits when observations were made.

The relationship between the SCOTS data and the typology

A relationship was found between the SCOTS data and the typology. The data revealed a clear link between the schools with corporate and co-operative plans and high scores in categories relating to 5 'organisation of work', 6 'industry' and 7 'interpupil co-operation' and some less conclusive evidence linking schools with these types of plans with high scores in categories 4 'teaching situation', 10 'pupil motivation', 11 'reinforcement', 13 'pupil self-discipline' and 15 'apparent teacher attitude to class'.

Indeed the analysis of the data appeared to indicate that there were links between schools with corporate and co-operative plans and scores for most of the SCOTS categories, except for category 3 'pupil choice of work activities'. What follows is a description of the classrooms related to the typology.

The rhetorical plan: School A

For the academic year 1992/3, the first class in this school was well organised and structured. This class of year-one pupils was always provided with plenty to do and exercised choice within carefully defined parameters such as choosing additional activities from a limited range when they had finished their main task. This classteacher scored highly in the categories 'organisation of work', 'pupil talk', 'pupil movement', 'intrinsic motivation', 'pupil/teacher social relationship' and 'apparent attitude to class'. The lower scores were for 'pupil responsibility for managing own work' and 'pupil choice of work activities'.

The learning environment was not as well structured for this class in 1993/4. Whilst there were similarly high scores for 'organisation of work', 'pupil talk', 'pupil movement', 'pupil/teacher social relationship' and, on one occasion, 'apparent pupil attitude to class' as well as one high score against 'teacher audibility', 'interpupil co-operation', 'pupil choice of work activities', 'pupil responsibility for managing own work' and 'control of pupils' learning activities', there were also significantly low scores in particular for 'teaching situation' and 'industry'. This classroom did not appear to have a hard working atmosphere. There was much time wasting and 'filler' activity.

For 1992/3 the second class in this school, a year-three class, was not well structured, though it scored highly on the teaching situation, which was interesting, and the teacher was enthusiastic. There was much talking and pupil movement, good use of praise and teacher encouragement of self-control by pupils, good pupil/teacher social relationships and the teacher did appear to enjoy working with the class.

In the second year of the study the class concerned had many low scores. These were particularly in the areas of 'control of pupils' learning activities' 'pupil responsibility for managing own work' 'organisation' and 'pupil movement'. There were some high scores for 'teaching situation', 'pupil talk', 'pupil movement', 'teacher audibility', 'pupil/teacher social relationship' and 'apparent teacher attitude to class'. This classroom appeared to lack a consistent approach to learning.

For this school the data revealed that only one classteacher was offering a learning environment which was consistent, well structured and organised and appeared to stretch the pupils.

The singular plan: School B

The two classes had a similar spread of scores across the two academic years. In 1992/3 for the first class of junior-aged pupils low scores against 'control of pupils' learning activities', 'pupil responsibility for managing own work' and 'pupil choice of work activities' were recorded. There was a spread of scores against 'pupil movement', 'pupil motivation' and 'teacher audibility' and high scores for 'pupil talk'. Other scores were mostly in the middle range.

In the second year of the study, when the same classteacher was working with the same pupils there was a similar wide range of scores allocated to priorities. Higher scores were allocated for 'pupil choice of work activities', 'organisation of work', 'interpupil co-operation,' 'pupil talk', 'pupil movement', 'pupil/teacher social relationship' and 'apparent teacher attitude to class'. Whilst this was one of the smallest classes observed, there were still pupils who appeared to waste considerable amounts of time. There was no sense that the pupils were being stretched. The atmosphere was pleasant and relaxed.

The second class to be observed in 1992/3 was a class of younger pupils. Low scores were noted for the same three categories as in the previous class. There was also a spread of scores against the category 'teacher audibility'. There were high scores for 'organisation of work', 'industry' and 'pupil talk'. Other scores were mainly in the middle range.

In the second year of the research project, this class was again working with the same classteacher as in 1992/3. Scores continued to vary with higher scores against categories concerned with 'organisation of work', 'pupil talk', 'pupil movement,' 'pupil/teacher social relationship' and 'apparent teacher attitude to class'. The learning environment was pleasant but teacher dominated and there was a lack of individualisation in the tasks set.

Across the two years the experiences open to the pupils observed in this school appeared to be rather limited. Whilst the classroom environments were ordered, there was a great deal of similarity in terms of the tasks being undertaken. The pupils did not appear to be intrinsically interested in their work but were adept at the traditional conventions of school behaviour.

The co-operative plan: Schools C to G

School C   In 1992/3, the first class in this school, which was a nursery class, scored highly with great consistency in all categories. The pupils were allowed a great deal of freedom and interventions by the classteacher or the nursery nurse were low. The pupils' interests were pursued and the learning situation was busy and interesting. There was always plenty of work to do and the pupils were enthusiastic and engaged. Pupil co-operation and pupil self-discipline were frequently encouraged and there was much talk and pupil movement. Intrinsic motivation was encouraged and there was a generally supportive atmosphere. The classteacher spoke quietly to the pupils and was very warm and friendly with them. She appeared to enjoy working with the class.

During the second year of the research project, the class continued to have a well-structured, organised, stimulating and interesting classroom experience. The only low scores were in the particularly context-specific areas of 'control of pupils' learning activities', 'pupil responsibility for managing own work', 'pupil choice of work activities' and 'pupil movement'.

In 1992/3, the second class in this school was taught by a less experienced classteacher whose scores using the SCOTS instrument were lower and somewhat more mixed. There was a spread of values allocated to the categories concerning 'control of pupils' learning activities', 'teaching situation', 'organisation of work', 'industry' and 'reinforcement'.

During the second academic year of the research project the pupils had a more experienced classteacher. There were high scores for 'pupil choice of work activities', 'organisation of work', 'industry', 'pupil motivation', 'reinforcement', 'teacher audibility', 'pupil/teacher social relationship' and 'apparent teacher attitude to class'. Low scores were particularly focused on those which were more context specific.

Three out of the four classroom environments which were observed in this school were pleasant, well structured and learning focused. The classteacher where the practice was less consistent was relatively inexperienced which could well have been the reason for some of the perceived difficulties observed. All classteachers appeared to enjoy working in the school.

School D　The first class to be observed in 1992/3 was a class of year-three pupils. The SCOTS data exhibited a number of differing scores but was characterised by a prevalence of low scores. Particularly low scores were recorded for 'pupil responsibility', 'control', 'pupil choice' and 'pupil motivation'.

The pupils' experiences in the second year of the research project were also disappointing. There were many low scores and although 'pupil/teacher social relationships', 'apparent teacher attitude to class', 'reinforcement', 'pupil talk', 'industry' and 'organisation of work' did have some high scores, there was still much low-level, undemanding work being conducted in a dull and unchallenging environment.

The second class to be observed in 1992/3, a year-four class, was again characterised by a wide spread of scores, but in comparison with the previous class the scores were higher with 3 being the average score. The lowest scores concerned 'control of the pupils' learning activities', 'pupil responsibility for managing own work' and 'pupil choice of work activities'. There was a happier working atmosphere in this classroom although sessions appeared to lack careful preparation.

In 1993/4, the pupils' classroom continued to be dominated by a mixture of low but a few higher scores. The atmosphere was pleasant and the classteacher made great efforts to provide the pupils with a well-ordered, structured, caring learning environment in which difficulties were openly discussed. There were high scores for 'organisation of work' and, on one occasion, for 'industry', 'pupil talk', 'pupil movement' and 'reinforcement'. All other scores were lower.

The classroom experiences of the pupils observed during the course of the two academic years were generally unsatisfactory. There appeared to be a lack of resources and display in the classroom was limited. Low expectations of the pupils' capabilities were apparent.

School E   The first class to be observed in 1992/3 was a reception class that was characterised by many different activities being undertaken simultaneously. There were some mixed responses but scores of 3 and 4 predominated. 'Pupil talk' scored highly (5) and in the case of 'organisation of work', although this category had a mixed score, it did contain two very low scores. Much pupil time was wasted through systems of working that either left pupils with nothing to do or compelled them to waste time by, for example, queuing for a long time for the teacher's attention. Time wasting was a major feature of the activity in this class.

In the second year of the research project, whilst there was still a complex organisation system in place, it did appear to be more ordered and more focused. There was more of an emphasis on working and less time wasting. The classroom layout and display were interesting and varied. High scores were allocated against categories concerned with the 'teaching situation' and 'organisation of work', 'industry', 'interpupil co-operation', 'pupil talk', 'pupil movement', 'reinforcement', 'pupil self-discipline', 'pupil/teacher social relationship' and 'apparent teacher attitude to class'.

The second class to be observed in 1992/3 was a year-one class. Again, this class received mixed scores both within and across categories. There was most variability in the categories concerned with 'pupil responsibility for managing own work' and 'organisation of work'. The category concerned with 'interpupil self-discipline' scored highly.

The two observations which took place in 1993/4 were of two different classteachers. The first observation was with the original 1992/3 classteacher. She then left the school and the second observation was of the replacement classteacher who had previously worked in the school. Despite this change, scores across the two observations were almost identical indicating considerable continuity over the changeover period. High scores were allocated for the same categories as observed during 1993/4 and there were two additional high scores for 'pupil choice of work activities' and 'teacher audibility'. This continued to be a well-ordered, pleasant classroom where the pupils were engaged in their work.

The observations in three of the four classrooms in this school scored consistently highly, whilst the fourth, though not as work focused also had much to recommend it. There was evidence of a focus on pupil-centred learning and all classrooms were well resourced, displays attractive and staff and pupils appeared to enjoy working in the school.

School F   The first class observed in 1992/3 was a class of year-five pupils and was taught by a relatively inexperienced classteacher. There were a number of categories where there was a spread of scores, most notably 'pupil self-discipline', 'organisation of work' and 'pupil movement'. This classroom was clearly structured and the pupils were engaged in their work. The classroom was filled with interesting displays of the pupils' work but was also rather untidy.

In the second year of the research project this class was taught by a more experienced classteacher who was very well organised and rigorous in her approach to teaching. The classroom display was exceptional. High scores were allocated against the majority of categories. The exceptions where lower scores were allocated were 'pupil motivation', 'teacher audibility' and 'pupil self-discipline'. Both the classteacher and the pupils were very focused on learning and on producing and engaging in high-quality work.

The second class to be observed in 1992/3, a year-four class, was also very well organised. Again, scores showed variation both within and across categories. Mixed scores were against categories concerned with 'control of pupils' learning activities' and 'interpupil co-operation'. 'Pupil choice of work activities' scored low as did 'pupil responsibility for managing own work' and 'pupil/teacher social relationship'. 'Organisation of work' scored highly. The classroom was very well organised, neat and tidy and displays of work were of a high quality. There was a very pleasant, caring, working atmosphere.

During the second year of observations with this class, the classroom environment and the work produced and on display were not of as high a standard. There were more lower scores. Those categories which did score highly were 'teaching situation' (on one occasion), 'pupil talk', 'pupil movement', 'reinforcement' (on one occasion), 'teacher audibility' and 'pupil self-discipline'. The classroom environment was pleasant but lacked in rigour and there was an emphasis on the same task for pupils of all abilities.

Three classes in this school scored highly and overall the practice appeared to be very sound and learning focused. The fourth class compared unfavourably with the other three. This was another school where the staff and pupils appeared to enjoy being and working together.

School G   The two classes, observed in this school in 1992/3, a year-four and five class and a reception and year-one class, were taught by newly qualified or inexperienced young classteachers. Whilst for both classes the scores were variable within and between categories, standards in both classes were high.

Mixed scores for the first class of older pupils were for 'control of pupils' learning activities', 'pupil choice of work activities', 'interpupil co-operation' and 'pupil self-discipline'. High scores were for categories concerned with 'organisation of work' and 'industry'.

During the second year of the research project this class was taught by a more experienced classteacher. The classroom had exceptionally good and interesting displays of work and the classteacher was very well organised. The pupils were able to pursue a rich, varied and rigorous programme of work. The categories allocated high scores were 'pupil responsibility for managing own work', 'teaching situation', 'organisation of work', 'industry', 'interpupil co-operation', 'pupil talk', 'pupil movement', 'teacher audibility' and 'pupil/teacher social relationship'.

The second class of younger pupils which was observed in 1992/3 scored highly against 'industry' and 'pupil talk' with mixed scores against 'control of pupil learning activities', 'pupil movement' and 'teacher audibility'. The 'pupil choice of work activities' had the lowest range of scores. This was another class where the resources and display of work were of an exceptionally high standard.

In the second year of observation, this class was taught by a very experienced classteacher. The class, in this year, did not score as highly as the other three classes in the same school. There were, however, some high scores against the categories of 'pupil talk', 'pupil movement', 'teacher audibility', 'pupil/teacher social relationship' and 'apparent teacher attitude to class'.

The classes in this school were providing the pupils with a high-quality learning atmosphere with the exception of the classteacher of the younger pupils in 1993/4, although there were some positive features. The staff appeared to be very hardworking and committed.

The corporate plan: Schools H and I

School H   The first class which was studied in this school in 1992/3, another nursery class, scored consistently very high scores. This was a very well-structured, planned and organised classroom which managed to be both lively and interesting and calm and caring. The classteacher and nursery nurse clearly worked as a team.

The pupils in 1993/4 also had a classteacher who scored highly against the majority of categories. The only lower scores were for the 'control of pupils' learning outcomes', 'pupil responsibility for managing own work' and, on one occasion, for 'pupil choice of work activities' and 'teacher audibility'. This was an interesting, stimulating and well-structured classroom run by a classteacher with considerable teaching experience.

The second class which was studied in the first academic year was a class of reception and year-one pupils. There was a wider spread of scores than in the previous class and the average score was a 4. Performance in this classroom did not always appear to be matched to the abilities of the pupils although there was much well-structured, high-quality work in evidence.

During the second year of the research project, the classroom atmosphere was again well structured and the pupils were engaged in challenging, interesting and high-quality work. The classteacher concerned was in her first year of teaching and her scores were consistently high except for the categories mentioned for the second year of the other class in this school.

All four classes observed in this school were high scoring. There was evidence of a high-quality learning environment and consistency and continuity between classes and from one year to the next.

School I The first class in this school which was observed in 1992/3 was a class of year-four pupils and revealed scores which varied across the four observation sessions and across the 15 categories measured, although 2 and 3 scores predominated. This classteacher was able to vary her teaching strategies and practice as the class settled down together. The classroom environment was stimulating and the atmosphere purposeful, orderly and focused on learning and high expectations.

During the second academic year, the scores were again varied and the learning environment was similarly pleasant and challenging. High scores were assigned against 'teaching situation', 'organisation of work', 'industry', 'inter-pupil co-operation', 'pupil talk', 'pupil movement', 'reinforcement', 'teacher audibility', 'pupil/teacher social relationship' and 'apparent teacher attitude to class'.

The second class to be observed in 1992/3 was a year-two class where again the practice attracted a wide variety of scores across the 15 categories measured. This classteacher was very well organised and activities were clearly structured. When it came to examining evidence relating to planning, practice and priorities, this was to be found in the pupils' books rather than display in the classroom. It was very noticeable that when a primary PGCE student had been on teaching practice in the school the quality and range of display in the classroom increased markedly.

During the second year of observations, the scores almost mirrored those of the other class in the school. There was a very similar pattern of both high and low scores. The only exception was a low score for 'teacher audibility'. The class continued to be lively, hardworking, interesting and well structured and organised.

All four classes studied in this school scored well. There was evidence of consistently high standards between classes and over time. Expectations for teachers and pupils were high. The pupils and classteachers concerned appeared to enjoy working hard within a pleasant learning atmosphere.

Conclusion

The SCOTS schedule provided useful data about the experiences of the pupils. There was considerable variation of practice within and between schools. It could be argued that this is a partial reflection of the autonomous nature of primary-school teaching. A relationship was found between the classroom experiences of the pupils and the typology. The two schools with a rhetorical and a singular plan respectively had a number of classes which appeared to be offering a learning environment which was – on a number of grounds – unsatisfactory. In addition, the classrooms in School D, where there was a co-operative plan in evidence, were also a cause for concern. This was the school which had experienced six years of rhetorical planning prior to the appointment of a new head-teacher who was now beginning to put in place a development plan which had the characteristics of a co-operative plan. There were six schools, but in particular schools H and I, where the experiences of the pupils appeared to be more positive and to be more consistent both between the same classes in the school and over time. It was these two schools that had a corporate type of plan.

THE OBSERVATION SCHEDULE DATA ANALYSIS

The section in Chapter 5 which describes the development of this instrument (see p. 52) provided details about its structure and content including the seven categories of evidence to be collected along with general information about the layout of the classroom and the composition of the pupils and adults working in it. This general information was completed first. This enabled the research officer to obtain a detailed impression of the classroom, allowed the classteacher, pupils and the research officer to adjust to the observation session and meant that the research officer could more easily identify evidence – or the lack of it – for priorities named in each school's plan for development. The first four pages of the instrument were designed to seek classroom evidence related to previous, ongoing, new and future SDP priorities which were identified in the written plan or its associated documentation, or through the semi-structured interviews with the headteacher and the two classteachers concerned. The lack of agreement in the priorities which were identified from these sources has already been commented upon. For the purposes of classroom observation, however, if a priority was mentioned either in the documentation or by the headteacher or any classteacher it was included as a focus for the collection of observational data.

The priorities which had been noted were categorised in the following way.

Curriculum and subject areas

1. The three core National Curriculum subjects of

   mathematics
   English (which included language, library and reading)
   science.

2. Other National Curriculum subjects

   history
   geography
   music
   art (which included display and aesthetics)
   physical education (PE)
   design and technology
   Religious education (RE).

3. Other subject areas

dance and drama
information technology (IT) and computing
personal, social and health education (PSHE, which included sex education, child protection and AIDS).

Other priority areas

1. Record-keeping and assessment, SATs and Records of Achievement.
2. Special educational needs (which included child abuse).
3. Community (which included preschool liaison, links with nursery, infant, junior and secondary schools, home/school links and liaison, parents, governors, cluster group, pastoral care, home/school reading arrangements, outings and links with educational psychologists).
4. Management (which included meetings, both general and departmental and notices, communication and school booklets, ethos, teams and staff policy, staffing and roles, induction, health and safety and first aid).
5. Professional development and inservice training (which included responsibilities and job descriptions, shadowing and curriculum leadership, staff development and training).
6. Appraisal.
7. Teaching and learning (which included policy documents and schemes of work, topic work, collaborative planning and observation, partnership teaching, audit of quality of work, continuity and progression, evaluation meetings, co-operative and collaborative learning, classroom management, curriculum planning, standards, expectations and attitudes, homework and assemblies).
8. Resources (which included stock).
9. Budget and LMS.
10. Equal opportunities (which included anti-racist and multicultural education, gender, individual needs and able pupils).
11. The use of Section 11 funding.
12. Building and premises (which includes maintenance, school environment, image and decoration).

An analysis of National Curriculum and other subject area priorities identified by the schools in 1992/3

Seven out of nine schools identified the three National Curriculum core subjects in some form in their plans either as a previous, ongoing, new or future priority, or as an area to be reviewed or as an area where there was activity concerning a policy. All schools referred to history, geography, music, art and

PE in their plans. Seven out of the nine schools noted design and technology. IT and computing were chosen by six schools. Four schools stipulated RE and dance and drama were identified by three schools. In addition seven schools included PHSE as a priority.

An analysis of National Curriculum and other subject area priorities identified by the schools in 1993/4

The pattern in relation to the prioritisation of core subjects was more varied in the plans for 1993/4. Only one school explicitly mentioned all three subjects. There was also more variation in priorities in relation to other subject areas, with just one school noting history, geography, music, art and PE. Attention to these subjects had noticeably declined as had a focus on priorities concerned with design and technology, IT and computing, RE, dance and drama and PSHE. The decline in coverage of subjects, particularly those included in the National Curriculum, was perhaps a reflection of the staged introduction of the National Curriculum and a reduction in the role of LEAs in establishing priorities for schools at a local level. This has implications for the number and type of changes and priorities that might be part of any school's development plan. Main priorities may only refer to new subjects of the National Curriculum being introduced or revised, reviewed and updated or to nationally directed or motivated priorities, for example, preparation for an Ofsted inspection. We had difficulty ascertaining from the plans how new developments were to be maintained after the initiation stage. The balance between review and development was also unclear. The balance and links between new priority developments and their subsequent maintenance and review seemed to be an important issue.

Other priority areas identified in documentation and by staff in 1992/3

All schools noted record-keeping, assessment and community as a priority. Eight identified teaching and learning, management, appraisal, special educational needs (SEN) and equal opportunities. Six schools mentioned professional development, INSET and resources, five identified building and premises and four mentioned budget or LMS.

Other priority areas identified in documentation and by staff in 1993/4

In common with curriculum subjects there was a decline in the number of other priority areas noted in the documentation and by staff for 1993/4. Record-keeping and assessment were still high priorities and were mentioned by seven of the nine schools as was teaching and learning. In contrast, 'community' was only mentioned by five schools. This was an interesting point because, as has already been established, involvement of members of the school community emerged as one of the characteristics of the most effective development plan. Equal opportunities were identified by six schools but management, building and premises were only in the plans of five schools. Professional development and inservice training were well down in 1993/4, being a focus of attention in only two schools. In contrast, appraisal continued to be a priority for six schools. Resources, budget or issues concerning the delegation of budgets through LMS were only explicitly mentioned in the plans of three schools.

New categories emerged in the documentation or from the interviews during 1993/4. Five schools identified school ethos, image or presentation. Three schools mentioned preparation for an Ofsted inspection. Two schools mentioned an LEA inspection and review procedures. Two schools said that there was to be a review of the aims of the SDP itself.

It should be remembered that our data on responses from headteachers and classteachers were not standardised. Headteachers were not, as classteachers were, explicitly asked what the main priorities in the SDP were. This information from the headteachers' perspective was gathered from their responses to related questions in their semi-structured interviews. The database is therefore partially incomplete although it still provided us with useful information.

How the instrument was used

The observation instrument was used on six separate occasions in all 18 classes. Four observations took place in the academic year 1992/3, two in the academic year 1993/4. This was one of the most detailed instruments used in the research project and it amassed large amounts of data on evidence which could be observed in the classrooms or through the examination of planning and record-keeping documents collected from the classteachers concerned. Each observation was for a complete session in the school day, for example, from the start of the school day until morning playtime, from morning playtime until lunchtime or after lunchtime until afternoon playtime or the end of the day. Each observation session lasted for at least one hour, the average time spent in the classroom being one and a half hours.

The first observation took place in the second half-term of the autumn term 1992, the second and third in the first and second half-terms of the spring term 1993. The fourth observation visit took place in the second half-term of the summer term 1993, the fifth in the second half-term of the autumn term 1993. Eight of the sixth and final observations were made in the first half-term of the spring term 1994. One of these observation visits was delayed by the school and therefore took place in the second half-term of the spring term 1994. Wherever possible visits were timed to avoid the first and last weeks of each half-term as these are often the weeks when pupils are either settling back into the routine of school or finishing off activities, and sometimes they have a different structure and content from the norm which we were more interested in observing.

A coding system was used to complete the observation schedule. To begin with, for the priorities identified, a score was allocated to indicate whether there was high, low or, indeed, no agreement about a particular priority between the documentation and the headteachers' and classteachers' stories. Similarly, high or low scores were allocated in respect of any link between evidence in the classroom concerned with work on display, be it on the walls or in pupils' books, resources available, teachers' record-keeping and assessment and classroom activities and each priority listed. The scores obtained by each teacher were totalled and compared and then these results were compared across the nine schools.

An unanticipated outcome of the use of this instrument was the ease with which it could be used to gather information on all areas of the National Curriculum and other subjects along with general aspects of classroom organisation and management. It proved very useful as a general classroom observation tool facilitating the collection of detailed data whilst still being simple and relatively quick to use. For the purposes of this book, however, only data linked to the priorities for development will be drawn upon.

Links between the classroom observation data and the typology

The first issue which emerged from an analysis of the evidence was confirmation about the lack of agreement about priorities for development which had already emerged as an issue from the headteachers' and classteachers' stories. The second issue to arise was the gap between stated priorities and evidence of their implementation in the classroom. From the scoring system used for the instrument, the overall scores did not always indicate a link with the different types of plans although the majority of schools with co-operative and corporate types of plans scored most highly. A clear pattern did emerge, however, between the typology and schools with high or low scores across subjects and other priority areas. For example, the work observed in the two classrooms of the school with a rhetorical type of plan bore little or no resemblance to priorities in the plan.

The analysis of the classroom data confirmed that, whilst the impact of development planning could be discerned in some classrooms, particularly those with a corporate type of plan, overall the lack of evidence of impact in respect of increased learning opportunities for pupils was a cause for concern. This raised questions about how priorities can be translated into actions which would have an impact on classroom experiences for teachers and pupils. In common with the analysis of the headteachers' and classteachers' stories in Chapters 7 and 8, it would appear that success criteria or performance indicators which focus on measurable outcomes for both teachers and pupils need to be developed.

12

THE GOVERNORS' STORY

This chapter begins with comments on the context of national legislation and the policies of the three LEAs in which the nine schools were located. In 1993 the chair of governors and a parent governor in each of the schools were interviewed about their school's development planning, and their responses are summarised together with an analysis of the relationship between these and the typology.

The powers of the elected members of LEAs in England and Wales have been eroded considerably by the 1988, 1992 and 1993 Education Acts, whilst the responsibilities of governors have been enhanced by the 1986, 1988 and 1992 Acts. If the rationale behind this changing balance is that the governors' role is crucial to the public accountability of schools, then it might be expected that this would be reflected in their involvement in school development planning.

The evidence both from the 1992 national survey of LEAs described in Chapter 6 and from our 1993 case studies of the nine schools indicated, however, that the expectations about the role of governors enshrined in legislation and elsewhere were not yet being achieved throughout the UK. This is supported in an Ofsted (1994, p. 5) publication which reported that governors 'are often unclear about their roles and that this is sometimes associated with a lack of purposeful planning'.

At LEA level, eight of the 118 LEAs in England and Wales indicated in their response to the national survey that they did not include in their policy for school development planning an expectation that governors would necessarily be involved in the planning process. Four of these LEAs were London boroughs, three were metropolitan districts and one was a county, and the political control of their education committees at the time of the survey ranged across the political spectrum.

The indication from the national survey was that the only county LEA in our sample was not typical of county LEAs in its approach to school development planning and governors. The other two LEAs were also unusual for smaller LEAs in significant ways – one had been involved in planning for much longer, and the other for much less time than the great majority of similar LEAs.

Two of our three case-study LEAs in the 1993 sample indicated that governors were not involved in formulating the plan. The LEAs considered that the extent to which governors were involved in monitoring the implementation of the plan varied between schools, and there were few cases where the outcomes or effects were said to have been evaluated.

Two interview schedules were designed by the research team in order to gain information about the governors and to ascertain their views about school development planning. One was for the chair of governors, the other for a parent governor. These two governors from each school were interviewed by an experienced researcher during the spring term 1993.

It appeared that about a third of the governors were not clear about their role in development planning, including three of the 18 that had not undergone training. Another third said they were thoroughly involved and appeared to be performing in the way that was intended under the 1986 and 1988 Acts. The other third seemed to be involved more sporadically, depending on the influence of other factors, such as the degree of satisfaction that they experienced in the role or on personal commitments.

Some of the questions concerned governors' perceptions of the role of the LEA. Three of the chairs of governors were councillors, and two of these were also on education committees. Two of the 18 governors (11 per cent) mentioned that the LEA had been a significant influence on the school. The same proportion considered that inspectors, advisers and officers had played a role in formulating and implementing the plan.

The perceptions that headteachers and governors have of development planning are likely to reflect their understanding of planning processes more than their experience in role. The relationship among the headteacher, the chair of governors and the LEA link person, and their cumulative experience of planning, seemed to us to be likely to affect such perceptions. In the nine project schools, headteachers had been in post for up to six years; the chair of governors up to 11 years; and the LEA link people up to seven years. It could well be that any school experiencing a change in more than one of these roles may tend to need more help from the remaining person. It was noticeable, at the time of our research, that LEAs were reducing their support for individual schools which meant that the relationship between the headteacher and the chair of governors is likely to become increasingly important. For example, where there are disagreements between the governors and the teaching staff about priorities, it is becoming less likely that the headteacher and the chair of governors will be able to seek as much external advice or support from the LEA as was possible in the past.

Governors are expected to know the school well to be able to contribute effectively to planning and other decision-making, and the frequency of their visiting is often used as one indicator of their involvement. We asked the 18 governors from the nine schools how often they had visited the school in the last year. Three-quarters of the visits (320 of 416 or 77 per cent) were carried out by one-third of those interviewed. In contrast, another third had only carried out 23 visits (6 per cent), including one who had not visited at all. Presumptions about the link between the quality of visits before and after training need to be based on detailed evidence about specific contexts and individuals. There is, however, increasing national evidence from governors' associations and from Ofsted (1993) that the way in which an experienced and trained governor can use time productively contrasts starkly with that used by the inexperienced and untrained. Seventy-eight per cent of the governors in our study claimed to have taken part in governor training activities, but these were not necessarily concerned with school development planning.

A SUMMARY OF THE RESPONSES FROM THE GOVERNORS ABOUT SCHOOL DEVELOPMENT PLANNING

We decided to focus on, and to analyse, responses to questions asked of each governor most likely to yield information about:

- the governors' sense of purpose and ownership of the SDP;
- their views about the leadership and management of the plan;
- the extent to which they felt that the SDP had had an impact on the school; and
- the nature of that impact.

Unlike the previous analyses of interview data, it was difficult to discern a definite relationship between the governors' responses and the typology although, for some answers, it was possible to recognise some of the characteristics. It became clear that the governors' story could have formed a study in its own right; more questions than answers were revealed.

As a group, the governors unanimously supported the idea of school development planning. In common with the headteachers and classteachers, SDPs were seen to be multipurpose in nature, although governors were not in agreement with one another about the purposes they served. Half the governors stressed their value as a management tool. They were said to be 'a means of forward planning, a focus for the future, an aid to the management of time'. Half the governors also talked about how SDPs provided a planned approach to improvements in teaching and learning. A third of the governors identified an accountability purpose for SDPs and stressed their usefulness in keeping governors informed about, for example, 'what the school's done and what's left to be done'. Five governors, including both from School G, specifically noted benefits for pupils. The overall impression gained from answers about the purpose of development planning was that SDPs appeared to give governors a sense of confidence that action was being taken, particularly by the headteacher, to improve the school.

Like the headteachers and classteachers, governors were uncertain about whether or not there was a formal, external requirement to have a development plan and, if so, by whom. Seventy-two per cent thought the school was required to have a plan; 39 per cent thought the DFE required a plan; and 61 per cent thought that the LEA did. Only one governor expressed the view that a plan was not required. In seven schools there was disagreement between the two governors over this issue.

In respect of whether, as a governing body, they required the headteacher to have a plan, five pairs of governors said no and in School E there was disagreement. Eleven of the 18 governors considered that there was no formal requirement for the plan to be submitted to them. It was interesting that, despite this, the headteachers from all nine schools provided a report to governors about the SDP, although it was very rarely a specific agenda item in its own right.

Whilst the governors generally supported development planning, it soon became clear that there were considerable differences between the governors in terms of their sense of ownership of the actual plan and that these differences did not relate to a particular type of plan. Responses ranged from one governor who was very distanced from the whole process and saw it as the headteacher's responsibility, to another who was very knowledgeable about the plan and wanted to become more involved. In general, the governors' knowledge about the content of the plan was limited. When asked if they could identify any current priorities, only a third of the chairs of governors had any knowledge of one or more priorities in the plan, compared with two-thirds of the parent governors, some of whom came into the school regularly because of their children.

Questions about governors' involvement in formulating and implementing plans, and about the role of others, revealed views about the leadership and management of SDPs. Governors from every school emphasised the importance of key leadership and management roles and that the responsibilities of the headteacher were considerable. Headteachers were perceived to have multiple roles and responsibilities and, as one governor described it, the headteacher was seen as the 'king-pin'. They all thought there was a role for teachers. The deputy head and curriculum and inservice training co-ordinators were also mentioned, in particular, by 11 governors. It was noticeable that the responses of the governors in schools involved in co-operative and corporate planning stressed the importance of staff involvement. The need for the headteacher to co-ordinate, facilitate, delegate and consult was mentioned by nine of these governors. At the formulation stage, 12 governors mentioned others who should be or were involved, for example, support staff, parents, pupils and the LEA. In contrast, only six governors noted such a role in the implementation of the plan.

The answers from the governors about their own role in the formulation and implementation of plans were somewhat surprising. In relation to the formulation of the plan, 13 governors, five of whom were the chairs of governors, said they were not involved. Of those who said they had been, three described informal meetings and two were on a governor curriculum subcommittee. When asked about their particular role, the general impression was that the majority of governors lacked confidence in their ability to contribute. Eleven did not identify a role for themselves and the main reason given was their perceived lack of expertise. For example, one said 'it is best left to the professionals', another that 'in theory yes, but the headteacher is the professional and it is difficult for governors'. Some governors, however, did identify support and advisory roles and one felt she should be much more informed and involved.

When it came to the implementation of the plan, 11 governors said they were not involved, with the lack of time being a noticeable excuse. Only one of those not involved said she would have liked to have been but had been given no opportunity. This was a governor from School E whose dissatisfaction with the whole process was a consistent theme and whose answers were totally at variance with the chair of governors from the same school. It was interesting that it was only School I where there was said to be no involvement of either governor in either formulating or implementing the plan. This was not for a negative reason, rather that both governors said they had full confidence in the headteacher. However, the chair of governors did feel that, in future, the governor role would increase, particularly in relation to their involvement in school-based inservice training related to the plan. One other issue worthy of comment was that there were six schools where both governors said that no financial resources were allocated to support the implementation of the plan, even though, in some of these schools, there was a governors' finance subcommittee.

Monitoring the implementation of the plan produced a more positive response. Whilst 12 governors mentioned this as an important element of the headteacher's role, it was this aspect of the process about which the governors felt they carried the most responsibility. Fourteen governors specifically made reference to this fact. However, from the responses given to us there was an indication that, again, governors lacked confidence in this area. This was confirmed in their replies to questions about how the plan was monitored and evaluated by governors. In eight out of the nine schools, at least one governor said that either monitoring was not taking place, or that they had ideas about how it ought to be done in theory, but that these had not yet been put into practice. The reliance on the headteacher and, in particular, on the head-teacher's report to governors as a means of enabling governors to be kept informed, was noticeable. Typical comments about monitoring were 'not done at present, not discussed'; 'done in report back from headteacher but we're not really doing it in any depth'; 'we get the plan, we get the report back and then we get the next plan'.

Responses to the question about how governors evaluated the plan revealed some concerns from the respondents. In 13 cases, evaluation was said not to be happening. Some examples of responses were 'we should have a small working group on it I suppose'; 'we don't evaluate, we just leave it to the headteacher'; 'we haven't done this, perhaps it should be a job for the curriculum subcommittee'. Two main reasons were given as to why evaluation was not taking place. It had either not been discussed by the governing body, or it was recognised that it was difficult and some tentative suggestions were made as to how it might be done. It was very evident that, whilst the majority of governors felt they should be monitoring and evaluating the plan, they were having great difficulty fulfilling this responsibility.

There was one exception, and that was School G. The responses from both governors were totally different in content and quality from all the other governors in the sample. It became clear that the headteacher had created a structure which enabled the governors to become involved and informed. She had established a means whereby they could monitor and evaluate progress achieved. With the headteacher's encouragement and support, a policy of termly, focused visits by a small group of governors had been negotiated. Through these visits, governors were able to see, for themselves, the implementation of the plan in practice. In particular, they could see its impact in classrooms. When asked about evaluation strategies, they said 'through our structured visits we can see the way the school has changed and the success rate and personal progress of pupils'. This sense of confidence in their responses was echoed in the replies they gave about the impact of SDPs.

We asked all the governors if the SDP had made a difference and, if so, in what way. The two governors from School G gave the most comprehensive response; a response which noticeably focused on pupils. For example, one of the governors listed the following improvements:

> continuity in teaching both in content and methods; planning and stages of development of pupils and therefore individual pupils have benefited; it makes sure the National Curriculum is delivered; common approaches to things like multiethnic education; improved inservice training, more finely tuned to the needs of the school; it has kept governors more in touch with the school and how it works, this is especially important for lay people.

The strong sense of ownership and involvement in the SDP by these two governors was self-evident, but they were in the minority.

In summary, only 28 per cent of the governors (5) felt they had been involved in some aspect of formulating the plan, though only 11 per cent (2) felt they had no role at that stage, and 17 per cent (3) felt they had no role in implementing the plan; 61 per cent (11) had seen the completed written plan; 33 per cent (6) considered that governors were not monitoring the use of the plan and 50 per cent (9) had not discussed any evaluation of the outcomes of the plan.

It was not surprising, given the weaknesses identified in the governors' responses about monitoring and evaluating, that they had mixed perceptions about the impact of SDPs. Eight out of nine chairs of governors felt that the plan had made a difference, the ninth thought it 'probably' had. There was a tendency, however, for their answers to be very general, not surprising given that very few of them knew about actual priorities for development. One governor, for example, said 'yes, I can't envisage a successful school without one, it is something to aim for', another that 'governors can now see what's happened, for the school it focuses them down on things'. The parent governors were less confident that the SDP had had an impact. Five said yes, and four that they did not know. As one governor put it:

> I think it has helped to tighten up and focus on one area but it is chiefly dealt with by the headteacher and deputy head. There is a dilemma because, as a parent governor, I only have a little knowledge and that can be a bad thing, but we're stuck with it and have to do our best.

When the responses of both governors were combined, four particular improvements were mentioned by five or more governors. Eight identified improvements in management and how the plan had provided a focus. Of these governors, five mentioned the value of a written commitment. Six said the governors had benefited because it had helped them to be better informed. Six also felt that there had been an improvement in the standards of pupils work. As has already been identified, however, the evidence base for such views was questionable. The responses, for example, from both governors of School A revealed just how problematical it is if governors rely solely on a headteacher's report. There was no indication from either governor that they were aware of any difficulties in relation to the rhetorical plan.

This analysis of the governors' responses about SDPs neither confirmed nor disconfirmed the typology. Instead, it raised a number of questions that merit more attention and further research. These are questions which reflect the difficult, somewhat vague situation in which governors find themselves in relation to the powers and responsibilities they have in respect of the general conduct and curriculum of the school; a concern which has been raised repeatedly (Auld, 1976; Taylor and Saunders, 1980; Kogan *et al.*, 1984; Deem, 1993).

The DES guidance on SDPs (1991a) describes one of the benefits of development planning as strengthening the partnership between staff and governors. Whilst suggestions are made about the contribution governors can and should make, the first sentence of the section reveals the dilemma: 'Each governing body must decide for itself how fully it should be involved in development planning' (*ibid.*, p. 13). The governors in our study clearly supported the idea of SDPs but were finding it difficult to become involved and informed despite the fact that all the headteachers, whatever the type of plan, had, to varying degrees, tried to engage governors in the process. Only one school had successfully managed to use the process to strengthen the partnership advocated by the DES. The subsequent Ofsted (1994, p. 52) publication states that 'Inspection evidence shows that where governing bodies are fully involved in their school's planning they have better informed and more effective oversight of the conduct of the school'. A list of questions related to the different aspects of the development planning process are provided in an attempt to guide governors. In the study only School G appeared to have found a way of successfully involving governors in the process of school development planning.

13

THE LEAs' STORY

This chapter describes the outcomes of the interviews with inspectors and officers in the three LEAs in our sample. It begins with the context and background of these LEAs before summarising their representatives' views of the three stages of planning – formulation, implementation and evaluation. This is followed by a synopsis of their comments. The chapter ends with conclusions which link with the typologies derived from the national survey of LEAs and from the nine schools.

Seven inspectors and officers in the three contrasting LEAs were interviewed in June and July 1993. All were linked with the nine schools participating in our project and the dual purpose of interviewing these personnel was to compare their views of

- LEA approaches with those expressed by respondents to the national survey a year earlier; and
- the project schools with those expressed by the headteachers, classteachers and governors in those schools.

A structured interview with each 'link person' was carried out in a venue of their choosing, generally in the offices of the three LEAs. The comments reported in this chapter reflect the perceptions of two or three senior staff in each LEA who had regular contact with the schools in our project.

The three LEAs were at various stages of adjusting to the separation of inspection and advisory services necessitated by the 1992 and 1993 legislation. Consequently, the description of the roles and titles of the officers varied more than would have been the case until recently. In one LEA they were still called inspectors, one respondent being a Senior Inspector and one a General Inspector. In the second LEA, the titles Chief Adviser and Assistant Director of Education describe two of the respondents, while the third was a Senior Manager responsible for a service. All three had become absorbed into the officer structure. In the third LEA, one respondent was an Education Officer, while the other's title had been changed from Inspector to Management Consultant.

Three of the seven had been appointed to their roles within the last year. The others had been in post for between three and seven years. Five of the seven had served in the same LEA for three or four years. The other two had served in the same LEA for 14 and 25 years respectively. Consequently, while all were experiencing structural changes, all had been serving their LEAs long enough to know the schools in the wider context of the services available within the LEA. Most had been responsible for significant aspects of the development and maintenance of such services. All but one had experienced development planning in other types of school and four of the seven had been involved in development planning in contexts other than primary schools.

The interviewees were asked if their LEA had a policy on school development planning. One of the three LEAs was said to have education committee endorsement of a policy about SDPs in primary schools. It was reported that the other two LEAs strongly encouraged schools to have such plans, both to help internal management and to meet external expectations arising from local management and from inservice planning as well as the inspection framework. These policies had not changed in the last year in two of the LEAs. In the third there had been a subtle change from a curriculum-focused plan towards a school management plan which identified resources to meet needs. Although the principles and processes had not changed, there had been an intention in this LEA to widen participation in planning so that governors and more staff became involved.

In practice, increasing government control and changing instructions over testing and the National Curriculum, together with financial cuts and the lack of guarantees about funds, were said to have encouraged short-term planning in schools. One interviewee considered that central government had made it harder for LEAs and headteachers to promote the concept of more strategic, longer-term planning. On the other hand, it was thought that the requirement for plans in the Ofsted inspection framework had formally raised the profile of planning documents and encouraged links among curriculum, staff development and LMS issues.

Each of those interviewed was linked with particular primary and secondary schools as well as having a general brief for schools throughout their LEA. Some were linked also with nursery or special schools. In two of the LEAs the number of link establishments ranged from four to nine schools. In the third the interviewees had become consultants for between 23 and 28 schools. The frequency of visiting reflected the number of link schools, with two visits a term being the most common pattern. Where particular problems existed, this frequency rose significantly according to the nature of the problem, and was said in some circumstances to involve many meetings with the headteacher, governors and staff. Conversely, visits were rare where the LEA person was linked with a large number of schools, had a major general responsibility and was confident from other contacts that a particular school did not require specific assistance. Nevertheless every school had been visited by the link person during the school year 1992/3.

Those interviewed said that they knew the headteachers well in virtually every school, and in most instances this knowledge was extended to the deputy and the senior staff. The interviewees considered that involvement in staff meetings or with issues involving particular post-holders led to getting to know staff better than was possible from only visiting classrooms. Access to data either in the schools or the LEAs presented no difficulties. Data used included reports to governors, statistical information about aspects such as finance or test scores and curriculum statements. All had regular access to the schools' development plans, except for one school with a recent change of headteacher in which the inservice diary had previously been the only plan. Practice varied between the LEAs, from one in which the plan was an up-to-date working document and the focus of work within the school, to the others in which the plan simply provided a context for LEA knowledge about the schools' priorities.

Development plans were seen to be multipurpose and were defined in various ways according to the perceptions and experience of the interviewee. It was considered that an SDP assisted in managing the school; clarifying priorities for development; reviewing progress; stimulating a shared process; and communicating with others. The following are examples of some of the phrases which were expressed during the interviews about the purposes of plans: 'a management tool to co-ordinate the work of the school'; 'an umbrella to bring together curriculum, professional, premises and financial planning'; 'a means of identifying pupil needs and matching these with institutional needs'; 'a framework for the individual development of teachers, for the allocation of resources and the better prioritisation of work'; 'a declaration of shared intentions to improve and move things forward'; 'a joint process with the governing body'; 'a record of achievements and successes'.

The headteacher was seen to have the key role in formulating the SDP, but it was accepted that this was interpreted in various ways according to his or her experience and circumstances. The headteacher was deemed to be responsible for the process and was said either to lead it or delegate it to the deputy or curriculum co-ordinator. This process included involving the staff and governors in the determination of priorities, encouraging a sense of ownership and fine tuning the plan into an effective written document. It was felt that headteachers who entrusted the key role to others usually ensured that their own views remained influential. The link person's relationship with the headteacher became particularly important in situations when the responsibility to plan was not recognised sufficiently, or when the process needed supporting.

The interviewees were asked who else, other than the headteacher, had a role in formulating the development plan. All included the deputy and the teaching staff, one stressed the need to consult the teaching staff about needs and another mentioned the curriculum co-ordinator in particular.

Opinion varied about involving others. In two of the LEAs it was said that support staff might be involved, and that this was more likely in infants' schools. One person mentioned that there might be resource implications in involving them. In two of the LEAs, inspectors, advisers and officers had been used, particularly in the early stages, as external consultants on planning processes. In these same two LEAs the involvement of governors was mentioned, for example in curriculum panels or inservice days focusing on planning. In one LEA the importance of pupils' views was mentioned, together with links between planning and records of achievement. Parents were not mentioned at all, except in their role as governors. The general picture appeared to be that the plan was considered a document for professionals and that, at present, others had only limited involvement in contributing to its formulation.

The respondents were asked explicitly about the role of governors in formulating a development plan. It was said that intentions were not yet fully realised, and responses indicated that the quality of the headteacher, of the chair of governors and of the governors was paramount in determining, at this stage, how far they were actively engaged. In one LEA they were said to be consulted and to see the draft. In another, the professionals produced the plan, a governors' subcommittee discussed it and the full governing body approved it in the way that a shareholders' meeting approves a report. The governors validated the priorities generated by the professionals. In the third LEA, the impact of inspection forced the governors to debate issues and drew them into making the recommendations that became incorporated into the plan as priorities. The learning curve of the governors was said to be particularly steep where schools were involved in an amalgamation.

The LEA link people were asked to comment on their involvement in development planning with the nine schools. In two of the LEAs, the interviewees had been informed about the formulation stages of the planning whereas in the third LEA they felt involved. In the latter case this included discussion with the headteacher during the decision-making process, or being involved in the annual training day at which the plans were formulated. However, this involvement was said to be diminishing in comparison to previous years. In this LEA there was a formal requirement that the plan should be submitted to the LEA, whereas in one of the other LEAs schools were encouraged but not required to do so. The completed written plan was seen by all the link people whether there was a requirement or not.

In all but one case, the reaction on seeing the plan was supportive and no further action was required. In the one case there was no proper plan, and the lack of it was but one indicator of a problem which, it was thought, might diminish with a change of headteacher. Reactions to the others included positive comments together with potential ways in which future plans could improve, for example, by including more explicit references to ways in which resources could be used to achieve objectives. One respondent mentioned that discussion of the plan was included as part of a continuing debate in the appraisal of the headteacher. All those interviewed said that they knew what the current priorities were, or had easy access to the headteacher and appropriate documentation, except where the headteacher had changed recently and the priorities were being reviewed.

The role of the headteacher in implementing the plan involved both management and leadership. The interviewees considered that it was the headteacher who had responsibility for identifying who is responsible for achieving the tasks, for setting a realistic timescale and for ensuring that the process kept to it. One headteacher had been overoptimistic about the time needed to achieve a particular change, but the interviewee considered that she now appreciated better the need for patience. The skill of judging pace and capability was said to be an important characteristic of competent school leadership.

The link people were in agreement that the headteacher needed to be able to articulate what was wanted and to empower people to get on with achieving it. He or she needed to promote a common vision about teaching and learning, and to provide a structure in which teachers were encouraged to support one another. One headteacher was described as being fairly non-directive, but achieving much more behind the scenes than was apparent to the superficial observer. One of the interviewees compared two headteachers' approaches, saying that one 'finds it in people' and the other 'requires it of people'. Both the schools were considered nice to work in, under contrasting leadership styles. In another school it was considered that staff experience with curriculum planning was contributing to the quality of development planning.

All the respondents said that the implementation of the development plan involved the deputy head and the teaching staff. All considered that support staff should be involved, but about half either indicated that this depended on the relevance of particular priorities, such as pupil behaviour or communications, or were uncertain whether a particular school involved such staff in implementing the plan. Similarly, most respondents indicated that parents would be involved where the priorities in the school included home-reading schemes or home/school liaison.

All but one of the plans were said to indicate that financial or other resources – notably time – had been allocated for implementation. The inservice element was clearest, with targeted inservice funding and training days or staff meetings devoted to identifying or addressing the priorities in the plan. The inservice co-ordinator was mentioned in one school as a key figure in formulating and implementing the plan, and in ensuring that staff shared expertise with colleagues after participating in professional development activities. In two schools mention was made of staff with responsibility to tackle priorities, and incentive allowances were allocated 'to move action' in one school. Another school was involved 'vigorously' in seeking funds from local industry as part of its priority to improve communications with the community.

Decisions about funding were taken by the headteacher, but there was said to be variation between schools and LEAs concerning who else was involved. The deputy was specifically mentioned in only one school. LEA advice was mentioned by only one respondent, which may reflect the extent to which confidence in financial decision-making was growing in increasingly autonomous schools. In one LEA, the headteacher consulted the teachers and gained the approval of the governors. Governors were not mentioned in another LEA. In the third LEA the governors were consulted in one school and in another they 'rubber stamped' the decisions of the headteacher and staff. The role of governors therefore in implementing the plan varied. In one school they were said to be directly involved in targeting finances. In most cases, however, this is delegated to the headteacher and professional staff. They receive reports of progress in each case and, in most, progress is monitored regularly.

All responded that LEA inspectors, advisory staff and officers would have a role in implementing the plan, though this would be less strong than in the past and would depend on the extent of devolution of previously centralised services. For example they would be involved in issues concerned with site development or special needs services under the Child Protection Act, and might be involved in linking with other services such as personnel, management development or inservice activities. In one LEA, the link people had been personally involved in supporting the school in conjunction with specialist colleagues, or in leading inservice sessions. In another, the link people acted as a bridge and promoted access to support services. They evaluated some programmes and were involved in piloting other developments, such as records of achievement. Appraisal of headteachers and governor training also brought LEA staff into contact with the needs of individual schools. Two respondents expressed a regret that other commitments inhibited their ability to support the management of the school.

The interviewees were asked if there had been any significant changes in the way in which the schools approached development planning in 1992/3 as compared with 1991/2. One school, in which the headteacher had changed, was reported as having made considerable changes, and the responses to the other questions indicated that such changes were considered long overdue. Another school which had experienced a change of headteacher in the previous year had also been changed by the headteacher increasing the involvement of teaching staff and governors in planning.

Improvements in a third school were said to have taken place in five areas: defining success criteria; evaluating why the plan had failed to meet a target and deciding what to do about it; making judgements; improving the coherence and sophistication of the process; and improving the confidence of the teaching staff each year. Some schools had found that changes in inspection requirements and LMS had caused them to modify their processes. Others had changed their priorities. In one case it was stated that they were already reviewing how the co-ordination of finance, resources and organisation could better deliver their objectives.

The LEAs varied in their monitoring of the implementation of the schools' plans. In one LEA, the general inspector's regular discussions with the headteacher included how far targets had been met, whether they were too ambitious and whether support was needed; an annual, retrospective meeting took place in September. Although there had been similar practice in the second LEA, the reduced capacity of the LEA now left the link person with the total role of identifying where there was cause for concern. One respondent considered that a more rigorous process than 'supported' self-improvement was needed in some schools. In the third LEA, the officer and the chair of governors were responsible for monitoring the implementation of the plan. The link consultant was expected to advise, on the basis of knowledge of the school, rather than to make specific judgements.

The evaluation of outcomes of the plan by the LEAs was said to be relatively rare. One LEA scrutinised links between inservice provision and the needs identified in the plan. A second LEA depended on feedback from link consultants and inspection processes. Responses varied from respondents in the third LEA. The Chief Adviser said that the LEA would no longer be evaluating outcomes. A Senior Manager said that links between evaluation policy and emerging inspection arrangements were not yet clear. The Deputy Director focused on the outcomes of school planning in monitoring the implementation of LEA policies across the whole authority.

Despite the variety of responses about the evaluation of the outcomes of the plan, each of the interviewees was in no doubt, on the basis of a range of detailed evidence gathered while inspecting and visiting regularly, that development planning had led to improvements in each of the schools. Thus there was an interesting mismatch, in some cases, between these perceptions and our findings.

It was argued that school development planning had provided a clearer structure within which to plan priorities. This – it was claimed – encouraged schools to identify realistic goals which were appropriate and achievable. Financial and physical resources, together with staff energies, had become focused on these consequences which benefited pupils' learning. It was thought that schools had a better sense of direction and now tended to evaluate better what had been achieved before moving on to other priorities.

It was reported that the importance of the influence of the headteacher's vision had become more widely recognised. As people appreciated that the plan and the planning process were integral parts of managing the school, support for the headteacher became more important. One respondent said he had never seen a good plan operate in a school with a weak headteacher.

The SDP had helped to raise the profile of the planning process. It was said to be a unifying and collaborative process for the staff as a whole which brought staff together yet reflected individual jobs. When decisions had to be made there was less concern if an agreed set of priorities had become a cohesive influence in the school. The framework of a plan provided the staff with a 'kernel of sanity' at a time of many externally imposed pressures, and helped to plug the gap between rhetoric and reality.

It was also said that the plan enabled schools to demonstrate their own development as organisations and to clarify where improvements were needed. Across the schools as a whole confidence was perceived to have been enhanced with the headteacher and the staff better able to meet their accountabilities. One respondent felt strongly that a commitment to development planning by the staff had made a difference. She considered that it had enabled people to clarify and articulate what it was that they were trying to achieve with pupils. Governors and parents were said to value the improved quality of information about what had been achieved and what was intended.

The interviewees were asked whether there were any links between school development planning and LEA development planning, and it was clear that the links varied between the three LEAs. In one there was no link with the budget cycle, and some officers, such as those involved with site development, had no contact with school plans. This LEA expected, but did not require, its core values and priorities to be reflected in school plans. In the second LEA, one respondent was unhappy that inservice planning was dictated by GEST priorities. Another said that the LEA's plan was developed as an amalgam of school plans, and the LEA tried to avoid mismatches in priorities between the LEA's members and officers and the schools' governors and headteachers. The third respondent in this LEA added that its plans were affected by the political process both at national and at local levels, and that local authority directorates other than education also influenced policy at corporate level, for example, over how far an 'agency approach' to selling services should be developed. The third LEA did not publish a plan, although units were involved in meeting the strategic needs of members, such as supporting assessment in the National Curriculum, or submitting the GEST return based on a staff development plan.

The interviewees were invited to comment on any other general aspects of school development planning. Some raised issues which had already been mentioned earlier by others, but some new issues also emerged. For example, one felt that continuity in a school was important and that a change of headteacher should not necessarily lead to a new plan. Indeed, in their view if priorities were only related to a specific headteacher, the process was flawed. The need to engage parents more in addressing priorities was also mentioned. It was considered that this might help them to feel more involved in discussing potentially conflicting priorities when decisions had to be made. Finally a view was expressed about the relationship between the Ofsted approach to whole-school inspections and school development planning. There was support for incorporating development plans into the inspection framework and requiring governors to have action plans. It was felt that although these inspections would be much less frequent than under present LEA processes, it was encouraging that such plans would be scrutinised for their effectiveness. This was likely to provide a much-needed impetus for a school which did not yet have a plan in place.

THE RELATIONSHIP BETWEEN THE RESPONSES AND THE SDP AND LEA TYPOLOGIES

One of the aims of analysing the responses of the LEA inspectors and officers was to compare the views expressed about each school's development plan with our findings about the four different types of development plan in evidence across the nine schools. We found that the perceptions of the LEA link people about the schools did not conflict with the strengths and weaknesses which we had identified, although the quality of the perceptions reflected the experience and type of contact developed by the individual inspector or officer. The views expressed by each interviewee also appeared to be linked closely with that person's seniority and responsibilities in the LEA. In some cases there were wider gaps between levels of understanding within LEAs than between those of officers and inspectors of a similar level in different LEAs.

Another purpose of analysing these data was to ascertain whether or not there was any apparent relationship between the views expressed, the typology of LEA involvement identified in Chapter 6 and the different types of plans. What we found was that the LEA's policies in general, and the strategies for supporting school development planning in particular, were loosely linked to the effectiveness of planning processes in the nine schools.

In one LEA, two of the schools had a co-operative plan and one, a corporate plan. This LEA displayed 'systematic' characteristics, and the various forms of evidence were more consistent with one another than in the other two LEAs. In the second LEA, two of the schools had a co-operative plan and one, a singular plan. The responses from the link people indicated that the LEA was shifting from a 'supportive' to a 'minimalist' approach. In the third LEA, one of the schools was classified as having a corporate plan, one, a co-operative plan and one, a rhetorical plan. The responses indicated that this LEA tried to be 'supportive'.

In all three LEAs there were suggestions that cuts in LEA resources were resulting in the reduction of inspectors, officers and advisory support staff. One measurable effect was the contracting extent and quality of management and inservice support available to schools. If the LEA typology incorporated a continuum from 'systematic' down to 'minimalist' support, financial pressures during the period of our project appeared to be causing each of the LEAs to move a few notches down the continuum. There were indications that they were not necessarily adapting sufficiently in this process to focusing support resources on schools with weaker management.

Overall, we did find that there was a correlation between the categorisation of LEA involvement and the typology of SDPs to the extent that the LEA with the most developed approach of the three (systematic) was also the LEA with the greatest proportion of schools with the most effective type of plans. This was an interesting finding given the limited evidence obtained from the schools of an LEA infrastructure of support. We concluded that LEAs should not claim too much for their guidelines or inservice activities on planning and that, conversely, headteachers should not underestimate the impact of the LEA's policies and strategies on their approaches in practice.

14

THE THEORETICAL IMPLICATIONS OF
THE RESEARCH FINDINGS

This chapter examines the theoretical implications of the research findings. It begins with a review of the characteristics of the typology which emerged in Chapter 9 followed by an analysis of the typology. The extent to which there is a relationship between the characteristics of the different plans and the findings of other researchers is then examined as a means of further testing the validity of the typology. Then, the relationship between the findings of the empirically derived hypothesis and the two hypotheses derived from the research literature identified in Chapter 4 is explored. Arising out of this analysis, the three hypotheses are reformulated as a set of theoretical propositions which, combined, are offered as a theoretical model of school development planning. The implications of the proposed model for further research are considered. So too are the implications of the findings for the general theoretical postulates identified at the outset of the research. Finally, the extent to which the findings of this study can be generalised is assessed.

Through a systematic analysis of the headteachers' and classteachers' accounts and a comparison of these with other sources of data, considerable evidence has been found to substantiate the hypothesis that four different types of development plans were in use across the nine schools and that it was possible to identify the type of plan in use in each school.

Some key findings emerged in relation to this typology. It was found that SDPs did make a difference and that they had the potential to make a very significant impact on the school. The nature of that impact, however, was determined by the type of plan. The consequence of this was that some plans were found to be more effective than others in respect of identifiable improvements for the school as a whole, for teachers in classrooms and for pupils. The rhetorical plan was found to be the least effective; the corporate plan the most.

The effectiveness of the plan was associated with a set of characteristics which delineated each type of plan. The characteristics represented a number of key factors that appeared to be generic across the plans. They were factors which concerned a combination of the use of the process itself, that was determined by the degree of shared ownership, purpose, leadership and

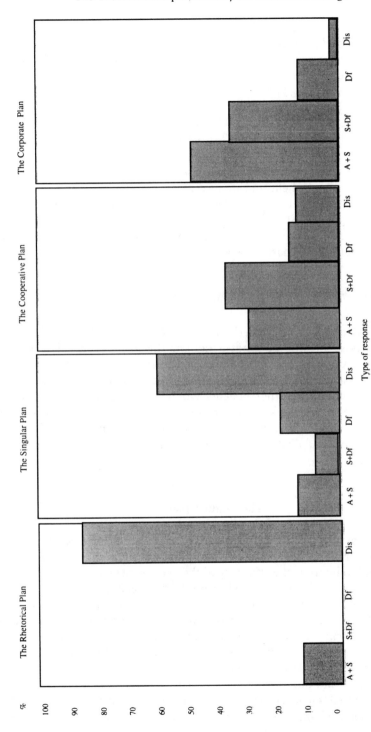

Figure 14.1   The four graphs of the percentage of agreement and disagreement and similarity and difference between the responses of the classteachers and headteachers engaged in the four different types of SDP

management of the plan, and the focus of the plan. It was the combination of these two factors which proved to be critical. The focus of the plan, not just the quality of leadership and management of the process, marks out the difference between the plans.

THE MAIN CHARACTERISTICS OF THE FOUR TYPES OF SDPs DERIVED FROM THE EMPIRICAL DATA

Figure 14.1 is a combination of the four graphs in Chapter 9 which represent the percentage of agreement and disagreement and similarity and difference between the responses of the classteachers and headteachers engaged in the four different types of SDP. The considerable differences between the four types are a reflection of the different characteristics of each plan. What follows is a description of those characteristics.

The rhetorical plan

The rhetorical plan was characterised by a lack of a shared sense of ownership and purpose by both the headteacher and the classteachers. The written plan was not a working document and the leadership and management of the process was weak. This resulted in a limited sense of control over the process and a lack of confidence that benefits would ensue. Neither financial resources nor INSET were linked with the plan and monitoring and evaluation strategies were weak. The impact of the plan was a negative one. Teachers became frustrated and disillusioned and the headteacher was distanced from the staff.

The singular plan

The singular plan was characterised by a sense of ownership and purpose by the headteacher alone. The purpose of the plan was singular in nature. It was used as a tool to improve the efficiency of the management and organisation of the school and provided a means whereby the headteacher could be accountable to governors. It instilled a degree of confidence in the headteacher but the sense of control over the process was minimal. The written plan was not a working document and the leadership and management of the process was limited; the headteacher assumed the main responsibility for both. There was little or no financial and professional development to support the implementation of the plan and monitoring and evaluation procedures were weak. The plan had a limited impact. It resulted in improved efficiency in relation to the overall management and organisation of the school, but there was no evidence of any impact on teachers and pupils.

The co-operative plan

The co-operative plan was characterised by a co-operative effort to improve. Whilst there was only partial shared ownership by the teaching staff of the content of the plan, there was a general willingness to participate in the process. The plan was perceived as multipurpose in nature. There was a dual emphasis on improving both the efficiency and effectiveness of the school with a noticeable focus on school-wide improvements and the professional development of teachers. The leadership of the plan was vested in the head-teacher. However, the management of the process was shared among some key staff, many of whom were members of the senior management team. The written plan tended to be a working document. The implementation of the plan was supported by financial resources and a linked programme of professional development. Teachers' learning was seen to be important. There was a sense of growing confidence and control over the process, although involvement in the implementation of the plan tended to be confined to the teaching staff. The process was perceived as a complex and continuous one, although monitoring and evaluation procedures lacked rigour. The impact of the plan was a positive one. It resulted in improvements in whole-school management and organisation, professional relationships and teachers' effectiveness in the classroom. There was limited evidence, however, of improvements for pupils.

The corporate plan

The corporate plan was characterised by a united effort to improve. There was a strong sense of shared ownership and involvement by the teaching staff and an attempt was made to include others in the process. The plan was seen to be multipurpose in nature and there was a sense of control over the process and confidence that it would lead to improvements in efficiency and effectiveness. The focus on teaching and learning, especially on improvements in the quality of pupils' learning, was a particular characteristic. The written plan was an open, working document and the leadership of the plan was shared among the senior management team. The complexity and continuous nature of the process were recognised and the management of the process was shared by all the staff. Financial resources and staff development were linked to the implementation of the plan and monitoring and evaluation strategies were sound. Teachers had a definite sense of responsibility for the outcome of the plan. The impact of the plan was significant across the school as a whole, for teachers in classrooms and for pupils' learning. A link could be discerned among school development, teacher development and pupils' development. There was evidence of a learning community within the school with headteachers and class-teachers exhibiting the characteristics of reflective practitioners, continuously seeking to develop and improve their practice.

An analysis of the typology

The characteristics of each plan represent a continuum from the least to the most effective type of plan: a continuum in respect of the nature of the impact of the plan, from one that is negative to one that is very positive. However, the typology does not represent a linear, developmental process. It is not a stage theory of development planning. It was schools with co-operative and corporate plans that revealed this finding, in particular, Schools G and H. These two schools were engaged in co-operative and corporate planning respectively, although they had had little or no previous experience of planning in this way. The schools involved in co-operative planning were also on a continuum themselves and demonstrated how schools can change from one type of plan to another. School D was new to this type of plan, having previously had a rhetorical one, whereas Schools F and G were already beginning to demonstrate some of the characteristics of corporate planning.

The characteristics of the typology indicate a differential awareness of the complexity of development planning, with the rhetorical plan the simplest, the corporate plan the most sophisticated. What was particularly surprising was the finding that the more effective the plan, the more complex the characteristics appeared to be. Whilst this contradicts the message of much of the guidance which has been published on school development planning described in Chapter 2, it confirms what is known from the literature about the complexity of schools. It was interesting that the actual number of components and priorities in the plan were not a determining factor. What was more important was the main focus of the plan and therefore the nature of the priorities and the integrated nature of the planning process, especially the extent to which financial resources and the professional development programme were linked with the implementation of the plan.

The characteristics revealed a link between the extent to which there was a shared sense of agreement between the staff and the headteacher about the purposes and priorities of the plan and the effectiveness of the plan. Not unrelated was the fact that the two schools with the most effective plans had both established a policy statement about the aims and practices of development planning. In these policy statements a link had been made between the school's overall aims and the role of development planning in fulfilling these. In these schools development planning had become embedded into the culture of the school.

Shared ownership and involvement and shared leadership and management were noticeable characteristics of the most effective plan. The corporate plan was characterised by the degree to which all the teaching staff were engaged in the process. There was evidence that, because the main focus of the plan concerned teaching and learning in the classrooms, and INSET was provided to support this, teachers were prepared to take a 'classroom exceeding perspective' (Hopkins, 1989). The teachers had experienced the benefits of taking such a perspective and of engaging in school-wide improvement efforts. This was reflected in the degree of confidence and control over the process. Another characteristic of the corporate plan was the wide range of qualitative and quantitative evidence gathered to assess the effectiveness of the plan and the monitoring role of the headteacher and other senior staff in relation to the gathering of this evidence. The implication of this finding is that not only is there a need for classteachers to develop a classroom exceeding perspective, but, correspondingly headteachers and senior staff need to develop a *classroom perceiving perspective*. This was demonstrated by the headteachers engaged in corporate planning. They had recognised the need to develop strategies to focus on classrooms to ascertain the impact of the priorities for development.

It was noticeable that a characteristic of the least effective plans was the weakness in respect of monitoring and evaluation strategies. What has emerged from the characteristics of the typology is that *self-management cannot be equated with self-improvement*. It was the findings in relation to the impact of the rhetorical and singular plans which exposed this issue. Without well-developed self-evaluation strategies, self-improvement will not be the outcome. The definition of the self-managing school, therefore, needs to incorporate a clear evaluation dimension. Without it, the implications of this study are that improvement in efficiency and effectiveness will not be achieved.

A common feature across the typology was the noticeable professional base of the plans. Whilst there was evidence from schools engaged in co-operative planning and in corporate planning in particular that they were opening up to include and take account of the views of others, such as support staff, parents and governors, the content of the plans was determined, on the whole, by the headteacher and also the teaching staff depending on the type of plan. The role of governors was revealed to be problematical and the LEA featured little in relation to the formulation of plans.

It could be the case that the concept of local management will, over time, change from self-management to community management, especially if the number of grant-maintained schools increases and market forces become more of a reality. If this happens, a fifth type of plan could emerge, namely, a community plan. Such a plan would be representative of the views and needs of the community which the school served. It could be, for example, that some secondary schools, particularly with the development of business partnership schemes, have already moved in this direction. In a concurrent Danish study on development planning (Kruchov and Høoyrup, 1994), the community plan is already a common feature because of the way the system is structured. Careful attention, however, would need to be paid to the focus of such a plan. There could be a danger that, in attempting to be so multipurpose in respect of taking account of multiple views, the focus on pupil learning could become blurred.

Whilst it was possible to identify the generic characteristics of each plan, what was interesting was that there was no one set of contextual characteristics which delineated one type of plan from another. For example, there were no links between the size, type and location of the school and the type of plan. The genesis of the plan was not a critical factor either. For example, for School H the plan had been initiated from outside by the LEA, whereas for School I, the notion of development planning had come from within the school itself. Despite this, both these schools were engaged in corporate planning. Nor was there a link, in all cases, between the length of experience of planning, either by the school or the headteacher, and the type of plan which was in use. The actual length of headship experience was not a factor either. It was also demonstrated, in the case of the rhetorical plan, that the appointment of a new headteacher is not necessarily associated with improvements in the development planning process. However, there was a link between the degree and nature of teacher involvement and collaboration across the types and the extent to which both headteachers and classteachers were able to learn from this experience and so continue to improve the process.

A characteristic noticeable by its absence was the role of external agencies. There was some evidence of the involvement of an outside agent in the form of the LEA. Some examples were provided by the schools of specific support with the implementation of plans, particularly in relation to the provision of inservice courses and the use of advisers in school. However, although the headteachers mentioned visits and inspections by the local inspectors and HMI, there was little or no evidence of the extent to which these were directly related to the SDP. The lack of clarity as to whether the plan had to be reported to the LEA, or the DFE, at either the formulation or the evaluation stages, was symptomatic of uncertainty about the role of outside agents. From the responses there was no sense of a systematic approach by the LEA to SDPs. This was perhaps a reflection of their rapidly changing circumstances at the time of the interviews. There did not appear to be an infrastructure at LEA level to support the implementation of the SDP. This is a particular cause for concern in respect of the rhetorical and singular types of plans. The negative effect of the former, and the limited impact of the latter, indicated the need for external intervention and support to ensure that the headteachers were able to change to a different, more effective type of plan. This finding has important implications for the national programme of inspections.

The relationship between the characteristics of the different types of SDPs and the research literature

A relationship can be found between the findings of this study and the research literature concerned with school improvement, school effectiveness and the change process. It was the characteristics of the co-operative and corporate types of plans that were the most revealing. The key characteristics related to these two types of plans find much support in the literature, as the following examination of each of them in turn indicates. Each of the characteristics has been rewritten as a theoretical proposition.

Plans which are complex in character are likely to be more effective

Studies of schools seeking to improve themselves confirm that the planning for that improvement needs to take account of, and reflect, the complex nature of educational change (Rosenholtz, 1989; Fullan, 1991; Hargreaves and Hopkins, 1991; Chrispeels, 1992; Louis and Miles, 1992). The inadequacy of a simplistic approach to improvement is a consistent theme in the literature (Cuban, 1988; Fullan, 1991; Louis and Miles, 1992). So, too, is the need for an approach to school improvement which brings about changes in the culture of the school, if the outcomes are to have any significant, long-lasting effect (Sarason, 1971; Rossman *et al.*, 1988; Hargreaves and Hopkins, 1991; 1993; Torrington and Weightman, 1993).

Plans which are multipurpose in nature are likely to be more effective

The need for planning which seeks to improve both the efficiency and the effectiveness of the school has been emphasised (West and Ainscow, 1991). So, too, has an approach to improvement which enables internal and external priorities to be integrated in a coherent, planned way (Hargreaves and Hopkins, 1991; Fullan, 1992a). It is also argued in the literature that self-development by schools can serve as a means of ensuring internal and external accountability (Bollen and Hopkins, 1987; Schlechty, 1990) and that these two purposes can be compatible (Stoll, 1991; Stoll and Fink, 1992).

The greater the sense of ownership and involvement by the staff and others, the more effective the plan is likely to be

Teacher involvement in decision-making about school policy and practice is recognised as one of the characteristics of effective schools (Smith and Tomlinson, 1989). Collegiality and collaboration are seen as important requirements in school improvement efforts (Little, 1982; Holly and Southworth, 1989; Rudduck, 1991; Fullan and Hargreaves, 1992). However, studies have shown that by themselves they do not necessarily lead to improvement (Nias *et al.*, 1989; 1992). What is also important is the extent to which shared goals can be identified (Rosenholtz, 1989), a clarity of purpose can be achieved (Fullan, 1991) and meaningful involvement can be secured (Hopkins, 1990; Biott *et al.*, 1994). The negative effects of the failure to secure ownership and involvement, as exemplified in the rhetorical type of plan, also finds support in the literature (Conley *et al.*, 1988; Constable, 1994).

A plan which is well led and which has shared leadership of the process is likely to be more effective

The quality of the leadership of the headteacher has long been established as a significant characteristic of effective schools (Mortimore *et al.*, 1988; Lezotte, 1989; Smith and Tomlinson, 1989), as well as of school improvement efforts (Hall *et al.*, 1980; Coulson, 1986; Leithwood and Montgomery, 1986). At the same time, there has been a growing recognition of the importance of a shared approach to leadership emanating from recent school effectiveness research (Bolam *et al.*, 1993) and school improvement case studies (Rosenholtz, 1989; Mortimore and Mortimore, 1991; Chrispeels, 1992; Louis and Miles, 1992). Some researchers have also stressed the need for leadership to be shared, not just within the school but to emanate from outside as well, if schools are to be supported in their change efforts (Fullan, 1991; Chrispeels, 1992; Stoll and Fink, 1992). Fullan *et al.* (1990, p. 16) argue that long-lasting improvement requires a systematic approach to school improvement which involves complementary restructuring at school, local and national levels: 'Leadership can, does, and must come from a variety of different sources . . . it must be mobilised on multiple fronts for long-term development to occur.' There was a distinct absence in the present study of a noticeable infrastructure of support for schools engaged in development planning either locally or nationally. This is of particular concern given the findings of researchers that schools left on their own have difficulties maintaining an improvement momentum (Sirotnik, 1987; Fullan and Hargreaves, 1992; Slater and Teddlie, 1992).

The more the management of the plan and the planning process is shared, and its complex nature understood, the more effective the plan is likely to be

The need to involve teachers in school-based management is a common theme in the literature (Lieberman, 1988; Rosenholtz, 1989; Jenni, 1991; Chrispeels, 1992). A number of studies have focused on the importance of teachers extending their responsibilities beyond the classroom (Pollack *et al.*, 1987; Casner-Lotto, 1988; Hopkins, 1989). Hargreaves and Hopkins (1991) identified different levels of understanding about development planning. Others have stressed the need for an approach to planning which reflects the complexity of change itself (Patterson *et al.*, 1986; Fullan, 1992b). The perception of the plan as a working, flexible document, and the process as a continuous one, finds support in the literature. It is not, for example, dissimilar to some of the principles underpinning school growth planning (Stoll and Fink, 1989; Fink and Stoll, 1992) and evolutionary planning (Louis and Miles, 1992).

A plan which links financial resources and a staff development programme to the priorities for development is likely to be more effective

Examples of the practical difficulties incurred by schools engaged in the implementation of improvement programmes are prevalent in the literature (Rosenholtz, 1989; Fullan, 1991; Fullan and Hargreaves, 1992; Louis and Miles, 1992). The need to integrate the different aspects of the management of the school in a planned way has been emphasised, particularly, financial management (Caldwell and Spinks, 1988) and staff development (Joyce and Showers, 1988). The importance of linking school development with teacher development is a common theme in the literature (Little, 1986; Fullan *et al.*, 1990; Hopkins, 1990; Levine and Lezotte, 1990; Fink and Stoll, 1994).

A plan which is systematically monitored and in which a range of evidence is used to evaluate outcomes is likely to be effective

It is argued that school self-evaluation is essential (Riddell and Brown, 1991) but problematical (Clift *et al.*, 1987; Stoll, 1991). School improvement studies reveal the importance of schools developing strategies for monitoring and evaluating the improvement programme (Chrispeels, 1992). The complex task of assessing the effectiveness of the outcomes, particularly in respect of pupil achievement, has been identified (Lezotte, 1990; Goldstein, 1991; Chrispeels, 1992; Gray *et al.*, 1993; Stoll and Reynolds, 1994).

The greater the sense of control over, and confidence in, the planning process, the more effective the plan is likely to be

Hargreaves and Hopkins (1991) argue that development planning can empower teachers. Other research studies have also identified this characteristic as a necessary feature of school improvement programmes (Furtwengler, 1990; West and Ainscow, 1991). Fullan (1991), however, emphasises the uncertainty that change programmes can generate and that it is necessary to plan for this. The Halton Study (Stoll and Fink, 1989) found that as the confidence of the school growth planning team increased, teachers assumed greater control over the change programme and also increased their ability to become the agents of change within the school (Fink and Stoll, 1994).

The more the planning process encourages and supports teachers' own learning, the more effective the plan is likely to be

There are many studies which have demonstrated the relationship between teachers' learning and school improvement (Rosenholtz, 1989; Chrispeels,

1992; Nias *et al.*, 1992). It is as a result of these, and other studies, that views about approaches to professional development have changed. Strategies for improving staff development programmes have been identified (Joyce and Showers, 1988), as have strategies for encouraging teachers to be more reflective and analytical (Good and Brophy, 1986; Rosenholtz, 1989; Joyce, 1991). The importance of a continuous, systematic approach to school improvement which centres on the teachers' own workplace and supports their own learning is a consistent theme (Rozenholtz, 1989; Fullan *et al.*, 1990; Chrispeels, 1992). The concept of the school as a learning community and the relationship between this and improving student outcomes has emerged in the literature (Barth, 1990; Schlechty, 1990).

Those plans which have improving pupil progress and achievement as a central focus and are able to link this with teacher development and school-wide development are likely to have the most significant effect

The focus of the plan in this study proved to be a critical factor. One of the key findings of Rosenholtz's (1989, p. 171) research was that 'if the school is a rich learning environment for students, it is also likely to provide learning opportunities for the staff'. There are those involved in school improvement work who argue that all important is the focus on pupil outcomes, in particular their academic achievement (Pollack *et al.*, 1987; Lezotte, 1990; Taylor and Levine, 1991; Chrispeels, 1992). At the same time, Murphy (1990) maintains that one of the most significant contributions of school effectiveness research has been to draw attention to the importance of pupil progress and outcomes. Chrispeels' study (1992, p. 167) strongly supports this contention: 'It is no accident that monitoring of student progress and academic focus are two key features of effective schools.' It is argued that school-based management should be data driven (Lezotte, 1990), particularly in relation to pupil outcomes (Pollack *et al.*, 1987). However, the need to gather both qualitative and quantitative evidence about a range of pupil outcomes has been stressed, and the need for indicators of effectiveness in relation to pupils have been suggested (Gray, 1990). The necessity to improve the identification of success criteria linked with priorities for development, and to broaden the range and type of evidence gathered about the focus for improvement, is one of the particular findings of this study. Research findings about differential achievement between, for example, different groups (Nuttall *et al.*, 1989) and school departments (Sammons *et al.*, 1995), has shown just how complex this issue can be.

The analysis of the relationship between the characteristics of the most effective SDPs and the general research literature lends considerable support to the findings of our study. It could also be argued that there appears to be a close relationship between our typology and Rosenholtz's (1989) concept of 'moving' and 'stuck' schools. For example, the rhetorical plan exemplifies a 'stuck' school, whereas the co-operative type of plan and the corporate one, in particular, demonstrate how school development planning can support and help to develop a 'moving' school in which shared goals, teacher collaboration, teacher learning and teacher certainty and commitment are some of the key characteristics. As in our present study, Rosenholtz found that there was a relationship between such characteristics and pupils' learning.

The analysis did reveal, however, some contrary evidence and exposed an anomaly. Despite growing research evidence of the need for external support to guide and sustain a school's own improvement efforts, such an infrastructure appeared to be absent for both the 'moving' and 'stuck' schools in our sample. This raises a question about the long-term impact of development planning given the findings of other related studies (Stoll and Fink, 1989), although, as Wallace (1991b) argues, the nature of the external support is an important factor.

THE RELATIONSHIP BETWEEN THE TYPOLOGY AND THE TWO HYPOTHESES DERIVED FROM THE RESEARCH LITERATURE

Two hypotheses were identified in Chapter 4 which were both derived from the detailed literature reviews in Chapters 2, 3 and 4. The validity of these hypotheses is now examined in the light of the empirical findings.

Hypothesis one

The impact of development planning on the school as a whole will be determined by

- *the purpose for which development planning is used;*
- *the internal and external context of the school;*
- *the understanding and application of the process; and*
- *the content of the plan.*

The characteristics of the typology reveal that there are factors related to all four of these dimensions of development planning which, when combined together, appear to have a determining influence on the effectiveness of the plan. Of particular significance is the relationship between the extent to which there is a shared sense of purpose, ownership, leadership and management of the process, and the actual focus of the plan. The link between this relationship and the differential impact of development planning is a key finding. The discovery that there were four different types of plans in use, and that each appeared to have a set of generic characteristics, meant that our original hypothesis needed to be revised. Our research has produced evidence to support the following theoretical proposition.

SDPs can make a difference, but the nature of that difference is determined by the type of plan in use. There are at least four different types of SDPs, each of which has its own set of generic characteristics. These concern factors related to the purpose, context and content of the plan, and the planning process itself. It is the particular characteristics of each type of plan which determine both the nature and the extent of the impact the plan has on the school as a whole.

Hypothesis two

The extent to which school development planning is a school improvement strategy will be manifested in changes in the culture of the school, in particular, changes in

- *professional relationships;*
- *organisational arrangements; and*
- *opportunities for learning.*

The positive impact of the co-operative and corporate types of plans provided evidence to substantiate the proposition that school development planning can be used as a school improvement strategy; a strategy which can improve both the efficiency and the effectiveness of the school. It was the combination of the quality of the leadership and management of the process, and the focus of the plan, which appeared to determine the nature of any changes that took place in respect of these three cultural dimensions of the school. The typology revealed that not all development plans improve the school. The difference between the negative effects of the rhetorical type of plan, compared with the very positive changes in the culture of the schools which had a corporate type of plan, was a substantial one. The characteristics of the different types of plans disclosed that only one kind of plan resulted in identifiable improvements in learning opportunities for pupils. With regards to this hypothesis, therefore, there was evidence to suggest the following theoretical proposition.

School development planning can be used as a school improvement strategy, but not all SDPs lead to school improvement. The type of plan determines the extent to which both the efficiency and the effectiveness of the school can be improved. Only certain types of plans have a positive impact on the culture of the school in respect of professional relationships, organisational arrangements and opportunities for teachers' own learning. Of these, only one type also leads to discernible improvements in learning opportunities for pupils.

A THEORETICAL MODEL OF SCHOOL DEVELOPMENT PLANNING

One of the key contributions of this study is the identification of the characteristics of the type of SDP which has the most significant impact on schools in respect of pupils' learning, teachers' own development and school-wide improvements. The findings indicate that it is the type of plan, not just the approach to planning, that is important. Our study has revealed that the development planning process can provide a systematic means whereby a school can improve its effectiveness.

A set of theoretical principles and propositions emerged from our analysis of the theoretical implications of the typology. They represent a combination of the three hypotheses we explored during the study which were themselves the product of an interaction between theory and empirical investigation. We have drawn these propositions together in the form of a theoretical model about the processes and impact of school development planning in the nine primary schools studied.

SDPs can make a difference but the nature of that difference is determined by the type of plan in use. There are at least four different types of SDPs, each of which has its own set of generic characteristics. These concern factors related to the purpose, context and content of the plan, and the planning process itself. It is the particular characteristics of each type of plan which determine both the nature and the extent of the impact the plan has on the school as a whole.

School development planning can be used as a school improvement strategy, but not all SDPs lead to school improvement. The type of plan determines the extent to which both the efficiency and the effectiveness of the school can be improved. Only certain types of plans have a positive impact on the culture of the school in respect of professional relationships, organisational arrangements and opportunities for teachers' own learning. Of these, only one type also leads to discernible improvements in learning opportunities for pupils.

The most effective plans have the following characteristics:

- They are complex in character.
- They are multipurpose in nature.
- There is a strong sense of ownership and involvement by the staff and others.
- They are well led and the leadership of the process is shared.
- The management of the planning process is shared, and its complex nature is understood.
- The implementation of the plan is supported by financial resources and a staff development programme.
- Progress is systematically monitored and a range of qualitative and quantitative evidence is used to evaluate outcomes.
- Those involved have a strong sense of control over, and confidence in, the planning process.
- The planning process encourages and supports teachers' own learning.
- Improving pupil progress and achievement is the central focus of the plan and this is linked with teacher development and school-wide developments.

THE IMPLICATIONS OF THE THEORETICAL MODEL FOR FURTHER RESEARCH

This model now needs to be tested and developed through further research studies. In particular, more research is needed about the characteristics of effective plans identified in this study and the role of outside agents in school development planning. The following are examples of the kinds of questions which need to be addressed:

- Are the characteristics generic?
- If the characteristics are generic, what are the implications for secondary schools? For example, can an institution-wide plan be achieved, or is the locus of planning more likely to be at the department or faculty level?
- In what ways can or should those other than teachers become involved?
- What is the best role for governors?
- How can schools be helped to change to a more effective type of plan?
- How can schools be helped to improve their own self-evaluation strategies in respect of school development planning?
- What should be the role of the LEA?
- What is the relationship between external inspection and the SDP? How can external evaluation and self-evaluation procedures become more closely inter-related?

The implications of the finding for the theoretical postulates proposed at the outset of the research

We examined in turn each of the original six theoretical postulates described in Chapter 5 in the light of the findings of our study.

Most staff and the headteacher can agree on a clear mission for the institution

The findings revealed a link between the extent to which there was a shared sense of agreement between the staff and the headteacher about the purposes and priorities of the plan and the effectiveness of the plan. It was the two schools with the most effective plans which had both established a policy statement about the aims and practices of development planning. In these policy statements a link was made between the school's overall aims and the role of development planning in fulfilling these. What the data did not reveal was whether, at the audit stage, the schools with a co-operative type of plan were making a definite link between the school's overall aims and the priorities for development agreed upon. In respect of the singular type of plan, the purpose of development planning was not to further the school's aims, rather, to improve school-wide management practices. Again, it was not possible to ascertain whether or not, unconnected with the development plan, the staff and the headteacher had agreed a clear mission for the institution. It is interesting that in Scotland, the planning process begins with a re-examination of the school's aims as the first step in the auditing process (SOED, 1993).

A systematic audit of current strategies and weaknesses is an important element

There was evidence from the way plans were formulated that those involved in co-operative and corporate types of plans were endeavouring to use the development planning process to identify, systematically, priorities for development. The data provided evidence of how the lessons headteachers and classteachers had learned were being used to help improve all aspects of the planning process. It was the schools in which headteachers and classteachers demonstrated a sense of control and confidence over the process which were able to use it as a systematic means of improving practice.

A change plan is thoroughly thought through

Again, the co-operative and corporate types of plans revealed a growing sophistication in the strategies used to implement the plan. In contrast, the singular and rhetorical types of plans showed serious weaknesses. A particular weakness, however, across almost all the plans, was the lack of identification of success criteria at the formulation stage in respect of the priorities for development chosen. Schools were seldom asking the question, for example, *how will the successful implementation of a particular priority be demonstrated?*

An outside agent is involved *and* the implementation of the change plan is supported by all appropriate external authorities

As described earlier in this chapter the limited involvement of outside agents was a particular cause for concern in the light of our findings. This has considerable implications for local and national strategic approaches to school improvement. For example, the kinds of external involvement and support required by a school with a corporate type of plan will be very different from those needed by a school with a rhetorical type of plan.

An evaluation of progress is used formatively to support the implementation

This aspect of the school development planning process was found to be the weakest. The absence of regular monitoring and well-developed evaluation strategies was a noticeable feature across a number of the schools. Those involved in co-operative and corporate types of plans were aware of the need to improve this aspect of the process. The schools engaged in the corporate type of plan were using the most comprehensive range of quantitative and qualitative evidence to support the implementation process. The headteachers and the classteachers in the schools were constantly evaluating progress and seeking to improve the process.

These postulates were focused on school improvement. They reflected aspects of planning concerned with the formulation, implementation and evaluation of SDPs which were deemed to be important conditions for success at the outset of the research. We found there was a relationship between those concerned with school-based actions by headteachers and classteachers and school improvement. They were factors which appeared to contribute towards the effectiveness of the plan. In respect of the two postulates concerned with external involvement and support, there was some evidence that schools valued and took advantage of professional development opportunities provided by the local authority. Beyond that we failed to find support which would involve the external evaluation of the plan and the strengthening of a school's own planning strategies and self-evaluation processes. Given the general finding about the differential impact of plans, and the specific finding about weaknesses in monitoring and evaluation strategies, this is a cause for concern.

The overall findings of our study about the characteristics of the different types of plans in use indicated that the original postulates generally held up but failed to reflect the complexity of development planning. Our findings revealed that the more effective the plan, the more complex were its characteristics.

A consideration of the extent to which the findings of this study can be generalised

It was recognised from the outset that our ability to generalise from the findings would inevitably be limited. The sample of nine primary schools was far from random, as described in Chapter 5. The size of the sample is also problematic not least because it did not allow for any extensive statistical analysis. Throughout the collection and analysis of the data, the potential shortcomings of the methodology were a constant concern. As far as possible, these concerns were addressed in the research design and the code of practice which we formulated. Inevitably, the findings in respect of the theoretical model must be tentative in nature, not least because of the inherent difficulties in establishing causal relationships. However, despite this, the findings, arrived at as a result of our systematic triangulation of the varied data, have found considerable support in the literature. A relationship between the characteristics of the most effective types of plans and the findings of international research studies of primary and secondary schools has been identified. There is strong evidence to suggest that these characteristics are generic in nature and, as such, are applicable to the generality of schools, although it is acknowledged that the size and organisation of secondary schools is likely to increase the complex nature of the development planning process. As a result of this supporting evidence, the final chapter uses the findings of our study to identify potential practical implications for schools; LEAs; higher education and other support agencies; the national programme of inspections; and international studies of school improvement and school effectiveness.

15

THE PRACTICAL IMPLICATIONS OF THE STUDY

This final chapter explores the practical implications of the characteristics of the most effective types of plans identified in the theoretical model proposed in the previous chapter. Implications in respect of policy and practice for headteachers and class-teachers are explored in detail, as it was these two groups which were the main focus of our attention. General implications for governors, LEAs, higher education and other providers, and for Ofsted, are also identified, including, where relevant, the findings of the LEA survey. The chapter concludes with a short commentary on the overall nature and findings of the study and raises issues for consideration by school effectiveness and school improvement researchers in the future.

THE IMPLICATIONS OF THE FINDINGS FOR THE HEADTEACHER AND STAFF

A key finding of this study is that SDPs make a difference, but the nature of that difference is determined by the type of plan in use. Development planning can be used as a school improvement strategy but not all development plans lead to school improvement. There is one type of plan that, because of its particular characteristics, can improve learning opportunities for pupils. This is the type of plan which seeks to develop strong links among pupil learning, teacher development and school-wide improvements. For secondary schools, the latter are more than likely to incorporate departmental and interdepartmental improvements, as well as whole-school conditions. The key characteristics of this type of plan, revealed and discussed in Chapters 9 and 14, concern issues to do with the extent to which there is a shared sense of purpose and ownership of the plan; the quality of leadership and management of the planning process; and the focus of the plan. These findings have considerable implications for headteachers, those with senior and middle management responsibilities and all classteachers. They also have implications for others who work in the school. These will be considered in respect of how plans are formulated, implemented, evaluated and reported.

The formulation of plans

One of the implications of our findings is that the formulation of a development plan is much more complex than the guidance available described in Chapter 2 suggests. Issues of particular importance concern the process of identifying priorities for development; who should be involved; the nature of the priorities for development chosen; the identification of success criteria; and the kind of document produced.

The audit

The identification of priorities for development is called, in the published guidance (DES, 1989a), the 'audit' stage. Our study has revealed that the content of that audit needs to be broadened. Headteachers and the senior management team need to ensure that the audit includes the following aspects:

- A review of the extent to which there is a shared sense of understanding about the purposes of development planning and an understanding that, although development planning is multipurpose in nature, the central purpose is to improve pupil progress and achievement.
- A review of the overall aims of the school and the relationship between these and the development plan. The review needs to ask the question, 'To what extent have the priorities in the plan which has just been implemented helped to further the aims of the school?'
- An identification of the type of plan currently in use, using the characteristics of the corporate plan, described in Chapter 14, to guide the analysis. For a new headteacher, it will be necessary to ascertain the type of plan used in the past. The action required as a result of this aspect of the audit will be determined by the type of plan identified. If it is a corporate plan, for example, it will be important to sustain and continue to improve the implementation and evaluation of the plan. If it is not a corporate type of plan, then this in itself should become a priority for change. The culture of the school in respect of professional relationships, organisational arrangements and opportunities for learning for teachers and pupils, as described in Chapter 4, will need to become the focus for improvement.
- An improved database for deciding priorities. To achieve and maintain a focus on pupil learning, evidence about the quality of teaching and learning in the classroom and the levels of achievement of the pupils, including differential levels of achievement across subjects and the school as a whole, needs to be gathered to enable future priorities for development to be identified and agreed by all. The study has revealed that during the implementation phase of the planning process, monitoring and evaluation strategies were weak in a number of the schools. This in turn means that limited information is available to feed back into the audit phase of the next planning cycle. Without sufficient information it is difficult for a headteacher or governing body to decide what needs to be developed next and what needs

to be done to sustain the improvements achieved so far so that the process really does become a continuous one.

Involvement in the audit

Included in the broadening of the audit process needs to be a reconsideration of who is involved in the process and the nature of that involvement. The study has shown that it is essential for teachers to have a shared sense of ownership of the plan. Without this, the plan is likely to have little or no positive impact and could result in a negative outcome as was the case with the rhetorical plan. The study has also revealed that the definition of involvement varies depending on the type of plan, as exemplified, for example, by the singular type of plan. To achieve a united effort to improve requires the kinds of strategies adopted by the schools engaged in corporate planning; strategies which enable teachers to play an active role in establishing priorities for development. We found that the involvement of teachers in the leadership and management of this aspect of the planning process was an important factor.

It is essential, however, that teachers do not perceive the plan as a threat to their professional autonomy. Rather, they need to be helped to understand and experience the benefits of taking a 'classroom exceeding perspective' (Hopkins, 1989) and collaborating with, and learning from, others across a year group, a department and the school as a whole as described by teachers engaged in co-operative and corporate plans. These should be the kinds of benefits which concern teachers' own learning and that of their pupils. It is argued in Chapter 14, however, that this should not be seen as a one-way process. At the same time, there is a need for headteachers and senior and middle management teams to have a *classroom perceiving perspective*. It is important for them to be able to focus on classrooms as part of the process of gathering evidence about aspects of teaching and learning which need to be improved further. Head-teachers and their management teams need to develop strategies for knowing more about what goes on in classrooms. In this way, the identification of priorities for development can become a shared two-way process across the teaching staff as a whole.

Strategies for involving others are needed if the school is to achieve a more corporate approach to development planning. The study has revealed that the content of the plans are determined, on the whole, by the headteacher and, depending on the type of plan, by the teaching staff. There was evidence, however, from schools engaged in co-operative planning, and in corporate planning in particular, that they were opening up to include and take account of the views of others, such as support or associate staff as they have been called (Mortimore *et al.*, 1994), pupils, parents and governors. In Chapter 14 a cautious reference was also made to the possibility of plans incorporating the wider views of the community. By engaging others in the audit and taking account of their views this should strengthen their sense of ownership, involvement and commitment to the plan.

The type of priorities for development chosen

One of the major findings of our study is that it is not the number of components and priorities in the plan but the focus for development chosen which appears to have an important bearing on the impact of the plan. This implies that when choosing priorities for development headteachers and teachers need to be clear about the distinction between *means and ends* in development planning. For example, whilst teacher development is, in one respect, an end in itself, it also needs to be seen as a means to improving pupil learning. Similarly, whilst improving organisational arrangements and professional relationships across the school as a whole and across departments are important priorities, the rationale for choosing these needs to reflect the extent to which such changes are likely ultimately to improve learning opportunities for pupils. The study has shown that the priorities chosen can enable the link between school-wide and departmental development, teacher development and pupils' own development to be strengthened and that this principle should guide the selection of priorities. Related to this, the study has also shown that when teachers recognise that there are priorities in the plan which will serve their own purposes in the classroom, they are more likely to be committed to their implementation.

The identification of success criteria

For the schools engaged in rhetorical, singular or co-operative types of plans, the identification of success criteria in respect of the priorities for development chosen is a weakness, despite its importance. It is the schools engaged in corporate planning which recognise the need to be more rigorous in deciding, at the outset, how the improvements sought are likely to be demonstrated in practice. They understand the necessity to select ways of assessing the subsequent effectiveness of the plan. Schools need to ask the question, therefore, 'How will we know we have made a difference?' The answer to this question will, in turn, indicate the nature of the evidence which needs to be gathered to monitor the implementation of the priorities for development and evaluate the outcomes of the plan.

The written plan

The evidence from our study is that the written plan needs to be formulated in such a way that it is an open, working document: a document which, rather than being a published finite statement of intent, is practical and flexible in nature and can be amended if necessary. We found that if this is the case it will be regularly referred to and progress and achievements will be recorded. It will thus be more likely to lead to the implementation of the chosen priorities for development. In several of the schools not only did individual members of staff have a copy of the plan but also a synopsis which was regularly amended and updated was on display for all to see. There also needs to be a shared understanding about who else needs to have a copy of the plan. The audience for the written plan and the purpose for providing it should determine its format and content. For example, agreement needs to be reached with governors as to whether or not they should receive the detailed operational plan or a synopsis. Similarly, the requirements of others, such as support staff, parents, the LEA or an inspection team, will also determine the nature of the written document they receive.

The implementation of the plan

The importance of the quality of the leadership and management of the implementation of the plan, and the extent to which this was shared by all the staff and others, proved to be one of our key findings. Practical issues of particular importance concern the establishment of an action plan; the identification of roles and responsibilities; the provision of financial support for the implementation of the plan; the provision of a programme of professional development for teachers; and the systematic monitoring of the process as well as the progress in implementing the priorities for development.

The action plan

All the schools recognised the need to establish an action plan which would enable the identified priorities for improvement to be realised in practice. However, it was only the schools engaged in co-operative and corporate types of plans which were able to draw up action plans in such a way that they led to improvements in the effectiveness of the school. An action plan, therefore, needs to include the identification of targets; tasks; roles and responsibilities; timescales; an effective communication system; and a system for regular review and monitoring. This has important implications in respect of the requirement to establish an action plan following an Ofsted inspection. Schools need to be clear about the relationship between this kind of action plan and action planning as part of the continuous development planning process. In practice the two should be combined and this will have considerable implications for the way the plan is led and managed.

Roles and responsibilities

Those engaged in co-operative and corporate types of plans recognised that integral to the success of the action plan is the identification and clarification of specific roles and responsibilities. These concern both the leadership and management of the process and a combination of shared and individual responsibility by all the teaching staff and, in some cases, other groups. This has important implications for the approach to leadership and management adopted by senior management and middle management teams and the extent to which this enables individual teachers to have delegated, personal responsibility for implementing an aspect of the development plan. The approach to leadership and management adopted by the headteachers engaged in corporate planning engendered in all those involved a sense of confidence and control over the process. For this to happen, there is a need for headteachers to delegate responsibility in such a way that those concerned not only have a remit to act and make decisions but also will be held accountable for the outcomes.

A problem common to all the schools is the limited time available for implementing the plan. All important, therefore, is the efficient management of the use of time. Those headteachers that had confidence in, and control over, the process, were constantly seeking ways of creating sufficient time for class-teachers, and teams of teachers, to fulfil their roles and responsibilities in respect of the plan.

Financial support

Financial support directly linked to the implementation of the plan was found to be a characteristic only of the most effective types of plans. Schools need to decide not only how much money to spend on development activities but also the type of support needed. Supply cover will be necessary, not just for teacher release to work with and alongside others and to attend inservice training sessions but also to enable individual and teams of teachers to fulfil their leadership and management responsibilities in relation to the implementation of the plan. In addition, depending on the priorities in the plan, both in connection with sustaining past developments and introducing new ones, money will be needed to augment classroom resources and support departmental activities as well as school-wide improvements.

Staff development

In common with the previous issue, a programme of professional development directly linked to the implementation of the plan was found to be a characteristic of the most effective types of plans. The inservice training programme needs to serve at least two purposes and to take a variety of forms. The development of knowledge and skills in relation to the priorities for improvement is important and will require attendance at school-based and offsite workshops and courses; opportunities for teachers to learn with and from one another through, for example, paired work and teams of teachers working together; and the use of consultants and advisory support both from colleagues and from those bought in from outside. At the same time, there will be those members of staff who, because of their particular roles and responsibilities in relation to the implementation of the plan and oversight of the planning process, will require management development opportunities including attendance at appropriate offsite courses.

Our finding that the more complex and sophisticated the plan, the more effective it is, also has important implications for the professional development of headteachers. They need to ensure that the professional development programme for the school includes opportunities for them to develop and extend their own approaches to leadership and management and to learn more about the characteristics of the most effective types of SDPs.

Monitoring the implementation of the plan

A number of weaknesses emerged in relation to this aspect of the planning process. There was an absence of monitoring in those schools engaged in rhetorical and singular types of plans. Although monitoring was recognised as important by the schools involved in co-operative plans, in the main it was only the headteachers who fulfilled this responsibility. By way of contrast, for those involved in corporate plans, be they headteachers, senior staff or class-teachers, monitoring was seen to be a shared responsibility requiring a range of strategies to reflect the different roles and responsibilities individuals held.

The implication of this finding is that strategies for monitoring the planning process itself, as well as progress in implementing the specific priorities for developments, need to be built into the action plan at the outset. A systematic set of procedures for regularly reviewing progress is essential. This emerged as an important lesson learned by those engaged in the more effective types of plans. The procedures need to include opportunities for different groups to meet on a regular basis. The size of the school, the management structure and the way responsibility for implementing the plan has been designated to different groups, as well as the number and range of priorities for development in the plan, will determine the frequency with which these groups will need to meet. The groups are likely to include the whole staff, the whole, or a subgroup of, the governing body, senior and middle management teams and task groups which may involve teaching staff and others, for example, associate staff, governors and pupils. These different groups need to have a clear monitoring role supported by an agreed system for communication and decision-making, to enable any problems to be overcome and any necessary changes to be made. The corporate plan demonstrates that the procedures also need to include opportunities for the exercise of individual responsibility in respect of monitoring a specific aspect of the plan. In this way, teachers' sense of ownership and involvement can be strengthened. Through such procedures regular feedback on progress is possible; the kind of feedback that not only identifies problems to be solved but also tasks successfully achieved. The latter should provide an important source of motivation for those involved.

The evaluation of the plan

In practice, as illustrated in the diagram reproduced from the DES guidance (1989a) on page 10, monitoring and evaluation need to occur simultaneously throughout the implementation of the plan. The reason for creating a separate heading for evaluation here is that, like monitoring, this aspect of the planning process was a noticeable weakness in some of the schools. As described in Chapter 14, it was found that self-management does not necessarily lead to improvements in the effectiveness of the school. For those involved in rhetorical and singular plans little or no evaluation took place. The only evidence alluded to by respondents concerned the achievement of tasks identified in the plan, not their evaluation. Evaluation appeared to be equated with monitoring the implementation of the action plan itself. For the schools engaged in co-operative and corporate plans, however, there is a clear recognition of the importance of gathering a range of quantitative and qualitative evidence to enable the impact of the plan to be evaluated. Chapters 7 and 8 described the specific kinds and sources of evidence collected by the schools. It is the typology which reveals important differences in the focus of the evidence in that it was only those engaged in corporate plans who had a strong emphasis on the collection of data directly related to the work of teachers and pupils in the classroom.

These findings have important implications for practice. Integral to the action plan, and closely linked with the success criteria identified at the formulation stage, needs to be the systematic collection of evidence to enable the impact of the plan and the planning process to be evaluated. The lessons learned, particularly by those involved in co-operative and corporate plans, provide useful indicators as to the different aspects of development planning which need to be incorporated within the evaluation process. The impact of the agreed priorities for development must be assessed. Also important is an assessment of the strategies used in the planning process itself and the extent to which any of these can be improved upon. A third dimension of the evaluation should concern the culture of the school. This study has revealed that development planning can have a positive impact on those aspects which are an observable demonstration of the culture, namely, professional relationships, organisational arrangements and opportunities for learning.

The evidence gathered in relation to these different kinds of evaluation needs to include a range of quantitative and qualitative data in order to enable a comprehensive evaluation to be achieved. The priorities for development will determine the nature of the information needed for the evaluation. The kinds of quantitative data should be a combination of documentary evidence such as policy documents, inspection reports, schemes of work and teachers' plans; evidence of pupil progress, such as samples of work and records of achievements; and statistical data including, for example, pupils' academic attainment, progress and attendance. Qualitative data also need to combine observable evidence, such as environmental changes, new classroom resources and organisation and the quality of pupils' work in books and on display, with data related to the priorities for development which concern the attitudes and expectations of, for example, pupils, teachers, governors, parents and external visitors to the school. As revealed in our study, the focus of data collection is a particularly important issue. It is essential to ensure that improvements in the quality of teaching and learning in the classroom are central to the evaluation. It is the outcomes of these data analyses which need to feed back into the audit phase as the next cycle of development is formulated. At the same time, the process of evaluation should be continuous throughout the implementation of the plan. This will enable changes deemed appropriate to be made and unexpected new demands to be addressed.

Reporting the outcomes

The headteachers' and classteachers' stories described in Chapters 7 and 8 respectively, and the governors' story in Chapter 12, reveal a number of issues concerned with who was informed about the outcomes of the development plan. At the end of the planning cycle all the headteachers said they communicated outcomes to governors. Beyond this, there is no unanimous agreement about other groups, although the LEA and parents were mentioned by at least two-thirds of the headteachers. By way of contrast, the teachers were noticeably unclear about this aspect of the process and there was considerable disagreement among them as to who, if anybody, was or needs to be informed.

Arising from this are two practical implications. The first concerns the need for a decision by the headteacher and senior management team about who should be involved in development planning and the nature of that involvement. The strong professional base of the plans has already been identified. As more groups become involved, such as associate staff, pupils, governors and parents, then communication about the progress and outcomes of the plan needs to be thought through and made clear.

The second implication concerns the multipurpose nature of development planning. Our study has confirmed that it can be used as a school improvement strategy. It has also confirmed that all the headteachers recognised that one of the purposes of development planning is to enable the school to become more accountable for its work. This was one of the reasons why all the headteachers reported outcomes to the governors despite the fact that not all the governing bodies required them to do so. The government-initiated national inspection programme will heighten the importance of the accountability aspect of development planning, not least because it forms part of the inspection procedures. More attention needs to be given as to how, and to whom, outcomes are reported. The governors, in particular, need to pay closer attention to this issue as it relates to their role in development planning.

THE IMPLICATIONS OF THE FINDINGS FOR GOVERNORS

The implications of this study are that governors find it difficult to become involved in, and informed about, school development planning, not least because of the lack of clarity in general about their role and responsibility in respect of the leadership and management of the school. There needs to be a shared understanding among governors, the headteacher and the senior management team about the purposes of development planning and the characteristics of the type of plan most likely to improve the effectiveness of the school. Governors should have a role in the formulation of the plan, not least to enable them to exercise their responsibility in respect of the curriculum, special educational needs and budgetary decisions linked with the priorities for development chosen. Ways need to be found to include governors in the auditing process if a more corporate approach to planning is to be achieved and if governors are to fulfil their new responsibilities in relation to the action plan which they are required to establish following an Ofsted inspection.

The involvement of governors in the implementation and evaluation of the plan was found to be problematical. There is a tension in the findings. On the one hand, governors were content for the headteacher and staff to exercise the day-to-day leadership and management of the plan. On the other hand, governors wanted a role in monitoring the plan. Linked with this was their limited ability to evaluate the impact of the plan and their heavy reliance on the headteacher's report of the outcomes. Ways need to be found to enable governors to be better informed about the impact of the plan. School G (see Chapter 12) provided a useful case study of how governors can fulfil a monitoring and evaluation role. In addition, further practical steps can be taken. In recognition that school development planning can be used as a school improvement strategy, the SDP needs to be a separate item on the agenda at governors' meetings. It should be an extended item at the formulation stage and when outcomes are reported by the headteacher and staff. In between, shorter items to review progress should suffice. The governors, in partnership with the headteacher and staff, need to clarify who else should be, if not directly involved, at least informed about the SDP. The governors' annual report to parents, for example, is a useful vehicle for disseminating information about the ways in which the school is improving as a result of development planning.

Finally, there are implications for governor training arising out of our study and a decision needs to be taken as to who provides that training. Some training could be provided by the school itself through joint workshops with staff. Other providers of governor training, such as the LEA and governors' associations, may find it helpful to take account of the findings of this study when providing advice and guidance on school development planning.

THE IMPLICATIONS OF THE FINDINGS FOR LEAs

Our national survey revealed four types of LEA involvement in development planning. However, despite the initial surge of activity and interest in relation to SDPs, which was indicated in the LEA survey, there is little evidence from our subsequent study of this being sustained. During the time of the data collection the role of LEAs was changing considerably as a result of the 1988 legislation about local management and the devolution of financial responsibility to schools. The subsequent legislation about school inspections was also beginning to have an impact. The interviews with the personnel in the three LEAs in our study reveal a change in the nature of LEA involvement in development planning with a noticeable shift from support to monitoring. It would appear that the local authorities in our study are no longer able to provide a coherent infrastructure of support for the schools in respect of advice and inservice training. The practical implications of this, given the findings of the study, are a cause for concern. Our research has revealed the differential impact of SDPs and the need for 'stuck' schools with, for example, rhetorical or singular plans, to have external support to enable them to change from the current type of plan to a more effective one.

Our study indicates that what is required is an external infrastructure of support which:

- enables those advising and inspecting a school locally to do their own audit of the type of development plan in use and the school's collective understanding of the complex nature of the development planning process. This, in turn, will determine the kinds of support and intervention required;
- complements, as well as helps to develop, a school's own self-evaluation procedures through the external evaluation of the planning process and its impact;
- provides opportunities for headteachers and teachers to engage in school development planning moderation whereby they can share and learn from one another; and
- provides an inservice education programme which meets three specific needs related to school development planning. Advisory support and professional development opportunities for teachers and others will be needed in respect of the specific focuses for development. Similarly, management development opportunities for staff assuming specific management responsibilities in relation to the plan will be required. For headteachers and those seeking headship, a professional development programme is needed which enables them to understand the complexity of development planning and to develop and strengthen their approach to the leadership and management of the plan.

The indications nationally are that LEAs are likely to find it increasingly difficult to establish and sustain such an infrastructure of support and that the percentage of LEAs involved in development planning in a 'proactive' or 'systematic' way has reduced since our national survey in 1992. This raises a question about the ability of, as well as the need for, other providers to offer the kinds of services schools require to maximise development planning as a school improvement strategy.

THE IMPLICATIONS OF THE FINDINGS FOR HIGHER EDUCATION AND OTHER PROVIDERS

For higher education there are implications for both research and teaching as a result of the findings of this study. Future research possibilities arising from this study were identified in Chapter 14. In respect of teaching and consultancy support, there are implications for the content of courses and the kind of consultancy advice needed by schools. For those institutions engaged in school improvement work, such as the Cambridge Institute (Hopkins, 1994) and the Institute of Education (Stoll, 1994), the findings in relation to this school improvement strategy are important and should help to enhance work with schools. The accreditation of school-focused development efforts by teachers also needs to be developed further.

The implications of our study also have a bearing on the work of other providers such as education consultants and the professional associations. It will be for them to consider the ways in which the findings can enable them to offer a better service to schools and to those who work in or are connected with them.

THE IMPLICATIONS OF THE FINDINGS FOR OFSTED

Inspecting the SDP is part of the inspection procedures identified in the *Handbook for the Inspection of Schools* (Ofsted, 1993). However, the main emphasis is on the efficient management of the plan, the deployment of resources and the achievement of the targets set. Our findings indicate that this is insufficient and suggests that the handbook needs to be revised. The central importance of the SDP as a means of improving the effectiveness of the school should be recognised. The complexity of the process and the importance of the focus of the plan needs to be reflected in the handbook. The criteria for assessing the SDP also need to take account of the characteristics of the different types of plans which we have identified. In the inspection report these issues should be taken into account when recommending action by the school or when suggesting ways in which the SDP can be improved. The implications of the action plan to be established following the inspection have already been alluded to. In our judgement the action plan needs to be integral to the development planning process so that it becomes part of the school's continuous process of self-improvement. There is a danger that, otherwise, the timescale for producing an action plan, coupled with an expectation that change will happen quickly, could have a serious impact on the long-term effectiveness of a school's development plan and the achievement and sustaining of a corporate type of plan.

CONCLUDING COMMENTS

The history of school development planning is relatively short. Since the recommendation by the Thomas Committee in 1985 that 'every school should have a plan for development . . . and the central purpose should be expressed in terms of the improvements sought in children's learning' (ILEA, 1985, para. 3.94), the LEA survey has revealed that school development planning has become part of the practice of schools in almost every LEA throughout the UK. International studies reveal their introduction and use in a number of other countries.

Underlying this rapid expansion of development planning is an assumption, made particularly by policy-makers, that SDPs will improve schools; they are the answer to self-management and as such will make schools more effective. The findings of this study challenge these assumptions.

Our study has revealed that development planning is much more complex than many of those advocating its use have recognised. Its complexity is, in many respects, a reflection of the complexity of schools and the change process itself. Hargreaves and Hopkins (1993, p. 239) argue that 'the advantage of school development planning . . . is that it provides a means whereby knowledge about school improvement strategies can be put to the test of practice'. This study, through its focus on the processes and impact of development planning in nine primary schools, has endeavoured to put that knowledge to the test. It has shown that school development planning can be used as a school improvement strategy, but that the extent to which this becomes a reality in practice is dependent upon the type of development plan in use. Of the four types identified, only one was found to have a positive impact on student, teacher and school-wide improvements. The main contribution of this study has been to identify the characteristics of this type of plan; characteristics which have implications for both the theory and practice of school improvement.

References

Ackroyd, S. and Hughes, J.A. (1981) *Data Collection in Context*, Longman, New York.

ACSTT/INIST (1976) Towards a national policy for the induction and in-service training of teachers in schools (mimeo no. 17), ACSTT/INIST, London.

ACSTT/INIST (1978) *Making INSET Work*, HMSO, London.

Alexander, R.J. (1992) *Policy and Practice in Primary Education*, Routledge, London.

Arnott, M., Bullock, A. and Thomas, H. (1992) The impact of local management on schools: a source book (mimeo), NAHT/Birmingham University, Birmingham.

Arnott, M., Thomas, H. and Bullock, A. (1994) *The Impact of Local Management on Schools*, NAHT, University of Birmingham, QEd, Lichfield.

Audit Commission (1989a) *Assuring Quality in Education: The Role of Local Authority Inspectors and Advisers*, HMSO, London.

Audit Commission (1989b) *Losing an Empire, Finding a Role: The LEA of the Future*, HMSO, London.

Auld, R. (1976) *William Tyndale Junior and Infants Schools Public Enquiry*, ILEA, London.

Ball, S.J. (1987) *The Micro-Politics of the School: Towards a Theory of School Organisation*, Methuen, London.

Barth, R. (1990) *Improving Schools from Within*, Jossey-Bass, San Francisco, Calif.

Beare, H., Caldwell, B.J. and Millikan, R.H. (1989) *Creating an Excellent School*, Routledge, London.

Bennis, W. and Nanus, B. (1985) *Leaders*, Harper & Row, New York.

Beresford, C. (1994) Strategic planning: local education authorities and primary school development, Unpublished PhD thesis, Institute of Education, University of London.

Biott, C., Easen, P. and Atkins, M. (1994) School development planning: participation and staff membership, in D.H. Hargreaves and D. Hopkins (eds) *Development Planning for School Improvement*, Cassell, London.

Block, P. (1987) *The Empowered Manager*, Jossey-Bass, San Francisco, Calif.

Bolam, R., McMahon, A., Pocklington, K. and Weindling, D. (1993) *Effective Management in Schools*, HMSO, London.

Bollen, R. and Hopkins, D. (1987) *School Based Review: Towards a Praxis*, ACCO, Leuven, Belgium.

Bottery, M. (1988) Education management: an ethical critique, *Oxford Review of Education,* Vol. 14, no. 3, pp. 341–51.

Bradburn, N. and Sudman, S. (1979) *Improving Interview Method and Questionnaire Design*, Jossey-Bass, San Francisco, Calif.

Brenner, M., Brown, J. and Canter, D. (1985) *The Research Interview: Uses and Approaches*, Academic Press, London.

Briault, E. (1974) *Allocation and Management of Resources in Schools*, Council for Educational Technology, London.

Bryman, A. (1988) *Quantity and Quality in Social Research*, Unwin Hyman, London.

Burns, J.M. (1978) *Leadership*, Harper & Row, New York.

Bush, T. (1986) *Theories of Educational Management*, Harper & Row, London.

Caldwell, B.J. and Spinks, J.M. (1988) *The Self-Managing School*, Falmer Press, Lewes.

Cannell, C.F. and Kahn, R.L. (1968) *Interviewing*, Addison-Wesley, New York.

Casner-Lotto, J. (1988) Expanding the teacher's role: Hammond's school improvement process, *Phi Delta Kappan*, Vol. 69, no. 5, pp. 349–53.

Chrispeels, J. (1992) *Purposeful Restructuring: Creating a Culture for Learning and Achievement in Elementary Schools*, Falmer Press, Lewes.

Clark, D., McKibbin, S. and Malkas, M. (1980) *New Perspectives on Planning in Educational Organizations*, Far West Laboratory, San Francisco, Calif.

Clift, P.S., Nuttall, D.L. and McCormick, R. (eds) (1987) *Studies in School Self-Evaluation*, Falmer Press, Lewes.

Cohen, L. and Manion, L. (1985) *Research Methods in Education*, Croom Helm, London.

Conley, S.C., Schmidle, T. and Shedd, J.B. (1988) Teacher participation in the management of school systems, *Teachers College Record*, Vol. 90. no. 2, pp. 259–80.

Constable, H. (1994) Three arenas of tension: teachers' experience of participation in school development planning, in D.H. Hargreaves and D. Hopkins (eds) *Development Planning for School Improvement*, Cassell, London.

Constable, H., Norton, J. and Abbott, I. (1991) *Case Studies in School Development Planning*, Sunderland Polytechnic, Sunderland.

Coulson, A.A. (1986) *The managerial work of primary school headteachers, Sheffield papers. Education Manager* 48, Sheffield City Polytechnic, Sheffield.

Cuban, L. (1988) Why do some reforms persist? *Educational Administration Quarterly*, Vol. 24, no. 3, pp. 329–35.

Cuttance, P.F. (1992) Evaluating the effectiveness of schools, in D. Reynolds and P. Cuttance (eds) *School Effectiveness: Research, Policy and Practice*, Cassell, London.

Cuttance, P.F. (1994) The contribution of quality assurance reviews to development in school systems, in D.H. Hargreaves and D. Hopkins (eds) *Development Planning for School Improvement*, Cassell, London.

Dalin, P. (1989) Reconceptualising the school improvement process: charting a paradigm shift, in D. Reynolds (ed.) *School Effectiveness and Improvement: Proceedings of the First International Congress*, Cardiff School of Education, University of [Cardiff] and RION Institute for Educational Research, The Netherlands.

Davies, B. and Ellison, L. (1992) *School Development Panning*, Longman, Harlow.

Deal, T.E. (1987) The culture of schools, in L.T. Sheive and M.B. Schoenheit (eds) *Leadership: Examining the Elusive, 1987 Yearbook of the Association for Supervision and Curriculum Development*, ASCA, Arlington, Va.

Deal, T.E. (1990) Reframing reform, *Educational Leadership,* Vol. 47, no. 8, pp. 6–12.

Deal, T.E. and Kennedy, A.A. (1983) Culture and school performance, *Educational Leadership,* Vol. 40, no. 5, pp. 14–15.

Deem, R. (1993) Educational reform and school governing bodies in England 1986–92: old dogs, new tricks or new dogs, new tricks? In M. Preedy (ed.) *The Effective School*, The Open University and Paul Chapman Publishing, London.

Dempster, N. and Drew, P. (1992) *A Limited Literature Review of School Development Planning* (Appendix 2), Faculty of Education, Griffith University, Australia.

Dempster, N., Kruchov, G. and Distant, G. (1994) School development planning: an international perspective, in D.H. Hargreaves and D. Hopkins (eds) *Development Planning for School Improvement*, Cassell, London.

Dempster, N., Logan, L., Sachs, J. and Distant, G. (1993) *Primary School Planning: Survey 1*, Faculty of Education, Griffith University, Australia.

DES (1972) *Teacher Education and Training*, HMSO, London.

DES (1978) *Primary Education in England: A Survey by H.M. Inspectors of Schools*, HMSO, London.

DES (1979) *Local Authority Arrangements for the School Curriculum: Report on the Circular 14/77 Review*, HMSO, London.

DES (1980) *A Framework for the School Curriculum: Proposals for Consultation by the Secretaries of State*, DES/Welsh Office, London.

DES (1981) *The School Curriculum*, HMSO, London.

DES (1985) *Better Schools*, HMSO, London.

DES (1988a) *Education Reform Act*, HMSO, London.

DES (1988b) *Education Reform Act: Local Management of Schools*, Circular 7/88, 6 September, DES, London.

DES (1989a) *Planning for School Development: Advice for Governors, Headteachers and Teachers*, HMSO, London.

DES (1989b) *The Implementation of the National Curriculum in Primary Schools*, Report 332/89, HMSO, London.

DES (1989c) *School Indicators for Internal Management: An Aide Memoire*, HMSO, London.

DES (1990) *Developing School Management: The Way Forward*, HMSO, London.

DES (1991a) *Development Planning: A Practical Guide*, HMSO, London.

DES (1991b) *The Implementation of the Local Education Authority Training Grants Scheme*, DES, London.

Eisner, E.W. (1979) *The Educational Imagination: On the Design and Evaluation of School Programs*, Macmillan, New York.

Eisner, E.W. (1985) *The Art of Educational Evaluation*, Falmer Press, Lewes.

Eraut, M. (1988) Learning about management: the role of the management course, in C. Poster and C. Day (eds) *Partnership in Education Management*, Routledge, London.

Etzioni, A. (1964) *Modern Organizations*, Prentice-Hall, Englewood Cliffs, NJ.

Fink, D. and Stoll, L. (1992) Assessing school change: the Halton approach. Paper presented at the International Congress for School Effectiveness and Improvement, Victoria, British Columbia.

Fink, D. and Stoll, L. (1994) Linking school and teacher development. Paper presented at the International Congress for School Effectiveness and Improvement, Australia, Melbourne.

Foster, W. (1989) Towards a critical practice in leadership, in J. Smyth (ed.) *Critical Perspectives on Educational Leadership*, Falmer Press, Lewes.

Fullan, M.G. (1985) Change processes and strategies at the local level, *The Elementary School Journal*, Vol. 85, no. 3, pp. 391–420.

Fullan, M.G. (1988) Change processes in secondary schools: towards a more fundamental agenda (mimeo), University of Toronto.

Fullan, M. G. (1991) *The New Meaning of Educational Change*, Teachers College Press, New York.

Fullan, M.G. (1992a) *What's Worth Fighting for in Headship*, The Open University Press, Milton Keynes.

Fullan, M.G. (1992b) *Successful School Improvement*, The Open University Press, Buckingham.

Fullan, M. G., Bennett, B. and Rolheiser-Bennett, C. (1990) Linking classroom and school improvement, *Educational Leadership*, Vol. 47, no. 8, pp. 13–19.

Fullan, M.G. and Hargreaves, A. (1992) *What's Worth Fighting for in Your School?* The Open University Press, Milton Keynes.

Fullan, M.G. and Miles, M.B. (1992) Getting reform right: what works and what doesn't, *Phi Delta Kappan*, Vol. 73, no. 10, pp. 744–52.

Furtwengler, W.J. (1990) Student participation in restructured schools. Paper presented at the American Educational Research Association, Boston, Mass.

Gardiner, J. (Chairman) (1994) *School Teachers' Review Body Third Report*, Cm 2466, HMSO, London.

Glover, D.C. (1990) Towards a school development plan: process and practice, *Educational Management and Administration,* Vol. 18, no. 3, pp. 22–6.

Goldstein, H. (1991) *Assessment in Schools: An Alternative Framework,* Institute for Public Policy Research, London.

Good, T.L. and Brophy, J.E. (1986) School effects, in M.C. Wittrock (ed.) *Handbook of Research on Teaching,* Macmillan, New York.

Gray, J. (1990) The quality of schooling: frameworks for judgment, *British Journal of Educational Studies,* Vol. 38, no. 3, pp. 204–23.

Gray, J. (1993) The quality of schooling: frameworks for judgment, in M. Preedy (ed.) *Managing the Effective School,* The Open University and Paul Chapman Publishing, London.

Gray, J. and Jesson, D. (1990) The negotiation and construction of performance indicators: some principles, proposals and problems, *Evaluation and Research in Education,* Vol. 4, no. 2, pp. 93–108.

Gray, J., Jesson, D., Goldstein, H. and Hedger, K. (1993) The statistics of school improvement: establishing the agenda. Paper presented at ESRC Seminar on School Effectiveness and School Improvement, Sheffield.

Gray, J. and Wilcox, B. (1993) Inspection and school improvement: rhetoric and experience from the bridge. Paper presented at the ESRC Seminar on School Effectiveness and School Improvement, Sheffield.

Hall, G. (1987) The principal as leader of the change facilitating team. Paper presented at the annual meeting of the American Education Research Association, San Francisco, Calif.

Hall, G., Hord, S. and Griffin, T. (1980) Implementation at the school building level: the development and analysis of nine mini-case studies. Paper presented at the American Educational Research Association Annual Meeting, USA.

Handy, C. (1984) *Taken for Granted? Understanding Schools as Organizations,* Schools Council/Longman, York.

Hargreaves, A. (1989) Cultures of teaching: a focus for change (Part 1 and Part 2), *OPSTF News,* February and April.

Hargreaves, A. (1991) Contrived collegiality, in J. Blase (ed.) *The Politics of School Life,* Sage, San Francisco, Calif.

Hargreaves, D. (1993) School effectiveness, school change and school improvement: the relevance of the concept of culture. Paper presented at the ESRC Seminar on School Effectiveness and School Improvement, Sheffield.

Hargreaves, D. and Hopkins, D. (1991) *The Empowered School: The Management and Practice of Development Planning,* Cassell, London.

Hargreaves, D. and Hopkins, D. (1993) School effectiveness, school improvement and development planning, in M. Preedy (ed.) *Managing the Effective School,* The Open University and Paul Chapman Publishing, London.

Hargreaves, D. and Hopkins, D. (1994) *Development Planning for School Improvement,* Cassell, London.

Hargreaves, D., Hopkins, D. and Leask, M. (1990) *The Management of Development Planning – A Paper for Local Education Authorities,* DES, London.

Holly, P. and Southworth, G. (1989) *The Developing School,* Falmer Press, Lewes.

Hopkins, D. (1989) *Evaluation for School Development,* The Open University Press, Milton Keynes.

Hopkins, D. (1990) Integrating teacher development and school improvement: a study in teacher personality and school climate, in B. Joyce (ed.) *Changing School Culture through Staff Development,* Association for Supervision and Curriculum Development, Alexandria, Va.

Hopkins, D. (1991) Changing school culture through development planning, in S. Riddell and S. Brown (eds) *School Effectiveness Research: Its Messages for School Improvement,* HMSO, Edinburgh.

Hopkins, D. (1994) Yellow Brick Road, *Managing Schools Today*, Vol. 3, no. 6, pp. 14–17.

House of Commons Expenditure Committee (1976) *Policy-Making in the DES*, HMSO, London.

House of Commons Education, Science and Arts Committee (1986) *Achievement in Primary Schools*, HMSO, London.

Hutchinson, B. (1993) The effective reflective school: visions and pipedreams in development planning, *Educational Management and Administration*, Vol. 21, no. 1, pp. 4–18.

ILEA (1977) *Keeping the School Under Review*, ILEA, London.

ILEA (1984) *Improving Secondary Schools*, ILEA, London.

ILEA (1985) *Improving Primary Schools*, ILEA, London.

Jenni, R.W. (1991) *Improving America's Schools*, Longman, New York.

Jordan, B. (1989) School development plans: an inside view, in I. Craig (ed.) *Primary Headship in the 1990s*, Longman, Harlow.

Joyce, B. (1991) The doors to school improvement, *Educational Leadership*, Vol. 48, no. 8, pp. 59–62.

Joyce, B. and Showers, B. (1988) *Student Achievement through Staff Development*, Longman, New York.

Kerlinger, F.N. (1986) *Foundations of Behavioral Research*, Holt, Rinehart & Winston, New York.

Kitwood, T.M. (1977) *Values in Adolescent Life: Towards a Critical Description*, School of Research in Education, University of Bradford, Bradford.

Kogan, M., Johnson, D., Packwood, T. and Whittaker, T. (1984) *School Governing Bodies*, Heinemann, London.

Kruchov, C. and Høoyrup, S. (1994) Development of the school system in Gladsaxe Municipality. Paper presented at the International Congress for School Effectiveness and Improvement, Melbourne, Australia.

Lagerweij, N.A.J. and Voogt, J.C. (1990) Policy-making at the school level – some issues for the 1990s, in B.P.M. Creemers and D. Reynolds (eds) *School Effectiveness and School Improvement*, Vol. 1, no. 2, pp. 98–120.

Leithwood, K.A. (1992) The move toward transformational leadership, *Educational Leadership*, Vol. 49, no. 5, pp. 8–12.

Leithwood, K.A. and Jantzi, D. (1990) Transformational leadership: how principals can help reform school cultures, *School Effectiveness and School Improvement*, Vol. 1, no. 4, pp. 249–80.

Leithwood, K.A. and Montgomery, D. (1986) *The Principal Profile*, OISE Press, Toronto.

Levine, D.U. (1994) Creating effective schools through site-level staff development planning and improvement of organisational culture, in D.H. Hargreaves and D. Hopkins (eds) *Development Planning for School Improvement*, Cassell, London.

Levine, D.U. and Lezotte, L. (1990) *Unusually Effective Schools: A Review and Analysis of Research and Development*, National Center for Effective Schools Research and Development, Madison, Wis.

Lezotte, L. (1989) School improvement based on the effective schools research, *International Journal of Educational Research*, Vol. 13, no. 7, pp. 815–24.

Lezotte, L. (1990) Lessons learned, in B.O. Taylor (ed.) *Case Studies in Effective Schools Research*, National Center for Effective Schools, Madison, Wis.

Lieberman, A. (ed.) (1988) *Building a Professional Culture in Schools*, Teachers College Press, New York.

Little, J.W. (1982) Norms of collegiality and experimentation: workplace conditions of school success, *American Educational Research Journal*, Vol. 19, no. 3, pp. 325–430.

Little, J.W. (1986) The persistence of privacy: autonomy and initiative in teachers' professional relations. Paper presented at the annual meeting of the American Education Research Association, San Francisco, Calif.

Louis, K.S. and Miles, M.B. (1992) *Improving the Urban High School: What Works and Why*, Cassell, London.

Maden, M. and Tomlinson, J. (1991) *Planning for School Development*, Trentham Books, Stoke-on-Trent.

McMahon, A., Bolam, R., Abbott, R. and Holly, P. (1984) *Guidelines for Review and Internal Development in Schools: Primary and Secondary School Handbooks*, Longman/SCDC, York.

Miles, M.B. (1987) Practical guidelines for school administrators: how to get there. Paper presented at the annual meeting of the American Education Research Association, San Francisco, Calif.

Miles, M.B. and Ekholm, M. (1985) What is school improvement? In W. van Velzen, M.B. Miles, M. Ekholm, U. Hameyer and D. Robin (eds) *Making School Improvement Work: A Conceptual Guide to Practice*, OECD, Leuven, Belgium.

Miles, M.B. and Huberman, A.M. (1984) *Qualitative Data Analysis: A Sourcebook of New Methods*, Sage, Newbury Park, Calif.

Miles, M.B. and Huberman, A.M. (1994) *Qualitative Data Analysis: An Expanded Sourcebook* (2nd edn), Sage, Calif.

Mortimore, P., MacGilchrist, B., Savage, J. and Beresford, C. (1994) School development planning in primary schools: does it make a difference? In D.H. Hargreaves and D. Hopkins (eds) *Development Planning for School Improvement*, Cassell, London.

Mortimore, P. and Mortimore, J. (eds) (1991) *The Primary Head: Roles, Responsibilities and Reflections*, Paul Chapman Publishing, London.

Mortimore, P., Sammons, P., Stoll, L., Lewis, D. and Ecob, R. (1988) *School Matters: The Junior Years*, Open Books, Wells.

Murphy, J.F. (1990) Effective schools: legacy and future directions. Paper presented at the annual meeting of the American Educational Research Association, Boston, Mass.

National Curriculum Council (1989) *National Curriculum: From Policy to Practice*, DES, London.

Newman, E. and Pollard, A. (1994) Observing primary school change: through conflict to whole school collaboration? In D.H. Hargreaves and D. Hopkins (eds) *Development Planning for School Improvement*, Cassell, London.

Nias, J., Southworth, G. and Campbell, P. (1992) *Whole School Curriculum Development in the Primary School*, Falmer Press, Lewes.

Nias, J., Southworth, G. and Yeomans, R. (1989) *Staff Relationships in the Primary School: A Study of Organizational Cultures*, Cassell, London.

Nuttall, D., Goldstein, H., Prosser, R. and Rasbash, J. (1989) Differential school effectiveness, *International Journal of Educational Research*, Vol. 13, no. 10, pp. 769–76.

OECD (1976) Report on Britain, *The Times Higher Education Supplement*, 9 May, reprinted in R. Raggatt and M. Evans (eds) (1977) *The Political Context*, Ward Lock, London.

Ofsted (1992) *Framework for the Inspection of Schools*, HMSO, London.

Ofsted (1993) *Handbook for the Inspection of Schools*, HMSO, London.

Ofsted (1994) *Improving Schools*, HMSO, London.

Ouston, J., Gold, A. and Gosling, P. (1992) The development of managers in education: do men and women differ? Paper presented at BEMAS Research Conference, University of Nottingham.

Paisey, A. (1992) *Organisation and Management in Schools: Perspectives for Practising Teachers and Governors*, Longman, London.

Patterson, J.L., Purkey, S.C. and Parker, J.V. (1986) *Productive School Systems for a Nonrational World*, Association for Supervision and Curriculum Development, Alexandria, Va.

Peters, T. (1987) *Thriving on Chaos: Handbook for a Management Revolution*, Pan/ Macmillan, London.

Peters, T. and Waterman, R. (1982) *In Search of Excellence*, Harper & Row, London.

Pollack, S., Chrispeels, J.A. and Watson, D. (1987) A description of factors and implementation strategies used by schools in becoming effective for all students. Paper presented at the annual meeting of the American Research Association, Washington, DC.

Powell, J. (1985) *The Teacher's Craft. A Study of Teaching in the Primary School*, Scottish Council, Edinburgh.

Powell, J. and Scrimgeour, M. (1977) *System for Classroom Observation of Teaching Strategies*, Scottish Council for Research in Education, Edinburgh.

Powney, J. and Watts, M. (1987) *Interviewing in Educational Research*, Routledge & Kegan Paul, London.

Puffitt, R., Stoten, B. and Winkley, D. (1992) *Business Planning for Schools*, Longman, Harlow.

Purkey, S. and Smith, M. (1983) Effective schools: a review, *The Elementary School Journal*, Vol. 83, no. 4, pp. 427–52.

Reid, K., Hopkins, D. and Holly, P. (1987) *Towards the Effective School*, Blackwell, Oxford.

Reynolds, D. (1976) The delinquent school, in P. Woods (ed.) *The Process of Schooling*, Routledge & Kegan Paul, London.

Reynolds, D. (1988) British school improvement research: the contribution of qualitative studies, *International Journal of Qualitative Studies in Education*, Vol. 1, no. 2, pp. 143–54.

Reynolds, D. (1992) *School Effectiveness and School Improvement in Great Britain*, Department of Education, Loughborough University.

Reynolds, D., Hopkins, D. and Stoll, L. (1993) Linking school effectiveness knowledge and school improvement practice: towards a synergy, *School Effectiveness and School Improvement*, Vol. 4, no. 1, pp. 37–58.

Reynolds, D. and Packer, A. (1992) School effectiveness and school improvement in the 1990s, in D. Reynolds and P. Cuttance (eds) *School Effectiveness: Research Theory and Practice*, Cassell, London.

Riddell, S. and Brown, S. (1991) *School Effectiveness Research: Its Messages for School Improvement*, HMSO, Edinburgh.

Rosenholtz, S. (1989) *Teachers' Workplace: The Social Organization of Schools*, Longman, New York.

Rossman, G.B., Corbett, H.D. and Firestone, W.A. (1988) *Change and Effectiveness in Schools: A Cultural Perspective*, State University of New York Press, Albany, NY.

Rudduck, J. (1991) *Innovation and Change*, The Open University Press, Milton Keynes.

Rutter, M., Maughan, B., Mortimore, P. and Ouston, J. (1979) *Fifteen Thousand Hours: Secondary Schools and their Effects on Children*, Open Books, London.

Sackney, L.E. (1986) Practical strategies for improving school effectiveness, *The Canadian School Executive*, Vol. 6, no. 4, pp. 15–20.

Sammons, P., Mortimore, P. and Thomas, S. (1993) Do schools perform consistently across outcomes and areas? Paper presented at the ESRC Seminar on School Effectiveness and School Improvement, Sheffield.

Sammons, P., Thomas, S., Mortimore, P., Cairns, R., Bausor, J. and Walker, A. (1995) Understanding school and departmental differences in academic effectiveness: findings from case studies of selected outlier secondary schools in inner London. Paper presented at the International Congress of School Effectiveness and Improvement, Leeuwarden, The Netherlands.

Sarason, S. (1971) *The Culture of the School and the Problem of Change*, Allyn & Bacon, Boston, Mass.

Sarason, S. (1990) *The Predictable Failure of Educational Reform*, Jossey-Bass, San Francisco, Calif.

Schein, E. H. (1985) *Organizational Culture and Leadership*, Jossey-Bass, San Francisco, Calif.

Schlechty, P. (1990) *Schools for the 21st Century: Leadership Imperatives for Educational Reform*, Jossey-Bass, San Francisco, Calif.

Sergiovanni, T. (1992) Why we should seek substitutes for leadership, *Educational Leadership,* Vol. 49, no. 5, pp. 41–5.

Sirotnik, K.A. (1987) *The School as the Center of Change* (Occasional Paper 5), Center for Educational Renewal, Seattle, Wash.

Skelton, M., Reeves, G. and Playfoot, D. (1991) *Development Planning for Primary Schools*, NFER/Nelson, Windsor.

Slater, R.O. and Teddlie, C. (1992) Toward a theory of school effectiveness and leadership, *School Effectiveness and School Improvement,* Vol. 3, no. 4, pp. 242–57.

Smith, D. and Tomlinson, S. (1989) *The School Effect: A Study of Multi-Racial Comprehensives*, Policy Studies Institute, London.

SOED (1993) *School Development Plans in Scotland: A Consultation Paper*, Scottish Office, Edinburgh.

SOED/HMI (1991) *The Role of School Development Plans in Managing School Effectiveness*, Scottish Office, Edinburgh.

Southworth, G. (1987) *Readings in Primary School Management*, Falmer Press, Lewes.

Southworth, G. (1992 unpublished) School leadership and school development: reflections from research, Cambridge Institute.

Stoll, L. (1991) School self-evaluation: another boring exercise or an opportunity for growth? In S. Riddell and S. Brown (eds) *Effectiveness Research: Its Messages for School Improvement*, HMSO, Edinburgh.

Stoll, L. (1994) Where next? *Report*, Vol. 16, no. 5, pp. 4–5.

Stoll, L. and Fink, D. (1989) Implementing an effective schools project: the Halton approach. Paper presented at the Second International Congress for School Effectiveness, Rotterdam, The Netherlands.

Stoll, L. and Fink, D. (1992) Effecting school change: the Halton approach, *School Effectiveness and School Improvement*, Vol. 3, no. 1, pp. 19–41.

Stoll, L. and Reynolds, D. (1994) Taking action to link school effectiveness and school improvement: practical ways forward. Paper presented at the Seventh International Congress for School Effectiveness and Improvement, Melbourne, Australia.

Stone, S. (1984) *Interviews* (CRUS Guide 6), British Library Board, Sheffield.

Taylor, B.O. and Levine, D.U. (1991) Effective schools projects and school-based management, *Phi Delta Kappan*, Vol. 72, no. 5, pp. 394–7.

Taylor, G. and Saunders, J. B. (1980) *The Law of Education: First Supplement to Eighth Edition*, Butterworths, London.

Taylor, W. (1976) The head as manager: some criticisms, in R.S. Peters (ed.) *The Role of the Head*, Routledge & Kegan Paul, London.

Torrington, D. and Weightman, J. (1993) The culture and ethos of the school, in M. Preedy (ed.) *Managing the Effective School*, The Open University and Paul Chapman Publishing, London.

Tuckman, B.W. (1972) *Conducting Educational Research*, Harcourt Brace Jovanovich, USA.

Wallace, M. (1989) Planning for multiple change in primary schools, *Education 3–13*, Vol. 17, no. 3, pp. 15–17.

Wallace, M. (1991a) Flexible planning: a key to the management of multiple innovations, *Educational Management and Administration,* Vol. 19, no. 3, pp. 180–92.

Wallace, M. (1991b) Development plans: an LEA solution causing a primary school problem? *Education 3–13*, Vol. 19, no. 2, pp. 39–46.

Wallace, M. (1994) Towards a contingency approach to development planning in schools, in D.H. Hargreaves and D. Hopkins (eds) *Development Planning for School Improvement*, Cassell, London.

West, M. and Ainscow, M. (1991) *Managing School Development – A Practical Guide*, David Fulton, London.

INDEX

accountability, 76–7, 101, 108, 115, 119, 126, 176, 178, 189, 194, 199, 215, 218

action plans, 16–19, 214, 216–17, 221

advisers, 6, 58–60, 62–3, 65–6, 70, 74, 76, 79, 85–6, 108, 131, 139, 142, 158, 177, 183–91, 198, 215, 220

appraisal, 172, 174

audit, x, 11–14, 19, 38, 81, 206–7, 211–12, 218–20

Australia, xi, 25

Canada, 28

change, 7–9, 12, 23, 25, 27, 34–6, 42, 75–6, 98, 107–10, 115–17, 140, 142, 173, 181, 188, 196, 198–201, 204, 207, 211, 222

  agents, x, 38, 198, 201, 203, 207

  external influences, 35, 78–9, 119, 134–5, 137–8, 141, 147, 178, 184, 189, 199, 208

  internal influences, 34–5, 119, 134–5, 137, 199

classroom exceeding perspective, 196, 212

classroom perceiving perspective, 197, 212

collaboration, 199, 212

collegiality, 40–1, 199

communication, 77, 79, 81, 83, 85–9, 91, 141, 146–8, 172, 185, 187, 214, 216, 218

community plans, 197, 202, 212

confidentiality, 43, 47, 50, 59, 69

continuity, 26, 146, 153, 172, 181, 190

culture, school, 23, 26, 28–9, 34–42, 78, 89, 119, 137, 148, 196, 199, 204–5, 211, 217

curriculum (*see also* National Curriculum), 2–3, 5, 7, 12–13, 31, 40–1, 61–2, 65, 67, 69, 82, 90, 92, 102, 111–14, 117, 124, 135–7, 139, 141, 146–8, 154, 171–3, 175, 182, 184–5, 187, 219

Denmark, 197

deputy heads, 83–4, 97, 105–6, 139, 145, 152, 179, 182, 185, 197

documents, school, 48, 50, 150–8, 211, 213–14

Education Reform Act 1988 (*see also* legislation), 25, 31, 60, 62, 64, 176–7, 220

effectiveness, school, ix–x, 6–7, 22–3, 25, 35, 68, 120, 140, 143, 148, 195, 197–200, 202, 204–5, 214, 217, 219, 221–2

efficiency, school, 119–20, 127, 140, 143, 145, 147–8, 194–5, 197, 199, 204

equal opportunities, 41, 90, 92, 154, 172–4

ESRC project, x–xi, 44

  classroom observation, 159–75

    analysis, 171–5

    use 174–5

  design, 43–57, 208

  governor responses, 176–82, 218

  headteacher responses, 72–93, 118–49, 175, 192, 218

    analysis, 72–3

    backgrounds, 74–5

    benefits of SDPs, 78

    content of SDPs, 90–2

    context of SDPs, 74–6

    impact of previous plans, 86–9

ESRC project (*cont.*)
  outcomes of SDPs, 92–3
  process of development planning,
    79–89
  purpose of development planning,
    76–9
  roles and responsibilities, 82–3, 87,
    89
  strategies, 82
LEA responses, 183–91
  aims and methodology of survey,
    58–9
  analysis of SDPs, 63–4
  content of SDPs, 61–2
  guidance in planning, 61–2, 66, 68,
    70
  involvement, 62–3, 69–70
  policy, 59–60, 62–3
  regional variations, 67–9
  typologies, 190–1
  use of SDPs, 65
methodology, 43–57, 208
  data analysis, 57, 118–49, 208
  data collection, 49–50
  development of, 50–5
  ethics, 43–4
  fieldwork, 55–7
  selection criteria, 44–7
  sources of evidence, 47–9
practical implications, 210–22
  governors, 218–19
  headteachers, 210–18
  higher education, 221
  LEA, 219–20
  Ofsted, 221
  professional associations, 221
  roles and responsibilities,
    214–16
  teachers, 210–18
teacher responses, 94–149, 175, 192,
    218
  backgrounds, 94–9
  content of SDPs, 112–14
  outcomes of development planning,
    114–17
  process of development planning,
    102–12
  purpose of development planning,
    110–2
  roles and responsibilities, 104–5,
    109
theoretical implications, 192–209
  analysis of typology of SDPs,
    196–209

characteristics of SDPs, 194–203,
    205
  model, 204–9
  typology of SDPs, 118–49, 157–8,
    163–71, 175, 178, 182,
    190–204, 217, 221–2
  analysis, 121–49
  co-operative, 121, 127–30, 135–6,
    138–49, 157–8, 163, 165–71,
    175, 179, 191, 193, 195–8,
    203–4, 206–8, 212–17
  corporate, 121, 123, 130–2, 135–6,
    141–9, 157–8, 163, 169–71,
    175, 179, 191–3, 195–8,
    203–4, 207–8, 211–17, 219,
    221
  rhetorical, 120–1, 123–4, 126, 129,
    131, 134, 136–8, 142–9,
    157–8, 164, 170, 175, 182,
    191–4, 196–9, 202, 204, 207,
    212–13, 216–17, 220
  singular, 120–1, 125–7, 130, 134,
    138, 142–9, 157–8, 165, 170,
    191, 193–4, 197–8, 206–7,
    212–13, 216–17, 220
  written plans, 150–8, 211,
    213–14
evaluation, x, 140, 142–3, 145–6, 154,
    156–8, 172, 177, 180–1, 189,
    194–5, 197, 207–8, 211, 213,
    216–20
evidence, 53–4, 107–8, 138, 140, 142,
    146–8, 171, 174–5, 189, 197,
    202, 205, 208, 212–14, 217
evolutionary planning, 200

feedback, 43, 89, 216
finance, 14, 29, 31, 61–2, 64, 68–9, 82,
    86–8, 90, 105–6, 109, 112,
    138–9, 141, 143, 154, 172–4,
    180, 184–5, 187–9, 191, 194–6,
    201, 214–15, 219–20

GEST, 60, 64, 67, 80
governors, 10, 45–6, 48, 52, 56, 61–3,
    66–7, 69, 75–87, 89–93, 104–5,
    108, 112, 126, 131, 135–7, 142,
    144–7, 149, 151–3, 155–8, 172,
    176–90, 194, 197, 206, 211–12,
    214, 216–19
  role, 177, 179–80, 186, 188, 206,
    219
  training, 178, 188, 219
  visits, 177–8, 181

GRIDS, 3, 81
GRIST, 60
growth, school, 200

headteachers (*see also* senior staff), 10,
    38–40, 45–6, 48, 51, 55, 62,
    66–7, 69, 72–94, 98, 101–2,
    104–6, 110–13, 118–49, 151–3,
    155–7, 171, 175, 177–91, 194–8,
    200, 206–8, 210–18

ILEA, 2, 4–5, 61, 65
image, school, 174
INSET, 2–5, 7, 18, 61, 76–7, 80, 87, 90,
    101, 104–5, 107, 109–10,
    135–42, 145–6, 148, 154, 172–4,
    180–1, 184, 187–91, 194, 196,
    198, 215, 220
inspection, 2, 6–8, 13, 52, 58–60, 62–3,
    65–8, 70–1, 76–7, 79–80, 85–7,
    104, 108, 149, 153, 158, 173–4,
    177, 183–91, 198, 206, 209, 214,
    217–21
interviews, 49–52, 55–6, 72–93, 177,
    183, 220

leadership, 41, 73, 82–3, 88–9, 92–3,
    98–9, 104, 119–20, 136–45, 147,
    153, 172, 178–9, 187, 192,
    194–5, 200, 203–5, 210, 212,
    214–16, 219–20
LEAs, 3–10, 13, 15, 27–8, 45, 49, 52,
    54–5, 56–71, 76–80, 82–3, 85–8,
    91, 104–5, 108, 112, 135, 137,
    146, 149, 151–4, 156, 158,
    173–4, 176–7, 179, 183–91,
    197–8, 206, 208–9, 214, 218–20
  involvement, 186
  policy, 184
  typologies, 190–1
  visits, 184–5
  learning opportunities and outcomes,
    ix–x, xii–xiii, 8, 12–13, 19, 24,
    33, 41–2, 79, 97, 107, 119–20,
    140, 142, 144–9, 175, 181–2,
    189, 195, 197, 201–5, 210–13,
    217, 222
LEATGS, 60
legislation (*see also* Education Reform
    Act 1988), 1, 5–7, 25, 31, 63,
    67–8, 70, 176–7, 183–4, 220
LMS, 5, 7, 60–4, 67, 70, 77, 90–1,
    134–5, 138, 146, 172–4, 184,
    188, 197, 220

management, x, 26, 36–40, 67–8, 70,
    73–4, 76–7, 82–3, 88–93, 98,
    111–12, 119–20, 124, 126–8,
    135–49, 152–3, 155, 157–8, 172–
    5, 178–9, 182, 184–5, 187–9,
    191, 194–6, 201–6, 210, 212,
    214–17, 219–22
  classroom, x, 172, 175
  models, 37–40,
  self, 1–2, 5, 11, 137, 197, 217, 222
  training, 38
mission, 206–7
monitoring, 65–7, 70, 77–8, 81, 83–5,
    87, 89, 105–6, 110, 115, 137–9,
    141–3, 145, 147, 151, 153–4,
    156–7, 177, 180–1, 188–9,
    194–5, 197, 201–2, 205, 207–8,
    211, 213–14, 216–17, 219–20
'moving' schools, 202–3

National Curriculum (*see also*
    curriculum), 5, 7, 12–13, 48,
    60–2, 64, 67, 70, 88, 90–1, 94,
    98, 110, 113–14, 135, 155,
    171–3, 175, 181, 184, 190
networking, 60, 70
non-participant observation, 160–1
Northern Ireland, 58–9, 62–3, 65–9

objectives, instructional and expressive,
    17
observation, classroom, 48, 50, 52–4,
    142, 148, 159–75
  coding system, 175
  timing, 174–5
Ofsted, 6–8, 18, 65, 173–4, 176, 178,
    182, 184, 190, 214, 219, 221
ownership, 119–20, 124, 126–8, 130,
    134–6, 138, 141, 143–4, 147,
    151–2, 156–7, 178–9, 181, 185,
    192, 194–6, 199, 203, 205, 210,
    212, 216

parent governors, 176–82
parents, 62–3, 67, 70, 75, 77, 79–84,
    86–7, 89–93, 104–6, 108, 112,
    135, 137, 142, 145, 147, 151–8,
    172, 179, 186–7, 190, 197, 212,
    214, 217–19
performance indicators, 6, 25, 62, 81,
    103, 141, 175
planning cycles, 9–10, 30, 70, 77, 80–1,
    87, 101, 103, 138, 145–6, 156,
    211, 218

power, 35, 38–40, 78, 82, 88, 147, 182, 187, 201
practice, classroom, 144–9, 159–71
premises, school, 61, 64, 69, 77, 90–2, 172–4, 185
priorities, 14–15, 31–2, 53, 64, 76, 81, 85–6, 89–92, 102–3, 110–11, 113–14, 117, 134–8, 140–1, 143–9, 151–7, 171–5, 177, 179, 181, 185–90, 196–7, 199, 201–2, 206–7, 211–17, 219
   root and branch, 14, 32
professional development (*see also* staff development), x, 7, 39–41, 91, 97–8, 139, 140–1, 143–9, 154, 172–4, 185, 187, 194–6, 202, 204–5, 208, 210, 212–16, 220
pupils, 75, 79–81, 84–7, 93, 103, 105, 107, 116–17, 137–8, 140, 144–9, 151, 153, 156–7, 159–71, 178–9, 181, 185–6, 190, 192, 194–5, 205, 212, 216–18

questionnaires, 50, 54–5

reporting
   outcomes, 108, 218
   procedures, 77

school development planning
   content, 31–2, 72, 133–7, 204–5, 212
   context, 27–9, 72, 74–6, 94–100, 133–7, 204–5
   growth of, 1–8
   guidance on, 5–6, 10–33, 76, 80, 182, 191, 196, 211, 216
   model, 204–5
   outcomes, 32–3, 72
   process, 9–21, 29–30, 72
   purpose, 24–7, 72, 119–20, 124, 127, 130, 204–5, 211
   research, 8, 11, 23, 25, 28, 33–42, 196–203
school development plans
   construction, 13–15
   evaluation, 19–21
   formulation, 11–16, 211–14
   implementation, 16–19, 214
   publication, 15–16

typology, 118–49, 157–8, 163–71, 175, 178
   written, 150–8, 211, 213–14
School Management Task Force, 38
Scotland, 25, 61–3, 65–8, 207
secondary schools, x, 7, 11, 197, 206, 208–10
self-evaluation, 201, 206, 208
self-improvement, 197
senior staff (*see also* deputy heads *and* headteachers), 11, 84, 106, 136, 139–40, 143, 147, 185, 195, 197, 210–12, 214, 216, 218–19
sharing, 119–20, 131, 143, 147, 153–5, 185, 194–5, 199–200, 203, 205–6, 210–15, 219
special educational needs, 42, 90, 92, 112–14, 117, 155, 172–3, 188, 219
stability, 26
staff development (*see also* professional development), 2–3, 6, 30–1, 62, 64–5, 67–8, 76, 79, 112, 136–7, 143, 147, 151, 154, 195, 201–2, 205, 215–16
'stuck' schools, 202–3, 220
success criteria, 17–18, 20, 32, 81, 84, 86–7, 89, 103–4, 107, 141, 147, 155, 157–8, 175, 188, 202, 207, 211, 213, 217
SCOTS, 50, 53–4, 159–71

target-setting, 82–3
teachers, 10, 20, 30, 33, 48–9, 51–2, 56, 66, 69, 72–3, 84, 93, 94–149, 151, 153, 155–71, 175, 178–9, 183, 185, 187, 192, 194–8, 200–1, 204–5, 207–8, 210–18
time, 29, 76, 78, 82, 84–6, 88–9, 105–6, 110–11, 117, 138, 140, 142, 145, 178, 180, 187, 214–15, 221

uncertainty, 201

value added, 19

Wales, 67
whole school, 76, 80–1, 83, 85, 87, 90, 99, 101, 105, 108, 112, 115–17, 140–9, 154–7, 189, 195–7, 202, 205, 210–11, 213, 215–16, 222